Lessons from the Great Depression For Dummies®

Cheat Sheet

A Dozen Key Gre___ ___ ___on Dates

October 29, 1929: More than $9 b_____n is lost in five hours on the New York Stock Exchange. The day becomes known as "Black Tuesday."

March 4, 1933: Franklin D. Roosevelt is sworn in as the 32nd president of the United States.

April 9, 1933: The first member of the *Civilian Conservation Corps* — a public relief program that hires unemployed men to work on resource conservation projects — is enrolled. By July, 274,000 boys and young men are enrolled.

May 12, 1933: President Roosevelt signs the Agricultural Adjustment Act, which pays farmers not to produce so much.

December 5, 1933: Utah becomes the 36th state to ratify the Twenty-First Amendment, thus repealing Prohibition.

January 1, 1934: The Federal Deposit Insurance Corporation begins insuring personal bank accounts for up to $2,500 per customer.

May 11, 1934: A dust storm that began in the Great Plains spreads across the eastern half of the United States and over the Atlantic Ocean.

May 18, 1934: President Roosevelt signs a package of 12 crime-fighting bills that includes making bank robbery a federal crime.

April 15, 1935: An Associated Press story uses the term "dust bowl" to describe a drought-stricken portion of five states: Texas, Oklahoma, New Mexico, Colorado, and Kansas.

September 8, 1935: U.S. Senator and presidential aspirant Huey Long is shot at the Louisiana Capitol. He dies two days later.

December 30, 1936: Workers at a General Motors plant in Flint, Michigan begin a 44-day sitdown strike that eventually paves the way for new contracts with other automakers.

June 25, 1938: President Roosevelt signs the Fair Labor Standards Act, which sets a federal minimum wage of 25 cents per hour.

Lessons from the Great Depression For Dummies®

Federal Laws and Programs with Roots in the Great Depression

The Federal Deposit Insurance Corp.: Created in 1933, the FDIC protects bank customer deposits (see Chapter 4).

Temporary Assistance for Needy Families: This name belongs to the latest iteration of an assistance program begun in 1935 (see Chapter 5).

Food stamps: This form of assistance, which helps low-income people buy food, has its roots in a program that began in 1939 (see Chapter 5).

Financial assistance for farmers: Beginning with the Agricultural Adjustment Act in 1933, federal farm programs provide subsidies, crop insurance, and conservation funds (see Chapter 6).

Federal minimum wage laws: The first such law appeared in 1938 (see Chapter 11).

Securities and Exchange Commission: This federal panel, which regulates the stock market and securities trading, was born in 1934 (see Chapter 13).

Unemployment insurance: This type of assistance was created in 1935 as part of the Social Security Act (see Chapter 13).

Social Security: The federal pension system, which also provides aid to widows, orphans, and the disabled, began in 1935 (see Chapter 13).

Depression by the Numbers

24.9 percent: The U.S. unemployment rate in February 1933
8.1 percent: The U.S. unemployment rate in February 2009

4,000: U.S. banks that closed in 1933
25: U.S. banks that closed in 2008

16.1: Percentage decrease of the gross domestic product from 1930–1931
6.2: Percentage decrease of the gross domestic product from 2007–2008

For Dummies: Bestselling Book Series for Beginners

Lessons from the Great Depression

FOR

DUMMIES®

by Steve Wiegand

WILEY

Wiley Publishing, Inc.

Lessons from the Great Depression For Dummies®

Published by
Wiley Publishing, Inc.
111 River St.
Hoboken, NJ 07030-5774
www.wiley.com

About the Author

Steve Wiegand has been an award-winning political journalist and history writer for more than 30 years. His journalism career has included stints at the *San Diego Evening Tribune, San Francisco Chronicle,* and *Sacramento Bee,* where he currently covers state government and California politics.

Wiegand is a graduate of Santa Clara University, where he majored in American literature and U.S. history. He also has a Master of Science degree in Mass Communications from California State University, San Jose.

Wiegand is the author of *U.S. History For Dummies,* which is in its second edition. He is also the author of *Papers of Permanence* (McClatchy) and *Sacramento Tapestry* (Towery Books), coauthor of *The Mental_Floss History of the World* (HarperCollins), and a contributing author to *Mental_Floss Presents Forbidden Knowledge* (HarperCollins).

He lives in Northern California.

Dedication

To my mom and dad, for having lived through the Great Depression, and my wife and daughter, for keeping me out of one.

Acknowledgments

Thanks first to acquisitions editor Lindsay Lefevere at Wiley for successfully pitching the idea for this book, and then catching my pitch to do it. A big thank-you also to Joan Friedman, who served double duty as project editor and copy editor (the readable parts are all due to her). Thanks also to art editor Alicia South for making the nice-looking parts nice looking, and to technical editor David Goldberg for making the correct parts correct. Everything else is my fault.

Publisher's Acknowledgments

We're proud of this book; please send us your comments through our Dummies online registration form located at `http://dummies.custhelp.com`. For other comments, please contact our Customer Care Department within the U.S. at 877-762-2974, outside the U.S. at 317-572-3993, or fax 317-572-4002.

Some of the people who helped bring this book to market include the following:

Acquisitions, Editorial, and Media Development

Project Editor: Joan Friedman

Acquisitions Editor: Lindsay Sandman Lefevere

Assistant Editor: Erin Calligan Mooney

Editorial Program Coordinator: Joe Niesen

Technical Editor: David Goldberg, PhD

Senior Editorial Manager: Jennifer Ehrlich

Editorial Supervisor: Carmen Krikorian

Editorial Assistant: Jennette ElNaggar

Art Coordinator: Alicia B. South

Cover Photos: © Index Stock Imagery

Cartoons: Rich Tennant (`www.the5thwave.com`)

Composition Services

Project Coordinator: Lynsey Stanford

Layout and Graphics: Christin Swinford, Christine Williams

Proofreaders: Laura Albert, Laura Bowman, Reuben W. Davis

Indexer: Dakota Indexing

Publishing and Editorial for Consumer Dummies

> **Diane Graves Steele,** Vice President and Publisher, Consumer Dummies
>
> **Kristin Ferguson-Wagstaffe,** Product Development Director, Consumer Dummies
>
> **Ensley Eikenburg,** Associate Publisher, Travel
>
> **Kelly Regan,** Editorial Director, Travel

Publishing for Technology Dummies

> **Andy Cummings,** Vice President and Publisher, Dummies Technology/General User

Composition Services

> **Debbie Stailey,** Director of Composition Services

Contents at a Glance

Table of Contents

Chapter 9: Demagogues and Desperadoes 145

Chapter 10: Having Fun in Spite of It All 159

Introduction

- -

*N*ot long after the U.S. stock market crashed in late October 1929, a reporter for *The Saturday Evening Post* asked the esteemed British economist John Maynard Keynes if he could think of another period in history that was as financially bleak.

"Yes," Keynes replied. "It was called the Dark Ages, and it lasted 400 years."

The Great Depression didn't last quite that long. It is generally considered to have begun in late 1929 and ended in 1940 and 1941, when the United States stepped up military production as the threat of war loomed.

But the influences of the period — from the existence of the Social Security system to federal government price supports of U.S. farm products to the insurance on bank accounts — are felt in nearly every aspect of contemporary life in the United States.

In fact, virtually every economic downturn since the 1930s has inspired comparisons to that earlier period and raised questions about what happened just before and during the Great Depression. In the last 90 days of 2008, for example, the term "Great Depression" appeared 270 times in *The New York Times* alone, most often in stories about the state of the 2008 economy.

In most cases, making such comparisons is a legitimate response because it's highly probable that no other period has had as much impact on the way government, business, labor, and the American people interact with their economy.

The Great Depression has also had personal impacts on many modern American families because of the wrenching effects it had on their parents, grandparents, or great-grandparents.

For example, I'm a Californian because my mother's parents moved in the 1930s from a dust-choked farm near Stillwater, Oklahoma, to the uncertain promise of a better life in Monterey, California. Tens of millions of Americans can relate similar stories about how the Great Depression affected their families.

About This Book

The Great Depression has long been a favorite topic for historians and history book writers. Except for the Civil War, probably no period in U.S. history has been written about more than the era of Black Thursday, the New Deal, FDR, John Dillinger, bread lines, and the Dust Bowl. (Don't worry if some of these terms aren't familiar — I explain them all in this book.) But *Lessons from the Great Depression For Dummies* takes a little different approach than other books about the era.

Here are my goals in this book:

- To give you a solid grounding in just what happened during the Great Depression, in the rest of the world as well as in the United States.

- To look at how the experiences of the 1930s stack up against the economic conditions of the 21st century.

- To assess just what has — and hasn't — been learned from the events of eight decades ago.

- To maybe spark a chuckle or an "I didn't know that!" through an anecdote or quirky fact about the people and the events of the period.

This book is not a textbook. If you're looking for in-depth dissections of Keynesian economics or exhaustive explanations of the environmental effects of the Tennessee Valley Authority, you're likely to be disappointed.

It's also not meant to be a polemic for any particular political perspective. However, while I've tried hard to be objective, it's possible my personal biases may have snuck in from time to time. If they have, I apologize. Just ignore them. I do.

Conventions Used in This Book

To help you navigate through the book, I've used the following conventions:

- *Italics* are used both to emphasize a word and to highlight a new word or phrase that is being defined.

- **Bold** highlights the keywords in a bulleted list.

What You're Not to Read

Here and there in this book you're going to see blocks of text in shaded gray boxes (called *sidebars*). They contain quotations, mini-profiles of interesting people from the period, anecdotes about certain events, or the origins of customs or other aspects of American life.

Think of them as side trips off the highway. You can skip right by them and stick with the main text, or you can stop for a minute before resuming the journey. You could even save them until you've read all of the main text and then go back to them. It's like two books for the price of one!

Foolish Assumptions

We all know that when you *assume,* you make an *ass* of *u* and *me*. (Well, it was funny in sixth grade.)

Notwithstanding that admonition, I'm making a few assumptions about why you picked up this book:

- ✔ You know little to nothing about the Great Depression, and you want to find out about it.
- ✔ You know something about the Great Depression, and you would like to know more.
- ✔ You know a lot about the Great Depression, and you want to see just how big an ignoramus the author is.

Seriously, the only real assumptions I make are that you're interested in U.S. history or you're concerned about what's happening with the current economy and you want to know how it contrasts and compares with the 1930s. If either or both assumptions are true, I think you have picked up the right book.

How This Book Is Organized

This book is set up so you don't have to start on the first page and go straight through to the last. If you scan the table of contents and Chapter 10's title jumps out and grabs you by the throat, feel free to read it first. You can always go back to Chapter 1 later.

Basically, the book is organized along a three-tier structure. The *parts* are collections of chapters grouped more or less around a central theme. Next are the *chapters* themselves, which contain aspects of a topic or time period. Finally, the *headings* and *subheadings* denote parts of the chapters that home in on specific subjects.

Oh, and starting with Chapter 3, there's a section at the end of each chapter called "Lessons Learned." This section looks at how events covered in the chapter relate to contemporary situations, and whether we do a better job of handling them now than we did then.

Here's a look at what's in the five parts:

Part 1: Heading into a Mess

The chapters in this part are sort of like the appetizer course. There's an overview of the book's contents (think of it as an annotated menu). Then there's a collection of explanations of economic terms and concepts that will make understanding the Great Depression easier.

This part is topped off by some pretty detailed background on what happened before the Great Depression that helped bring it about, from making too many things to having too little money to buy them.

Part 11: Getting Depressed

This part covers just how hard the Great Depression's hard times were — and who they were hard on, particularly in the three years after the stock market crash in late 1929.

It explores the events that helped trigger the Great Depression; how it changed Americans' relationships with each other; how people coped with virtually no help from the government; the plight of rural Americans (who were doubly hit by the economy and Mother Nature); and what was happening in the rest of the world.

Part III: Living Through the Great Depression

Part III looks at the mass exodus of rural Americans from the drought-stricken Great Plains to the West. It also houses collections both of characters that made their livings with guns and of characters that made their livings with their big mouths. I explain how Americans tried to make the best of the gloomy economic times by escaping to radio shows or the movies, as well as how organized labor got stronger during the era.

Part IV: Fixing Things

This part focuses on the two presidents who played very different roles in the Great Depression: Herbert Hoover, the accomplished humanitarian who became the Great Goat; and Franklin D. Roosevelt, the polio-stricken patrician who simultaneously became the best-loved and most-hated man of the era. I examine the presidential campaign of 1932 and the transition between the two men, as well as Roosevelt's New Deal cures for the Great Depression — how well they worked and their lasting impacts. I conclude this part with a summary of what's different and what's similar about the economies of the 1930s and the 2000s.

Part V: The Part of Tens

Ah, the ubiquitous *For Dummies* Part of Tens. This particular collection includes a look at ten good movies set in the Great Depression, ten things invented or popularized in the period, and ten things about the 1930s that weren't so depressing after all.

Icons Used in This Book

Those little round pictures in the left-hand margins are designed to give you a heads-up as you are meandering or racing through the book.

This icon indicates a quote from an article, speech, or document.

 If you see this icon, you're looking at the origin of a law, custom, or other aspect of life.

 This icon alerts you to a fact or idea that you may want to stash away on your brain's hard drive.

 If you see this icon, there's a factoid about contemporary economic conditions lurking about, usually juxtaposed with how things were in the 1930s.

Where to Go from Here

You can go anywhere you want from here. You can start with Chapter 1 or skip around the book. That's how *For Dummies* books are built. Me, I almost always go straight to "The Part of Tens" and then head back to Chapter 1.

But heck, it's your book. Enjoy.

Part I
Heading into a Mess

The 5th Wave   By Rich Tennant

In this part . . .

*T*he Great Depression wasn't nearly as simple an historical period as some people make it out to be. It wasn't just a case of the stock market going down and everyone in the United States going broke.

In this part, you get an overview of the period to whet your appetite for other parts of the book. And before you dine on what comes next, this part gives you a menu of economic terms and concepts that can be useful in understanding the era.

I top off this part with a summary of the country's economic rough times prior to the Great Depression and a fairly detailed look at the decade just before things really got rough.

Chapter 1

It Was a Dark and Stormy Decade

In This Chapter

▶ Getting into a depression

▶ Dragging nearly everyone down

▶ Coping with life on the economy's edges

▶ Trying to make things better

*I*n August 1928, a few months before winning the U.S. presidency, Republican candidate Herbert Hoover boasted that "we in America are nearer to the final triumph over poverty than ever before in the history of any land."

Boy, was he wrong.

Less than a year after Hoover assumed office, the United States was plunged into the deepest and longest economic recession in its history. It wasn't called the *Great Depression* for nothing.

This book tells the story of this period in U.S. history (from the end of 1929 to the country's entry into World War II in late 1941) by looking at the different elements that gave the era its shape, as well as some of the lessons and legacies that the era left us. This chapter tells you what those elements are and where to find out more about them.

Before the Beginning

Every era has a beginning and an end (although historians often disagree about just when they occur). But nothing, not even history, happens independently of everything else.

The first part of this book takes a look at events before the Great Depression, to put the era in context and explain how those events affected things after the depression began. It also provides some explanations of terms and concepts that may prove helpful in understanding the era.

Defining the Great Depression

While the Great Depression was a political, social, and cultural event, as well as a financial calamity, its roots were economic. To have some understanding of what happened, you need to have a grasp of basic economic terms and processes.

On your to-know list: the difference between a depression and a recession; the methods the federal government uses in fighting economic downturns; how the Federal Reserve System works; what role the stock market plays in a recession; and how inflation and deflation factor into recessionary economics. I explain all these terms and concepts in Chapter 2.

Tracking events that led to the Great Depression

The Great Depression wasn't the first time that the U.S. economy hit the skids. In fact, recessions seem to come along with disconcerting regularity. But they do vary in their causes (foreign wars, broken-down railroads, even presidents who don't like banks), their duration, and their lasting impact.

In the period between the end of World War I and the onset of the Great Depression, the United States for the most part enjoyed economic good times under a string of Republican presidents who thought that what was good for big business was good for the rest of the country. There were new or improved products to buy (especially cars), lots of advertising to help talk people into buying them, and easily obtained credit with which to buy them.

But behind the façade of fiscal fun lurked indications that the U.S. economy was living on borrowed time. Large groups of Americans — farmers, minorities, and low-income workers — were not sharing in the good times. The stock market was dangerously overheated, and eventually it melted down.

I offer details of the times before the Great Depression, along with a look at modern stock market crash safeguards (as well as modern credit risks) in Chapter 3.

Sharing the Suffering

While relatively few Americans lost money directly when the U.S. stock market crashed in October 1929, the pain of the general collapse of the economy that followed was felt by almost everyone.

Part II of this book looks at the crushing blows suffered by various groups of people, from bankers to farmers.

Going hungry and jobless as the banks collapse

Trying to figure out why the Great Depression occurred has sparked debate among economists and historians for decades. It's a safe bet there was a combination of reasons for it, from farm failures to too many poor people.

Whatever its causes, the Great Depression's consequences were devastating. While government officials and business leaders initially tried to gloss things over, the U.S. banking system teetered on the edge of collapse. It took a change of administrations and an extended "bank holiday" to pull the banking industry back from the edge.

Unemployment soared, a swelling number of homeless people seemed to occupy every street corner, children went hungry, and World War I veterans marched on Washington, D.C.

To find out more, read Chapter 4, which also looks at the federal program that protects most bank deposits and the three-pronged approach the government has taken since World War II to prevent recessions from becoming depressions.

Looking for help, and striving to help themselves

The Great Depression damaged not only Americans' wallets and purses but also their pride. They had been used to fending for themselves, their families, and their friends. But many of them got into such deep holes that to get out required help on a much larger scale.

The failure to help themselves did not result from lack of trying. People did whatever they could to make money, but most often they fell short. Local governments and private charities did what they could, but it took a change of presidents — and a lot of gritting their teeth — for people to get and take meaningful help from the federal government.

In the meantime, people tried to create jobs and make do with what they had. The result was often a severe blow to their self-esteem and a source of stress in relationships. And hurting the most, as usual, were the nation's minority groups.

Details on all these topics are in Chapter 5, where you'll also find information on the country's 21st-century social services safety net, and how efforts to pay women what they are worth have fared since World War II.

Suffering on the farm

Times were tough among U.S. farmers even before the Great Depression started. They were in some ways victims of their own success: Overproduction of crops led to low prices and small or no profits.

Farmers got little help from the federal government until Franklin D. Roosevelt was elected president in late 1932. While they were waiting, some farmers took things into their own hands by staging mini-revolutions.

Then the Roosevelt administration came up with a plan to help farmers, in large part by paying them not to farm so much. But the federal government couldn't do much about the drought, dust storms, and insect invasions that plagued the agriculture industry during the Great Depression.

You can find out lots more in Chapter 6, along with how U.S. farmers are faring in the 21st century.

Exporting our economic woes

The United States wasn't the only country whose economy was hurting as the 1930s began. In fact, most of the world was feeling financial pain by the end of 1930.

Chapter 7 looks at the international state of things after World War I, including efforts to make things better and efforts that only made things worse.

In that chapter, I explain the role the gold standard played in the world economy, offer a country-by-country view of the Great Depression, and describe how nations that were under the thrall of dictatorships fared. I also introduce two international organizations working in the 21st century to foster economic cooperation among nations.

Coping with Hard Times

The Great Depression was populated with a lot of disparate characters, from the "boxcar children" (kids who hit the road looking for a future) to murderous bank robbers to Shakespeare-spouting labor leaders. Part III of the book covers these characters, as well as discussing migrant farm workers, historic labor strikes, and more.

Looking for better times down the road

While most Americans stayed close to home during the Great Depression, a sizeable number packed up what they had and hit the road. Chapter 8 describes the three groups in which most of those wanderers fell: men looking for work; young people looking for somewhere they wouldn't be a burden and would have a chance at a decent life; and families headed for the "promised land" of California, only to find the promise was mostly false. The desperation of these people is caught in the famous portrait of a migrant woman with her children, shown in Figure 1-1.

Chapter 8 also looks at an ambitious federal program that put Depression-era young men to work improving the national parks and wild lands: the Civilian Conservation Corps. And I discuss the plight of migrant farm workers, and how they are (and aren't) protected differently today.

Photo by Dorothea Lange/Getty Images

Figure 1-1: Migrant mother Florence Thompson with three of her seven children at a farm workers' camp in Nipomo, California.

Making noise with speeches, rallies, and machine guns

Unlike the citizens of some other countries, Americans never rose up in huge numbers to protest the state of things in the Great Depression (unless you count the election of Franklin D. Roosevelt in 1932 and 1936 as a protest).

That doesn't mean, however, that there weren't individuals with big visions, big mouths, and substantial followings. Chapter 9 looks at some of these characters, such as Louisiana Governor and Senator Huey Long and Roman Catholic priest/radio commentator Charles E. Coughlin.

Chapter 9 also covers efforts by communists and Nazis to gain a foothold in the U.S. political scene, as well as the fascination with criminals (both on the movie screen and in real life) during the era and the correlation between recessions and crime.

Putting smiles on depressed faces

One of the sterling qualities of the American character is a refusal to stay down just because things aren't going well. Even in the Great Depression, Americans found ways to have fun.

As Chapter 10 reveals, the most popular ways to fill an increasing amount of leisure time were to listen to the radio and go to the movies. But there were also comic strips, comic books, and pulp magazines to peruse; a new kind of music to listen to; legal liquor to drink; and better cars to drive.

Developing organized labor

Many sectors of the U.S. economy came out of the Great Depression better than they went into it, but perhaps none more so than organized labor.

Of course there were downs as well as ups. As Chapter 11 shows, it took thousands of strikes, scores of deaths, and three new major federal laws for labor to secure a significant role in U.S. politics and economic policy.

Chapter 11 also examines the history of the federal minimum wage since its inception in the Great Depression, and the role of labor in the first decade of the 21st century.

Finding a Way Out of the Great Depression

It took years for the United States to get into the Great Depression and years to get out of it. Part IV of this book examines the two men who bore the most responsibility for turning the country around in the era: President Herbert Hoover and President Franklin D. Roosevelt.

This part also looks in detail at the ambitious agenda of Roosevelt during his time at the helm, and what the effects of that agenda were on later generations. It ends with a look at what can be learned from the Great Depression and applied to other economic crises in U.S. history, particularly in the 21st century.

Swapping leaders mid-Depression

Herbert Hoover and Franklin Roosevelt had very different backgrounds, so perhaps it's not surprising that they took different approaches to dealing with the Great Depression. How well they succeeded, or how badly they failed, is still a source of debate among historians and economists.

Chapter 12 delves into what life experiences each man brought to the White House and how the two approached finding cures for the country's economic illnesses. I also look at their 1932 presidential race and how they handled the handing-off of power from one to the other.

Curing the Great Depression with a New Deal's worth of alphabet soup

Outside of a war, it would be hard to think of another period in U.S. history when so much federal government effort went into solving a problem as during the Great Depression.

The era was a great period for acronyms. There were federal programs from AAA (Agricultural Adjustment Act) to WPA (Works Progress Administration). Heck, even the president had one: FDR. Roosevelt's efforts were called the *New Deal,* even though most historians would say that there were really two New Deals.

A lot of historians would also say that the New Deal(s) had a lot more lasting impact on the role of the federal government in American life than it had an immediate impact on the Great Depression. Read Chapter 13 and decide for yourself. And then read a summary of the status of Social Security and Medicare in the early 21st century.

Lessons and Legacies from the Great Depression

Economically speaking, the worst thing that ever happened to the United States was the Great Depression. But it wasn't the last bad thing to happen to the U.S. economy.

In Chapter 14, I offer a summary of what helped to trigger the Great Depression and what came about as a result. I also review the 11 recessions that have come along since World War II and look at the differences between the mess that started in 1929 and the one that began in late 2007.

Chapter 2

Economic Basics: You Say "Depression," I Say "Broke"

. . . .

. . . .

*I*f you already know the difference between *general equilibrium analysis* and *multilateral trade conventions,* go ahead and skip this chapter because you clearly have a firm grasp of economic theory.

If you're like me, however, you have a tough time figuring out if "three for a dollar" is better than "40 cents each." If that's the case, stick around and peruse some basic economic terms and concepts that will give you a better grasp of what happened in the Great Depression and how things have changed since then.

Depression: A Recession on Steroids

There's an old economists' joke (told mainly by old economists) that a *recession* is when your neighbor loses his job and a *depression* is when you lose yours.

Actually, that's pretty accurate because the major difference between the two is that a depression is more severe than a recession, and thus a bigger economic calamity. Think of a depression as a recession on steroids.

Defining a recession

So what's a recession? Depends on whom you ask. The layman's definition is that a recession occurs when a country's *gross domestic product* (GDP) — the value of all the reported goods and services produced by a country — goes down for two or more consecutive quarters (which means for six months or more).

But the "two quarters or more of declining GDP" definition of a recession is much too simple for many economists. In fact, the official decision as to whether a recession is occurring is left to a private, nonprofit, nonpartisan organization called the National Bureau of Economic Research (NBER). Founded in 1920, the NBER uses data from more than 1,000 university professors and researchers who look at factors such as manufacturing sales, personal income levels, and unemployment rates.

Of course, gathering all that data and analyzing it takes a while, so recessions can be months old before the NBER gets around to telling us one is occurring (or has already been here and gone).

However they're defined, recessions are pretty common, and most economists consider them a natural part of the business cycle. For example, the NBER says the United States had recessions in the first half of 1980; from July 1981 until November 1982; from July 1990 until March 1991; from March to November 2001, and from December 2007 through at least the first quarter of 2009 (the time of this writing).

Sinking into a depression

A recession becomes a depression when things get so bad that a country's GDP drops by more than 10 percent. The last time that happened in the United States, we called it the Great Depression — and not because it was a lot of fun.

To get technical, the Great Depression was really two depressions:

- ✔ From 1929 to 1933, the GDP of the United States plunged 27 percent, or 10 times as much as during any recession since World War II.

- ✔ From 1937 to 1938, after a bit of a rally, the GDP dropped 18 percent.

Compare those numbers to the 1.5 percent decline in the GDP during the 1990–1991 recession or the 0.6 percent it went down in the 2001 recession, and you have some idea how severe the situation was in the 1930s.

Quibbling over definitions

"Let it show on the record that when the American people cried out for economic help, Jimmy Carter took refuge behind a dictionary. Well, if it's a definition he wants, I'll give him one. A recession is when your neighbor loses his job. A depression is when you lose yours. And recovery is when Jimmy Carter loses his."

— 1980 Republican presidential candidate Ronald Reagan, responding to criticism from opponent Carter that Reagan had misused the term "depression."

To be clear, a depression can still happen in modern times. In the 1990s, Finland's economy went into a depression. The Finnish GDP dropped 11 percent after the Soviet Union fell apart and Finland lost its best market for exporting its goods. (And since we've gone international for a minute, a *global recession* is said to occur when global economic growth drops to less than 3 percent.)

Considering Economic Cures

Ordinary recession symptoms are, well, depressing. People buy less stuff because they feel less confident about making money in the future. Factories make less stuff because people are buying less. It can be harder to get credit. Unemployment rises, and the stock market sags. (But as I explain in Part II, the Great Depression's symptoms made an ordinary recession look like a day at the beach.)

Since one of the purposes of having a federal government is to have someone to blame when things go wrong, it seems only fair that we look at methods the federal government can use to try to pull the economy out of a recession.

Setting fiscal policies

Fiscal policies are basically the guidelines the government follows to collect and spend our money. To combat recession, it can take the following steps:

- **Cut taxes** so people and businesses keep more cash for spending on goods and services.
- **Increase spending** on government projects to spur employment.
- **Widen "safety net" programs** such as unemployment insurance.

Adjusting monetary policy: The Fed

The United States pretty much wandered through its first 87 years as a country without a functional national banking system. The First Bank of the United States (1791–1811) and the Second Bank of the United States (1816–1836) were the only sources that issued and backed official U.S. currency. All other banks either operated under state charters or were strictly private enterprises. Each bank issued its own notes, which made for a chaotic system.

In 1863, Congress took the first step toward standardizing banking by passing the National Bank Act. The act established rules for lending practices and required minimum bank reserves. It also slapped a 10 percent tax on state bank notes, which made it financially impractical to use anything but federal currency.

In 1913, Congress created the Federal Reserve System, better known as *the Fed.* The system is essentially the federal government's bank. It oversees 12 Federal Reserve banks located around the country, issues currency, regulates banking operations, and oversees consumer credit rights.

The Fed is in charge of *monetary policy,* which means it helps regulate the economy by manipulating the money supply. In a recession, the Fed can boost economic growth by lowering the amount banks have to keep in reserves, which puts more money in circulation. It can directly pump more money into the economy.

The Fed can also lower the *federal funds rate* (the rate banks charge each other for short-term loans), which means that they can then charge lower interest rates on loans they make to their customers. In the recession that began in late 2007, for example, the Fed cut the federal funds rate nine times in 15 months. It dropped from 4.75 percent to between .25 percent and zero, the lowest in its history.

In 2008, the Fed broke out other tools at its disposal to try to open up the country's credit market. Those tools included buying Treasury bonds to prop up investment in the federal government and buying up loans that private entities had made so they could make new loans without being overburdened with debt.

But keep in mind that at the onset of the Great Depression, the Fed was only 16 years old, and like most teenagers, it didn't always make the best decisions. Moreover, most small banks weren't members of the system, mainly because the Fed snubbed them in favor of big commercial institutions. Both factors turned out to be disastrous, as I explain in Chapter 4.

Sizing Up the Stock Market's Role in a Downturn

The maxim that it takes money to make money has a corollary: Without money, you can't make money. One exception to the corollary is the stock market. If you're willing to gamble, you can make money by borrowing from someone else. But, of course, you can lose money the same way — and lots of it. In this section, I explore the role the stock market can play in exacerbating an economic downturn.

Buying on margin

Let's say you want to buy 1,000 shares of Acme Widget Corp., which is trading at $10 a share. You need $10,000, but you have only $5,000. No problem: You buy on *margin*.

What that means is you borrow the other $5,000 from your stockbroker. Now let's say Acme goes up in price by a dollar a share. Now your 1,000 shares are worth $11,000. You pay back the $5,000 you borrowed, and pocket your original $5,000 plus all of the $1,000 in increased value (minus any broker fees). You have thus profited on twice as many shares as you could have bought on your own.

Of course the reverse is true as well. If the price goes down, the broker may ask you to put some more money into your account as collateral for the amount you borrowed. That's called a *margin call,* and it sort of takes the fun out of buying on margin.

In the 1920s, it was common for investors to leverage as much as 90 percent of a stock purchase. Broker loans rose from $2.5 billion in 1926 to $8.5 billion in October 1929. Brokers charged interest rates of as much as 20 percent. No one cared because stock prices were going up so fast that everyone was making money.

But what was making the market go up so fast was the huge amount of money people were in effect borrowing by buying on margin. They used that money to bid up the price of stocks far out of proportion to the real value of the company issuing the stock. The Radio Corporation of America (RCA), for example, went from $85 to $420 in 1928 despite the fact that it had never paid a dividend.

When the overheated market dropped and margin calls were placed in droves, few people could repay what they had borrowed. "Buying on margin" became a recipe for disaster (see Chapter 3).

Samuel Insull

He began as a protégé to Thomas Edison and ended up face down in a Paris subway. In between, Samuel Insull was a hero of U.S. capitalism — and a villain of the Great Depression.

Insull was born in London in 1859. At 21, he came to New York and became Edison's private secretary and right-hand man. After helping to launch what would become the General Electric Co., Insull moved to Chicago and began building an electric utility super company. By the end of the 1920s, Insull's electric empire stretched to parts of 32 states and had 4 million customers.

To build his company, Insull sold low-priced stocks and bonds in various holding companies he controlled. More than a million people invested. But when the stock market crashed in October 1929, the empire went belly up, and investors lost more than $700 million. Subsequent investigations found an elaborate shell game in which one Insull company would sell property to another Insull firm at a large "profit." Then the property would be sold again to a third Insull firm. The profits, however, existed only on paper.

Insull, who had been on the cover of *Time* magazine in 1929 as a captain of industry and patron of the arts (he gave $20 million to build the Chicago Civic Opera House), found himself on the cover of *Time* in 1934 as the defendant in a fraud and anti-trust case. Although he was eventually acquitted, he was financially and personally ruined, and he left the country. He died in a Paris subway station in 1938 after suffering a heart attack. As a final indignity for a 1920s tycoon, his wallet was stolen from his body.

Nowadays, the U.S. Securities and Exchange Commission, the Federal Reserve Board, the stock exchanges, and the brokerage firms themselves set rules on which stocks you can buy on margin, what the minimum percentage is that investors must put up, and when brokerages must make margin calls. In 2008, investors had to put up a minimum of 50 percent of their own money to buy on margin. That regulation discourages wild speculation and also helps keep such speculation from artificially driving up stock prices.

Making pooled investments

If buying on margin seems a little risky, but you still want to invest in a variety of stocks with just a little money, the solution may be to pool your investment with a bunch of other small investors, give it to a stock-picking professional, and sit back and wait for the profits to roll in. That's basically what a mutual fund is. Mutual funds have been around in their current, regulated form since 1940. In 2008, there were more than 8,000 of them in the United States, with a total investment value of more than $12 trillion.

The 1920s versions were called *investment trusts,* but they were actually more like pyramid schemes than mutual funds. An average investor would buy shares (often on margin) in, say, Big Ed's Investment Trust. Big Ed and other trusts would buy shares of an even bigger trust, which would buy shares in an actual company.

The insidious part of the trusts — beside the incredible risk factor — was that they tied up much of the nation's investment capital. Instead of money going into businesses so that they could expand, make new products, and hire more people, much of that money just floated between trusts for speculation schemes.

Not everyone thought the investment trusts were a wonderful system. President Herbert Hoover called the trust system "an orgy of mad speculation" and noted that "there are crimes far worse than murder for which men should be reviled and punished." But most people shrugged off any criticism.

Factoring in Inflation and Deflation

Inflation is basically a sustained rise in the prices of goods and services. In the United States, the inflation rate is most generally measured by something called the *Consumer Price Index* (CPI). The CPI gauges what a collection of goods and services at the moment, compared to what it cost at a fixed point in the past, which is set at 100. For example, a CPI of 120 would mean the goods and services that used to cost $100 now cost $120 — a 20 percent inflation rate.

Most economists agree that a low inflation is best. In the United States, inflation rates stayed between 1.6 percent and 3.3 percent from 1991 through 2008.

The gold standard: Keeping inflation in check

Since the cost of goods rose more than 1,000 percent in the last 60 years of the 20th century, it's hard to believe that for most of history, inflation hardly existed. In the last third of the 19th century, for example, prices on many things in the United States dropped by nearly 50 percent as advances in transportation and technology made making and moving products cheaper.

Another reason inflation didn't pose much of a problem until the 1920s was that most countries (at least most Western countries) were on the *gold standard.* That term refers to a country tying its currency directly to the amount of gold it holds. The idea is that someone could go to the country's treasury and exchange paper money for an equivalent amount in gold. It also means that countries did business with each other by transferring gold rather than currency. Because the supply of money was limited to the amount of gold a country had on hand, prices and wages tended not to increase dramatically.

The gold standard more or less worked until after World War I, when some countries were so broke that they needed to print more money than they had gold to support. That led to severe inflation, as governments began churning out currency to help people with rising prices on scarce commodities. In post-war Germany, inflation got so bad that people literally had to carry their cash in wheelbarrows so they could buy a loaf of bread. (See Chapter 7 for a discussion of when and why the United States broke away from the gold standard.)

Battling deflation

The opposite of inflation — known as *deflation* — can be even more damaging to an economy. Deflation occurs when prices persistently fall. This decline usually reflects a drop in demand for goods and services. That situation causes oversupplies, which leads to slowed production, which leads to rising unemployment, which leads to even less demand.

Credit shrinks as a result of heightened fears that loans won't be repaid. Consumers stop buying because they're afraid they'll need the money even more in the future, or because they think prices will be even lower tomorrow. And the downward spiral continues.

Because prices drop in a deflationary period, people who bought things on credit — such as houses — find themselves in a bad way. After the October 1929 stock market crash, for example, housing prices dropped steeply. People found they owed more on their homes than they were worth. As unemployment rose, families who could no longer meet their mortgage payments found themselves homeless, as well as jobless.

Chapter 3

Prelude to Disaster: The Economy Prior to 1929

*T*he Great Depression didn't just get great overnight. It took years of events — some related to each other, some not — to give it form, and even then its enormity wasn't recognized right away.

In this chapter, I look at the up-and-down cycles of the U.S. economy prior to the Great Depression; the prosperity of the Roaring Twenties (both real and imagined); the hidden chasm between the rich and the poor that grew during that period; and the "everyone should be rich" ethos that helped trigger the stock market crash at the end of the decade.

Riding the Economic Cycle

Since the birth of the United States, its economy has tended to run in cycles, with periods of somewhere between 10 and 20 years of moderate-to-good times, interspersed with a few years of hard times.

Prior to the rise of capitalism, recessions were usually triggered by a specific external event, such as war, crop failures, or natural disasters. In capitalist economies, however, the causes of hard times are often attributed to the forces of the marketplace: supply and demand, consumer spending and saving, and the vagaries of people's responses to economic events.

Whatever the cause (and there is ceaseless debate among economists about precisely what causes recessions), the advent of hard times is often preceded by calamities in the banking industry and stock market. Hard times also often come hard on the heels of over-speculation in land or securities. Creditors call in loans, money supplies get tight, and businesses close.

"It has been a history of extravagant expansions in the business of the country, followed by ruinous contractions," said President James Buchanan in 1857. "At successive intervals the best and most enterprising men have been tempted to their ruin by excessive bank loans of mere paper credit, exciting them to extravagant importations of foreign goods, wild speculations, and ruinous and demoralizing stock gambling."

But we always seem to get over it.

Some hard times before World War 1

The precise beginnings and endings of recessions are as elusive as their exact causes. Keeping that in mind, though, following is a look at a half dozen tough economic times that the United States went through prior to World War I.

You can't tax the Feds (1819–1824)

The end of the War of 1812 (in 1815) left the United States feeling financially frisky. U.S. goods were selling well in Europe. Banks were liberal in their lending, especially to finance the sale of public lands in the West. Public land sales rose from $4 million in 1816 to $13.6 million in 1818.

Things were going so well, in fact, that stock traders on New York's Wall Street were compelled to take their business literally off the street in March 1817, moving it indoors and forming the New York Stock Exchange.

But a number of factors conspired to create this country's first great economic crisis. Perpetual wars between France and England finally ended in 1815, spurring economic growth in those countries that competed with U.S. production. U.S. banks issued their own currency with little ability to back it in *specie* or *hard money,* meaning gold and silver coins. When they needed more money, they simply printed more, which resulted in rapid inflation.

In 1816, Congress established the Second Bank of the United States (the first went out of business in 1811) in an effort to rein in the independent banks and establish some uniformity to currency. In 1819, the Bank began calling in loans it had made to state banks, and it demanded hard money as payment. (Part of the reason was that the United States needed to pay back — in gold — foreign loans it had received to finance the Louisiana Purchase in 1803.) The state banks, in turn, began calling in loans they had made, and many debtors couldn't meet their obligations. Wages fell, businesses failed, and banks closed.

Several states tried to counter the Bank's calling in of loans by imposing taxes on the Bank's assets within their borders. But in 1820, the U.S Supreme Court ruled that while the federal government had the constitutional authority to tax state and private banks, the states did not have the right to tax a federal institution. It wasn't until the mid-1820s that things leveled off.

The president who didn't like banks (1837–1843)

Through the last half of the 1820s and first half of the 1830s, the U.S. economy chugged along. By 1834, the national debt had been paid off. Roads, railways, and canals were being built at a rapid pace. Public lands in the West were being snapped up, in large part by speculators. Land sales soared from around $2.3 million in 1830 to $24.9 million by 1836.

To finance all that activity, banks were issuing loans like crazy. Not only that, but they were also still printing their own currency to lend. Inflation resulted, but few people minded because there seemed to be plenty of cash to cover things.

One guy who did mind was the president of the United States. Andrew Jackson had an antipathy to banks in general, in part because he had once lost a lot of money in one. He particularly disliked the Second Bank of the United States, believing it was unconstitutional. As a westerner, he also disliked what he viewed as the Bank's favoritism toward the desires of northeastern financiers and speculators.

So in 1832, Jackson vetoed a bill that would have extended the charter of the Bank past its 1836 expiration date. He also withdrew the federal government's money from the Bank and deposited it in "pet banks" chartered by various states. In July 1836, Jackson delivered another financial body blow by issuing the "Specie Circular," or Coinage Act. It decreed that the federal government would accept payment for public lands in gold or silver coin only. Jackson's idea was to end rampant speculation and inflationary practices spurred by banks that printed notes.

By the time Jackson left office in March 1837, the economic bubble had begun to burst. Foreign investors decided they wouldn't accept U.S. paper either, and they called in their substantial loans. U.S. banks, in turn, called in their loans to people who had nothing to repay them with but paper. By April, businesses were failing. Unemployment reached 10 percent, and about 800 banks closed. With little hard money in circulation, deflation took over for inflation, and wages and prices dropped.

Jackson's successor, Martin Van Buren, took the heat for Jackson's actions. Van Buren lost his 1840 reelection bid, and the economy stayed in the tank until 1843.

Bad news travels fast (1857–1859)

While it didn't last as long as the recessions of 1819 and 1837, the 1857 downturn was remarkable in several other aspects. The immediate sparks were the failure of the New York branch of a major financial company called the Ohio Life Insurance and Trust Company, due to embezzlement; and the sinking of the *SS Central America,* which was carrying 30,000 pounds of gold from the San Francisco mint to eastern banks.

Both events took place within three weeks of each other in late summer, and news of both was quickly spread around the country by the telegraph, still a relatively new medium. The immediacy of the news heightened the events' impacts.

But there were more fundamental causes for the recession. The end of the Crimean War between Britain and Russia drove down demand for U.S. grain. The panicked stock selling that followed news of the trust company collapse and gold ship sinking induced British investors to withdraw funds from U.S. banks.

The recession was notable for one other reason. The downturn had less of an impact on the South, where the cotton industry was solid. That encouraged many southerners to believe they could make an economic go of it without the North, should the country split up.

The Railroad Depression (1873–1879)

Following the end of the Civil War in 1865, the U.S. economy found itself driven by a boom in railroad construction. Between 1866 and 1873, 35,000 miles of track were laid. Railroads trailed only agriculture in importance to the country's financial well-being.

In 1873, however, Congress passed a bill that called for backing U.S. currency with gold only. Silver coins were out, and the Treasury quit buying silver at a fixed price. The move depressed silver prices, reduced the money supply, and created uncertainty in the economy.

On September 18, 1873, uncertainty turned to panic when a major bank, Jay Cooke & Co., declared bankruptcy. The firm, which became prominent marketing Union bonds during the Civil War, was pushing a plan to build a second transcontinental railroad. Unable to attract enough backing, Cooke collapsed.

The failure started a deluge of panicky unloading of stocks. A stunned New York Stock Exchange closed for ten days. About 25 percent of U.S. railroads went belly up, thousands of auxiliary businesses failed, and unemployment rose to 14 percent by 1876.

The job losses, combined with wage reductions, spurred labor unrest around the country. Acrimony between labor and management lasted well beyond the end of the depression, which lasted until 1879.

When the gold ran out (1893–1897)

The depression that began in 1893 in many ways paralleled the downturn of 1873. In February 1893, the largest railroad company, the Philadelphia and Reading, went bankrupt. More railroads and other businesses went under. Unemployment percentages climbed into the teens. Hard times in Europe dried up investment from other countries.

But there was a wrinkle to the 1893 depression that hadn't happened before, and it had to do with the U.S. money supply. In 1890, Congress had decided to require the U.S. Treasury to buy silver with notes that could be redeemed in gold.

Coupled with a demand by European investors to be paid only in gold, the policy resulted in shrinking U.S. gold reserves. In April 1893, officials announced that the nation's gold supply had dipped below the $100 million minimum that federal law required be kept on hand. Panic set in. Nervous investors, fearful they would be paid in silver rather than gold, began runs on banks. The stock market crashed as banks collapsed. Violent labor strikes paralyzed railways, as they had in the 1870s.

Ultimately, the Treasury sold bonds to obtain enough gold to build up its reserves, and the law requiring the federal purchase of silver with gold-backed certificates was repealed. But the country didn't fully recover until 1897.

The bankers' panic (1907–1908)

As recessions go, the Panic of 1907 was relatively short-lived. But its eventual impact was significant. It started when two Montana mine owners and a New York City banker tried to corner the national copper market in October 1907.

The effort by F.A. Heinze, his brother Otto, and Charles W. Morse involved taking control of banks and trusts, and using their assets to take over the copper market. Doing so would allow them to set any price they pleased for the metal. But the scheme failed. As a result, the companies involved suffered huge losses. People began pulling money out of banks and the stock market, which lost half its value.

Enter an unlikely hero: 70-year-old financier J.P. Morgan. The richest banker in the country pledged huge personal sums to shore up shaky banks. He dragooned other financiers to do the same and was joined by the U.S. Treasury. The rescue plan worked. But the episode rekindled debate about the lack of a U.S. central bank to oversee the money supply and coordinate bailouts in dire times.

In 1908, Congress established a National Monetary Commission, charging it with finding a way to regulate U.S. banking. It took until 1911 for the commission to craft a plan, and another two years for Congress to approve it. On December 22, 1913, President Woodrow Wilson signed the bill creating the Federal Reserve System. Before it passed the measure, however, the Senate removed a provision that would have offered some insurance for bank depositors. That change would cost a lot of people a lot of money in coming years.

Not much fun after World War 1

The First World War (1914–1918) had a major impact on the U.S. economy — and a big role in the creation of the Great Depression.

The United States stayed out of the first three years of the war, which pitted the Allies (chiefly Britain, France, and Russia) against the Central Powers (chiefly Germany, Austria-Hungary, and the Ottoman Empire). U.S. manufacturers and farmers took advantage of Europe's simultaneous preoccupation with the war and demands for food and goods by in essence becoming the war's supermarket. Between 1914 and 1918, U.S. steel production doubled, and farm exports tripled.

When the United States finally entered the war in April 1917 on the side of the Allies (in part because they were better customers), the U.S. economy was bolstered by a wave of government spending, which rose from $1.3 billion in 1916 to a hefty $15.6 billion in 1918. The government raised revenues by increasing taxes and selling bonds. The Feds also basically took over the running of the economy. Federal boards and commissions oversaw food production and pricing, fuel allocation, railroad operations, and labor relations.

Organized labor didn't mind the federal oversight because it gave some protection to those trying to organize labor unions. Union membership increased by 40 percent between 1915 and 1918. The labor shortage caused by the military draft brought significant numbers of women into the workforce, and some 500,000 African Americans migrated from the South to take jobs in the North and Midwest. Wages went up, and life wasn't bad on the home front.

Then the war ended in November 1918. More than $3 billion in federal war-related contracts were canceled almost overnight. Several million soldiers and sailors became civilians again, looking for jobs. Racial tensions rose as black workers were shoved out of jobs to make room for returning white workers. Scores of strikes sparked charges that unions were in league with communists.

The switch from a wartime economy to a peacetime economy triggered a sharp recession in 1920. An oversupply of food and other products caused severe *deflation* (a big drop in prices, followed by stalled production, rising unemployment, and even less demand). The unemployment rate reached 11 percent by 1921.

Prodded by his Secretary of Commerce, Herbert Hoover, President Warren G. Harding convened a meeting of 300 business and banking leaders in September 1921 to discuss the unemployment problem. The Unemployment Conference eventually organized state and local relief efforts such as public works projects and "work sharing" programs. This was the first time a major federal effort was made to try to assuage the pains caused by a recession.

Things did get better, as they tend to do. Manufacturers retooled from wartime products to consumer goods. Women went home, opening jobs for returning veterans. By 1923, the economy was humming again, at least for most people.

But the war left lasting marks on the U.S. economy. Technological advances necessitated by wartime demands increased productivity. That spurred the development of new products or improvements on old ones, which in turn spurred consumer demand.

The role of the United States in the world economy also changed. Prior to World War I, it had been a *debtor* nation, meaning its overseas investments were smaller than the investments other countries had in the United States. That changed after the war, as huge public and private U.S. loans to war-torn European countries made us a *creditor* nation. New York replaced London as the Western world's financial center. And that was fine, as long as the U.S. economy remained healthy.

Sharing the Good Times with "Silent Cal"

Warren G. Harding campaigned for the U.S. presidency in 1920 using a slogan he coined himself: "A return to normalcy." He had meant to say "normality," which should give you some idea of what a nincompoop Harding was. Still, the slogan struck a chord with voters. After the war and the post-war struggles, Americans were ready to kick up their heels a bit and enjoy life. Harding was elected in a landslide, and the Roaring Twenties started getting noisy.

Harding himself missed most of it, having had the good sense to die in August 1923 and thus escape an administration notable mainly for political scandal. But his successor, Calvin Coolidge, shared Harding's political philosophy that the chief role of the government when it came to the economy was to foster business growth.

Known as "Silent Cal" for his aversion to speechmaking, Coolidge did manage to observe aloud that "the chief business of the American people is business," and "the man who builds a factory builds a temple, and the man who works there, worships there."

All three Republican administrations during the 1920s (Harding's, Coolidge's, and Herbert Hoover's) did what they could to foster business growth. Tariffs were raised to protect U.S. manufacturers. Tax rates for the wealthy were lowered, purportedly to encourage them to invest more. The Federal Reserve Board kept interest rates low, so money was easier to borrow.

The presidents' perspectives reflected a highly popular sentiment of the times, which was reflected by the title of a 1929 article in *Ladies' Home Journal:* "Everybody Ought To Be Rich." In an era known at the time as "the Coolidge Prosperity," the acquisition of wealth to finance the acquisition of consumer goods, from electric irons to mouthwash, became tantamount to being a good American.

"As consumers of wealth, we exhibit mental and moral solidarity," asserted Franklin Giddings, a Columbia University sociologist, in 1922. "We want the same things. We have the same tastes."

The United States did seem richer. The gross domestic product grew from $51 billion in 1920 to $97 billion in 1929. *Disposable income* (the amount left after taxes are paid) increased from $33.3 billion in 1918 to $77.5 billion in 1928. And there was no consumer item more attractive to disposable income in the 1920s than the automobile.

Driving to the good life

In October 1923, *National Geographic* ran an article reporting that there were 13 million "motorcars" on U.S. roads. The author gushed, "The demand for initiative and enterprise in those who own and operate an automobile are giving to the American people a training the value of which cannot be estimated in dollars and cents."

Notwithstanding the author's sentiment, the dollars-and-cents impact the automobile had on 1920s' America was pretty hefty:

- By the end of the decade, one in every eight U.S. jobs was related to the automobile, from the people who made tires to the people who ran roadside motor hotels, or "motels."

- By 1925, there were 17.5 million motor vehicles registered in the country, and by 1929, there were 27 million — or one for every five Americans. Estimates showed there were more cars in New York than in all of Europe.

- Production methods had improved so much that a car that took 14 hours to build in 1913 was coming off the assembly line at a rate of every 10 seconds by 1925. The production speedup was reflected in lower prices. A car that cost the equivalent of two years' average wages before World War I cost about three months' worth in 1929.

But the *National Geographic* writer was correct in that the value of a car transcended its price for most Americans. They were no longer captives of the streetcar or bus schedule. They could live farther away from work, shop in distant stores, and take motor vacations.

Early cars had been simple transportation machines, with no frills. Automaker Henry Ford reportedly said that Ford buyers could have a car in any color they wanted "as long as they wanted black" (which dried faster than other colors and thus speeded up production). But as they became more acquisitive, Americans wanted more from their autos. Cars became an extension of a family's lifestyle, a status symbol. "[H]is motor car was poetry and tragedy, love and heroism," Sinclair Lewis wrote in his 1922 novel *Babbitt*.

Ford stubbornly stuck to no-frills cars (although he did close down for six months in 1927 to retool his factory for production of a new model — the Model A). However, Ford's rivals, particularly William C. Durant at General Motors, began offering extra features for extra money. The company began offering upscale models that made them stand out from the neighbors' cars.

And if someone couldn't afford to pay cash for a car, no problem. In 1919, GM started the General Motors Acceptance Corporation (GMAC) to let buyers purchase on the installment plan. By 1926, 75 percent of all auto buyers were buying on credit.

A dollar down, a dollar a week: Living on credit

In 1919, the same year that General Motors Acceptance Corporation began offering credit to car buyers, GM bought a small refrigerator company called Frigidaire. Realizing that a refrigerator, like a car, was basically a big box with a motor, GM began adapting its methods of making and selling cars to making and selling refrigerators. That included letting customers buy on credit.

Americans had traditionally viewed buying anything other than real estate on credit as something between embarrassing and shameful. But in the 1920s, Ben Franklin's "a penny saved is a penny earned" maxim seemed old hat. A 1928 business yearbook noted that installment buying "is now recognized as an integral part of our economic life."

By the end of the decade, more than 60 percent of appliances and furniture was being bought on installment plans. Consumer debt rose from $2.6 billion in 1920 to $7.1 billion in 1929. Installment buying at such high levels kept product demand — and thus production — at higher rates than the amount of real money in the economy could sustain indefinitely. The result was a situation that could — and did — lead to severe deflation.

In late 1928, the National Association of Credit Men, a group of 30,000 merchants and manufacturers, warned that "making it easy for people to buy beyond their needs or to buy before they have saved enough to gratify their wishes tends to encourage a condition that . . . supports a form of transaction for which credit buying is not primarily intended." But not many people were listening.

Creating demand for needless things

One of the challenges in a consumer-driven economy is to convince people that they need to keep consuming. That's where advertising comes in, and in the 1920s, it became both an art and a science.

Traditional advertising had merely suggested the *availability* of a product. But in the 1920s, ads earnestly explained the *necessity* of a product, even when the necessity was wholly fabricated. Normal health and hygiene conditions were elevated to serious-sounding maladies: bad breath became "halitosis," sour stomach was "acidosis," and stinky feet "bromodosis," all of which were curable by some product or other.

The economist Stuart Chase observed in 1925 that advertising "creates a dream world: smiling faces, shining teeth, school girl complexions, cornless feet, perfect fitting union suits, distinguished collars, wrinkleless pants, odorless breath, regularized bowels (and) happy homes in New Jersey — 15 minutes from Hoboken."

The ad game became a sophisticated avocation. Its most successful practitioners included Bruce Barton, who invented the baking icon Betty Crocker and wrote a best-selling book called *The Man Nobody Knows*. The book, which sold a staggering 700,000 copies between 1925 and 1927, portrayed Jesus Christ as a "super salesman" and "the father of modern business." There was also Edward Bernays, who had honed his pitchman's skills by spending summers in his youth with his uncle, Sigmund Freud. Bernays is credited — or blamed — for breaking down the taboo against women smoking in public by promoting cigarettes as "torches of independence" for the modern female.

Advertisers used sex, celebrities, and pseudo-science to sell, and they utilized newspapers, mass-circulation magazines, and the ubiquitous and new-in-the-1920s medium of radio to make their pitches national. In 1919, total advertising in the United States cost an estimated $684 million. By 1929, it was a $3 billion-a-year business — and inspiring a whole lot of consumption, much of it on credit.

Getting Richer, or Staying Poor

While it may have appeared on the surface that 1920s America was installment-buying itself a life of ease and comfort, the reality was far different.

Most working people still put in six-day weeks. Paid vacations and pensions were rare. The U.S. Supreme Court struck down minimum wage laws for women and children during the decade. Job security was rare. A man held his job until he was too old or infirm to be as productive as a younger man, and then he was out the door.

Some employers adopted paternalistic practices (known as *welfare capitalism*) to keep unions at bay. Henry Ford, for example, periodically raised wages and shortened workweeks. There were sometimes fringe benefits, such as company picnics. But when company profits slipped, the fringe benefits quickly disappeared.

A much worse problem was the mountainous disparity in the distribution of wealth, as evidenced by some statistics:

- ✔ The wealthiest 1 percent of Americans saw their incomes increase 75 percent in the 1920s, while the average worker's income rose just 9 percent. The 24,000 richest U.S. households controlled as much combined wealth as the 11.5 *million* at the bottom.

- ✔ While 0.1 percent of U.S. households had 34 percent of the country's savings, 80 percent had no savings at all.

- ✔ About 40 percent of American families in 1929 earned less than the $1,500 annual income that the federal government deemed the poverty level. That compares to 8.4 percent living at the federal poverty level of $15,000 in 2006. In 1929, only 2.3 percent earned more than $10,000 a year. In 2006, 24.2 percent earned more than $100,000, a comparable inflation-adjusted figure.

As ominous for the economy was the growing gap between productivity and wages. From 1923 to 1929, productivity per hour (the amount of goods made) rose 32 percent. During the same period, wages rose just 8 percent.

What that meant was there were too many things being produced and not enough people with the money to buy them. A person earning $100,000 a year was making 50 times more than the person earning $2,000 a year. But the wealthier person wasn't likely to buy 50 times as many cars or radios or refrigerators, or to spend 50 times as much for them.

So the rich put much of their excess money into luxury items (the making of which didn't employ a lot of people) or into investments. That led to more productivity but not more money in the pockets of average Americans.

Feeling downtrodden on the farm

If the average urban worker wasn't exactly rolling in clover during the 1920s, he had it made compared to his cousin on the farm. In fact, the best days for U.S. farmers had come and gone by the time the 1920s started.

Sweet deals in the Sunshine State

The stock market wasn't the only place people were looking to get rich in the 1920s. For example, there was the Florida land boom of 1925–1926.

An estimated $450 million poured into the state, lured by promoters who promised lush waterfront paradises or lively resort cities. Many of those who bought didn't care if they were actually buying fetid swampland, as long as they could resell at a higher price to someone else. And enough were able to do just that, keeping the scheme going for months.

Eventually the speculative bubble burst, just as two hurricanes slammed into the state, killing some 400 people and leaving 25,000 people homeless. By 1928, more than a hundred Florida and Georgia banks that grew fat on speculation money went under, taking much of the money with them.

The ridiculousness of the situation wasn't lost on the Marx Brothers, who lampooned it in their 1929 film *The Coconuts:* "Why, you can get stucco," leers pitchman Groucho in one scene. "Oh, how you can get stucco."

During World War I, the U.S. government encouraged farmers to produce as much as they could to help feed the country's European allies. So farmers mortgaged more land, doubling their total mortgage debt between 1910 and 1920. As mechanized vehicles such as trucks and tractors replaced horses and mules, 25 million acres once used to grow animal feed were put into crop production for humans.

But when the war ended, the European markets dried up, and prices dropped. Cotton that had sold for 35 cents a pound during the war slumped to 16 cents in 1920. Corn that had sold for $1.50 a bushel slipped to 52 cents. Farm income during the decade dropped 50 percent. Bankruptcies in the Midwest alone quadrupled, and more than 3 million people left farms for towns and cities.

In the South, half of the farmers lived on rented land. Those who lacked their own capital had to pledge shares of their crops as payment for rent and supplies. Most of these sharecroppers were African Americans, and almost all of them were desperately poor.

Congress made some effort to help, twice passing bills that would have established "parity" programs in which the federal government would buy surplus crops at guaranteed prices, and then sell them overseas for whatever the market would pay. But Coolidge vetoed both bills. "Farmers have never made money," he said. "I don't believe we can do much about it."

When Hoover became president in 1929, he pushed through Congress a bill that called for government price subsidies for farm products. Within months, however, the rural depression of the 1920s collided with the Great Depression of the 1930s, and life for U.S. farmers only got worse.

Immigrants and African Americans: Getting by at the bottom of the heap

Following World War I, America's distaste for foreign entanglements led to a series of laws limiting immigration. Even so, the 1930 Census showed that 10 percent of the population was foreign-born. Handicapped by language and cultural barriers, immigrants got the worst jobs and lived in the worst parts of towns and cities. As the Great Depression took hold in the early 1930s, many of them would turn around and go back where they originated.

Tightening immigration quotas meant U.S. industry had to find a new source of workers. A half million African Americans left the South for factory jobs during the war. Another 1 million would do the same during the 1920s. But they remained second-class citizens. Infant mortality rates for African Americans were twice those of white Americans. Life expectancies were 15 years shorter.

In the Southwest, a half million Mexicans, whose country had been exempted from the immigration restrictions, came for work, most as migrant farm laborers. Like African Americans, the Mexicans were generally tolerated, more than accepted, as a source of labor, and their lots would get worse as the 1920s ended.

Crashing with the Market

Few Americans actually had a direct stake in the stock market in 1929. About 3 million people, or about 2.5 percent of the country's population of 120 million, owned shares. Only half of those who did own stocks owned enough to involve a brokerage account. Playing the market was mostly a rich person's game, with 30 percent of all 1929 dividends going to families with annual incomes of more than $100,000.

But if they weren't actually in the stock market, it seemed everyone talked about it. A visiting British journalist noted that whatever topic a conversation started with, "in the end you had to talk about the stock market, and that was when the conversation became serious."

Buying into the market on credit

Both the wealthy and the wannabe wealthy often bought stock on credit. By putting just 10 percent down on a purchase, for example, a stock buyer could buy 10 times as much stock as he could afford out of his or her own pocket. (See the Chapter 2 discussion on buying on margin.) That was all right with brokers and other lenders because they were borrowing money from Federal Reserve banks at 5 percent and charging 12 percent or more to their clients. The total loaned by brokers rose from $4.4 billion at the beginning of 1927 to $8.5 billion in the fall of 1929.

The problem was that if brokers called in their loans, investors had to sell their stock at whatever price it was trading at to repay the money. If the stock was down, both the lender and the borrower could be in big trouble.

But there was certainly money to be made, at least for a while. The Dow Jones Industrial Average (a weighted average of 30 major companies' stock prices) doubled from the beginning of 1928 to September 1929. But the market was fueled by speculation, not value. As long as stock prices kept going up, people weren't much interested in what a company produced or if its products were turning a profit. So money kept pouring into the market.

"The ranks of the inexperienced — the 'suckers' — were swelled by numbers of men who had been attracted by newspaper stories of the big, easy profits to be made in a tremendous bull market," a brokerage house observer wrote in a 1928 article in *The Nation*. "These amateurs were not schooled in markets that had seen stringent, panicky drops in prices. They came in on a rising tide."

There were warnings that the tide of rising stock prices must inevitably recede. In March 1929, respected financier Paul M. Warburg wrote that "if orgies of unrestrained speculation are permitted to spread too far . . . the ultimate collapse is certain not only to affect the speculators themselves, but also to bring about a great depression involving the entire country."

Getting gored by the bulls

October 24, 1929, was a cool and overcast Thursday on New York's Wall Street. Inside the New York Stock Exchange, the morning's session began more or less as usual. Then, at about 11 a.m., people began selling. And selling. And selling.

"The deluge broke," *New York Times* reporter Elliott W. Bell wrote some years later. "It came with a speed and ferocity that left men dazed . . . it was the most terrifying and unreal day I have ever seen on the Street."

When the session closed, a record 12.9 million shares had sold — so many that the ticker tape machine that relayed market prices around the country was more than four hours behind by the end of the day.

As the market sank on October 24, which came to be known as "Black Thursday," a half dozen Wall Street bankers tried to calm things down by buying up shares. One of the bankers, Thomas W. Lamont, calmly told reporters "it seems there has been some distress selling in the market."

The bankers' effort failed. On October 29, which became known as "Black Tuesday," another stock-selling stampede broke out. More than $9 billion (about $113 billion in 2008 dollars) was lost in a single five-hour period, and 16.4 million shares were sold, a record that would stand until 1978. Figure 3-1 offers a glimpse into the chaos that erupted that day. Before the market hit bottom in July 1932, its *stock index* (a measurement of the market's value) fell from 452 to 58. It would take more than a decade to fully recover.

Figure 3-1: Workers flood New York City streets in a panic following the Black Tuesday stock market crash.

Contrary to popular myth, there was no mass exodus of despondent brokers and speculators through skyscraper windows. But it's a safe bet that few investors felt like singing along to a new tune that had debuted at a Manhattan ballroom that week.

It was called "Happy Days Are Here Again."

Lessons Learned

Following are two key lessons that Americans learned — or should have learned — from the events leading up to, and including, the stock market crash of 1929.

It's easy to borrow, hard to repay

If there is one lesson to be learned from the 1920s, it's that using credit to buy things can be a slippery slope to chronic debt.

When the Great Depression ended with the start of World War II, Americans who had lived through the hardest of hard times did become a nation of savers. Personal savings as a percentage of personal wealth reached a heady 26 percent during the war.

But after the war, consumerism collided with the ascension of credit cards that allowed repayment in installments. In 1978, a U.S. Supreme Court decision made it easier for banks to charge higher interest rates on credit cards and cross state lines in pursuit of customers. In the 1980s, rapidly rising inflation made the use of credit cards an attractive way to buy things before their prices went up. In the 1990s, home equity loans allowed consumers to tap money that they couldn't otherwise access without selling their houses.

By the beginning of the 21st century, Americans didn't even have to seek credit — it sought *them* through endless offers that even included paying off old credit cards with new ones. Many consumers developed a sense of entitlement. One college professor reported that his students referred to credit cards as "yuppie food stamps."

The resulting numbers were both stunning and sobering:

- ✔ Consumer credit, not including mortgages, jumped from $700 billion in 1988 to $2.6 trillion in 2008. Over the same period, the average personal savings rate dropped from 8 percent to less than 1 percent.

✔ In 2007, U.S. families were devoting 14 percent of their disposable income to paying off debt, the highest rate ever.

✔ From 2005 to 2008, the amount of credit card debt reported in personal bankruptcy filings tripled, to $61,000.

When the 2007 recession began, however, consumer credit began to dry up. Credit cards became harder to get, late payment fees increased, and down payments rose. In August 2008, consumer borrowing fell for the first time in a decade, indicating that — maybe — the credit lesson of the 1920s may be sinking in.

The stock market can go down

Could a big stock market crash happen again? Well, measured just by the size of the one-day decline in the stock market, it already did. On October 19, 1987, the market dropped 22.6 percent, far more than the 12.8 percent it dropped on October 29, 1929.

But after the 1987 crash, the various stock exchanges installed safeguards to protect against a complete meltdown. The safeguards included limiting computerized transactions in overheated selling sessions, requiring the markets to close after they fall by certain levels over a specified time, and requiring trading firms to have more capital available if there's a run on the market. Congress has also created two agencies that keep an eye on things:

✔ The **Securities Investor Protection Corporation:** Established in 1970, the SIPC doesn't provide insurance against broker fraud, but it does help investors recover their securities or cash when a brokerage firm is closed due to bankruptcy.

✔ The **U.S. Securities and Exchange Commission:** Formed in 1934 to restore public confidence, the SEC regulates the stock market and the securities industry. The five-member commission oversees requirements that publicly traded companies disclose accurate information about their firms. It also investigates and brings civil prosecutions in fraud cases.

But even with all these safeguards available, it's worth noting that a whole lot more people have something at stake: In the 1920s, around 2 percent of households had a stake in the market. In the 2000s, more than 50 percent did.

Part II
Getting Depressed

The 5th Wave   By Rich Tennant

In this part . . .

Most Americans had no direct stake in the stock market crash of late 1929 and consequently had no idea what kind of economic tsunami was about to come down on them.

All too soon, they found out.

In this part, I look at both the causes of the Great Depression and the consequences, including the near-collapse of the nation's banking system, record unemployment, and the resulting crushing poverty that followed. I focus on the impact on the American family, the devastation suffered by U.S. farmers, and — oh yeah — how the rest of the world was getting along.

Chapter 4

Going Bust: A Depression Is Born

*T*he Great Depression may have started with the stock market crash in October 1929 (see Chapter 3), but the crash didn't shoulder all the blame.

In this chapter, I look at some of the contributing factors to the creation of the Great Depression, the early and abortive attempts to deal with it, the collapse and resurrection of the U.S. banking system, and how the consequences of the crippled economy played out in the first few years after the stock market crash.

Analyzing What Happened

Explaining precisely what caused the Great Depression is like trying to nail an egg to the wall: messy and unfulfilling. In fact, historians and economists have argued with each other almost since the Great Depression started about precisely what caused it, and no one has yet come up with a universally accepted explanation.

It's reasonably safe to say that a combination of factors contributed to the sharp economic downturn that began in late 1929, including the bursting of the speculation bubble in the stock market, a drop in consumer spending, a rotten banking system, and too many poor people.

These factors were aggravated by tardy, insufficient, and misdirected efforts to fix things. The result was that a nasty recession turned into a ten-year economic ordeal.

Here's a look at some of the ingredients that created this economic stew:

- ✔ **The stock market crash:** In addition to financially wiping out tens of thousands of individual investors and speculators, the collapse of the market crippled banks that had made loans secured by stocks. It also greatly reduced public confidence in the economy, which meant people reduced their spending and investing.

- ✔ **Too much stuff:** In the 1920s, technological advances and innovative manufacturing techniques, such as mechanized assembly lines, meant U.S. workers were making things faster. In fact, they were making things too fast. Estimates indicate that by 1929, the country was producing 17 percent more than it could buy. The result of all this overproduction was a sudden halt to manufacturing in many areas when the economy slowed. That halt led to layoffs and higher unemployment, which naturally led to even less buying.

- ✔ **Too many poor people:** Most of the nation's personal wealth was concentrated in the pockets of relatively few people. In 1929, 40 percent of U.S. families had annual incomes below the federal poverty level. They could buy very little, and richer people couldn't buy enough to make up the difference. By 1930, the result was deflation: oversupplies of goods, lower prices, lower wages, and higher unemployment. See Chapter 3 for more details on the over-concentration of wealth.

- ✔ **Failure on the farm:** Agriculture was a major element of the economy. In 1929, 25 percent of U.S. jobs were still on the farm. But overproduction, low crop prices, foreign competition, disastrous weather, and lack of credit all combined to make a mess of agriculture. See Chapter 6 for a longer look at the fate of farmers in the Great Depression.

- ✔ **Other countries:** Much of Europe suffered a major economic hangover throughout the 1920s from the horrors of World War I. The United States made efforts to cure that hangover with loans during and after the war — $27 billion from 1914 to 1929 — most of which weren't repaid. But U.S. loans began to dry up in the late 1920s as American dollars were diverted into the overheated stock market.

That situation made it hard for other countries to buy U.S. products. The problem got much worse in 1930, when Congress approved a bill that steeply raised *tariffs* (taxes charged on imported goods). Other countries retaliated with their own tariffs, and international trade slowed to a trickle.

Putting a Happy Face on a Gloomy Economy

In June 1930, a group of clergymen visited the White House, hoping to persuade President Herbert Hoover to expand a federal public works program and put more people to work.

"Gentlemen," Hoover told them, "you have come 60 days too late. The depression is over."

It wasn't, of course. But Hoover wasn't alone in his cheery statements in the months following the collapse of the stock market. Other officials and academics pronounced that the "economic correction" (Hoover used the term "depression" because he thought it sounded better than "panic" or "crisis") would start getting better any day. They pointed to a brief — and only temporary — rally in the market in spring 1930 as proof things were turning around. Business leaders made public pledges to enlarge their enterprises. Henry Ford even pledged to raise wages for his workers to $7 a day.

The media did its part to accentuate the positive. *The New York Times* declared the most important story of 1929 was not the stock market crash but the Antarctic expedition of Admiral Richard Byrd. In its December 1930 issue, *Fortune* magazine hyperbolized that "to compute the total construction investment of U.S. industry in 1930 would be a mathematical undertaking of colossal complexity."

But the numbers told a much less rosy story. Private capital investment (money spent for fixed assets such as land, buildings, or machinery) fell from $35 billion in 1929 to $23 billion in 1930, on its way to an emaciated $3.9 billion in 1932. One survey showed the earnings of 200 non-automotive companies declined 19 percent in the first three months of 1930 compared to 1929. Auto company earnings plummeted 40 percent in that same period.

While Ford did raise wages, he did so by giving raises to some workers and laying off others. Then he contracted the work of those people who had been laid off to other companies, which paid their workers as little as $1 a day. Such tactics helped nearly triple the number of unemployed Americans, from 1.5 million in 1929 to 4.3 million in 1930.

As the reality of the situation began to sink in, many of Hoover's top aides, particularly Treasury secretary Andrew Mellon, advised the president to do nothing. Business leaders joined the chorus.

"The fact that we have let nature take its course may augur well for the ultimate prosperity of the country," said New York Stock Exchange president Richard Whitney. Others saw that approach as a convenient cover for not having a clue how to fix things. "The great advantage of allowing nature to take its course is that it obviates thought," observed economics writer Stuart Chase.

Hoover did make some efforts (which are covered in more detail in Chapter 12). He tried to coax business leaders into maintaining wage rates. He expanded federal public works projects. He asked the Federal Reserve System to ease credit requirements and lower interest rates. He promoted a national charity drive in the winter of 1929–30 (which raised an anemic $15 million).

But nothing seemed to help. In mid-January 1931, former President Calvin Coolidge came up with the understatement of the decade in his syndicated newspaper column. "The country," he wrote, "is not in good condition."

Banking in Ruins

The U.S. banking industry wasn't in such great shape even before the onset of the Great Depression. Between 1865 and 1920, banks had closed at an average rate of about 57 a year. In the Roaring Twenties, however, the average jumped to 635 closures a year.

Most of the banks that closed were small rural operations that were usually underfunded and overly ambitious when it came to investments. These banks were often operated by people who were crooked, stupid, or both. Senator Carter Glass of Virginia sniffed that such banks were "pawn shops (run) by little corner grocery-men calling themselves bankers."

Reacting to the crash

After the stock market crash, things only got worse for banks. Some of those that had made large investments in the market or issued loans to brokers and speculators closed. That made depositors at other banks nervous, and they began withdrawing their money to store it under the mattress or bury it in the backyard.

Banks tried to meet the demand for cash by selling off their bonds and real estate holdings, often at a loss, which made their financial condition even worse.

The number of failed banks soared to more than 1,300 in 1930, 600 of them in the last two months of the year. More than 2,000 failed in 1931, and more than 3,000 in 1932. In those three years, they took with them more than $2 billion in depositors' savings — $28.4 billion in 2008 dollars.

Many of the banks were small and in rural areas or small towns and cities. But on December 11, 1930, the Bank of United States in New York City closed. The failure wiped out $200 million belonging to more than 400,000 depositors, many of them immigrants. It was the largest commercial bank failure in U.S. history.

The bank might have been saved with help from other banks in the city, but the other banks refused. Some historians have attributed the refusal to the fact that the Bank of United States's principals, as well as many of its customers, were Jewish. Whatever the reason, the failure only increased the public's distrust of banks — and its dislike of bankers.

A popular joke at the time went, "Don't tell my mother I'm a banker, it would break her heart. She thinks I play the piano in a whore house." A British visitor related that U.S. bankers were "the most despised and most detested group of men" in the country.

Digging a deeper hole

Some of the public's antipathy was justified. At a U.S. Senate hearing in January 1933, more than a few bankers admitted they had used bank funds to speculate in stocks, made unsecured "loans" to bank officials, evaded taxes, and used bank assets to set up outside companies they controlled.

The 16-year-old Federal Reserve Board could have helped by pumping more money into the economy and lowering interest rates to make it easier for banks to borrow. But unsure of its authority and disinterested in the plight of smaller banks that were not members of the system, the Fed failed to act decisively.

President Hoover first tried to get banks to help each other. When that effort failed, he pushed through the creation of the Reconstruction Finance Corporation. The RFC was designed to make loans to banks and other financial institutions so they could make loans to businesses. But businesses needed credit less than they needed customers, and banks weren't anxious to extend themselves further by making loans.

So things got worse. People withdrew their money in fear their banks would close, often demanding payment in gold. Bank lobbies were jammed with panic-stricken customers.

The situation fostered some innovative thinking. A Utah bank manager tried to minimize the damage by instructing tellers to count out withdrawals as slowly as possible. A woman in New York City rented her baby to other customers for 25 cents: Holding a child in their arms entitled them to move to the front of the long lines.

But the crowds didn't work out to everyone's advantage. A would-be robber in Arkansas was thwarted because the bank was so crowded he couldn't cover everyone: A customer slipped out and got the sheriff.

So much money was withdrawn and hoarded, it's estimated that one-third of the nation's money supply was out of circulation by the beginning of 1933. Some communities, such as Salt Lake City, resorted to creating their own currency, which was used to pay workers and was accepted by local businesses.

"Our banking system was the weakest link in our whole economic system," Hoover later wrote in his memoirs. "(It was) the worst part of the dismal tragedy with which I had to deal."

It was soon part of his successor's new deal.

Taking a great bank holiday

As 1933 began, the country's financial system was on the verge of collapse. In the first two months of the year, more than 4,000 banks closed their doors. In mid-February, Michigan Governor William A. Comstock declared a banking moratorium for the entire state. He called it a "bank holiday."

Other states followed. By March 4, the day Franklin D. Roosevelt was sworn in as the 32nd president of the United States, 38 of the 48 states had declared partial or total "bank holidays."

Roosevelt made it unanimous. The day after taking office, the new president issued an executive order closing banks across the country and banning the export of gold. The order was, legally speaking, a bit of a stretch of presidential power, so FDR also called Congress into special session to ratify his order.

In the meantime, Americans began coping with a severe cash shortage caused by the banks being closed. Remember, this was in the days before ATMs and credit cards:

- A boxing tournament at New York's Madison Square Garden accepted false teeth, spark plugs, Bibles, and a box of egg noodles, among other things, in lieu of the 50-cent admission fee.

- A professional wrestler in Wisconsin signed a contract to perform in exchange for a can of tomatoes and a peck of potatoes.

- A newspaper in Ohio offered to trade ad space for produce.

The lack of change was a particularly vexing problem. Manhattan hotels sent bellboys to nearby churches to exchange bills for coins from the collection plates. Storekeepers in Elgin, Illinois, flocked to the house of a 16-year-old boy who, according to a local newspaper story, had collected 11,357 pennies toward his college education. And the country chuckled when it heard that for lack of change, the notoriously tight-fisted tycoon John D. Rockefeller had been forced to tip his golf caddy a dollar instead of his customary dime.

Federal bank officials, meanwhile, were trying to figure out how to get people to bring back to the banks all the gold and gold certificates they had withdrawn. On March 8, the Federal Reserve Board announced that lists would be made of everyone who had withdrawn gold after February 1 and not redeposited it by March 13. The announcement sounded ominous, although there wasn't any legal penalty for not redepositing the gold.

Breathing new life into the banks

On March 9, Congress approved the Emergency Banking Act of 1933 — and it did so with lightning speed. Congress spent only 35 minutes debating and voting on the bill, which was signed by FDR eight hours after it had been introduced.

The act authorized what Roosevelt had already done. It also declared that banks could not be reopened until they had passed muster from an army of federal auditors that already had been dispatched to the nation's 18,000-plus banks. The act extended the president's authority over credit and currency and gave him the power to set gold and silver prices. It authorized the Reconstruction Finance Corporation to buy stock in banks to help shore them up. And it approved the printing of $2 billion in new currency, backed not by gold but by the assets of the banks. Naturally, the new bills were sent only to the banks that proved they had assets.

The Bureau of Engraving and Printing roared to life. By March 11, planes were lifting off from Washington, D.C., to deliver the money. The next evening, Roosevelt spoke to the nation, via radio, to explain what had happened and to ask people to go back to the banks.

"I can assure you, my friends, that it is safer to keep your money in a reopened bank than it is to keep it under the mattress," the president told an estimated audience of 60 million. "You people must have faith . . . we have provided the machinery to restore our financial system, and it is up to you to support and make it work."

It worked. Hoarded gold and notes poured back into the banks. One Arizona bank reported taking in $640,000 in deposits the day after FDR's speech, while paying out only $32,000 in withdrawals. By March 15, 69 percent of the country's banks had reopened.

In June, Congress passed the Glass-Steagall Act, which established the Federal Deposit Insurance Corporation. The FDIC was given authority to insure bank deposits up to $2,500 per depositor per bank. Federal oversight was extended to all commercial banks. The FDIC was funded by charging fees to financial institutions.

For all his zest for reforms, Roosevelt didn't like the Glass-Steagall Act because he thought it represented too big a commitment for the federal government to make. But he signed the bill anyway, and it worked. Between 1921 and 1933, bank depositors had lost an average of $156 million a year. In 1934, the amount lost dropped to less than $1 million.

Becoming Jobless, Homeless, and Hungry

On June 18, 1931, U.S. newspapers carried a brief story from the West African country of Cameroon. The story reported that members of the Bulu tribe had raised $3.77 and had given it to a Presbyterian Missions Board to help the down-and-out people in the United States. The gesture was made after the residents of Cameroon had read in a local paper that "there are actually people in America who do not have enough to eat."

While the gesture may have amused some, what had motivated the Cameroonians was undeniably true: Some Americans were hungry, homeless, and unemployed. And it seemed that more people joined their ranks every day.

The writer Sherwood Anderson described watching "men who are heads of families creeping through the streets of American cities, eating from garbage cans; men turned out of houses and sleeping week after week on park benches, on the ground, in the mud under bridges . . . our streets are filled with beggars, with men new to the art of begging."

Watching jobs disappear

As the Great Depression ground on, the grim employment statistics piled up:

- ✔ The number of businesses in the country dropped from 2.2 million in 1929 to 1.9 million in 1933.

- ✔ Unemployment rates inexorably climbed: 1.5 million in 1929; 4.3 million in 1930; 8 million in 1931; 12 million in 1932; 12.8 million in 1933. By 1933, 24.9 percent of the entire civilian labor force was jobless.

- ✔ Total wages dropped from $50.4 billion in 1929 to $30 billion in 1932.

- ✔ Inflation-adjusted per capita income slumped from $681 in 1929 to $495 in 1933. At the Depression's depths, 28 percent of Americans had no income at all.

The effects on some regions and communities were even more depressing than the big-picture numbers. By the end of 1931, unemployment in Chicago was at 40 percent, and it stood at 50 percent in Detroit. In the steel town of Donora, Pennsylvania, it was estimated in 1932 that only 277 of the town's 14,000 residents had jobs.

The interrelationships of industries exacerbated things. Steel production dropped because railroads shrank. In the 1920s, U.S. rail companies had purchased 1,300 locomotives a year. In 1932, they bought none. As farming shriveled, demand for fishmeal fertilizer and livestock feed waned. As a result, sardine prices dropped from $11 a ton to $6 a ton. As construction fell, lumber production declined with it. Washington State had produced 7.5 billion board feet in the mid-1920s; in 1932, it produced 2 billion.

It was a buyer's market for employers. New York City department stores, for example, required elevator operators to have college degrees and had no problems filling the jobs. Other employers cut wages to microscopic levels. Hourly rates fell to 10 cents for lumbering and 6 cents for brick-making. Garment workers were paid $2.39 for a 55-hour week.

The 50 percent of coal miners who weren't out of work were paid $10.88 a month. And some weren't even paid in U.S. currency, but *company scrip,* which could be spent only at company-owned stores.

In 1931, a Harlan County, Kentucky, miner wrote to federal officials: "We are half fed because we can't feed ourselves and families with what we make. And we can't go to a cut rate store and buy food because most all the company forbids such trading. If you got the cash. But now we have no cash. And the companies keeps their foodstuffs at high prices at all times. So you can not clear enough to go anywhere. And if you do go some where and buy food you are subject to be canned."

If wages weren't cut, the hours worked were. In 1932, U.S. factory workers averaged 32 hours of work a week, down from 44 in 1929. Other companies cut jobs in half, figuring it was better to employ two people half-time than have one go jobless.

While some employers cut wages and hours just to keep the doors open, others were unapologetic about exploiting the situation. The president of the National Association of Manufacturers, J.E. Edgerton, told a Senate committee that "I've never thought of paying men on the basis of what they need. I pay for efficiency. I attend to all those other things, social welfare stuff, in my church work."

An apple a day

In the fall of 1930, apple growers in the Pacific Northwest found themselves with a bumper crop. So someone at the International Apple Shippers Association came up with an idea: Why not marry the excess fruit, in an economic sense, with all those jobless people in the big cities of the East?

The idea caught on. People could buy a crate of about 60 apples for $1.75. At a nickel each, they could gross $3 a day and net $1.25. It wasn't much, but it beat nothing at all.

By November 1930, city streets were packed with apple sellers. In New York City alone, there were an estimated 6,000, "some so near each other they could hold hands if they weren't competitors," in the words of one writer.

Journalist Frederic J. Haskin noted that "in the great industrial cities where thousands have been walking the streets, some for months, in search of work, apple selling is going forward briskly. One cannot walk a city square without encountering vendors of the fruit."

In Akron, Ohio, city officials heard that some apple sellers were making $50 a week. So officials required the sellers to give up their spots every two weeks and let someone else have a chance.

Apple selling lasted only until the big crop ran out. A sign displayed by one seller summed up the experience: "We used to have to eat an apple a day to keep the doctor away. Now we have to sell a few apples a day to keep the wolf away."

President Herbert Hoover held a variation of that sentiment. He disliked wage cuts but disapproved of government interference in setting wages. But in June 1930, Hoover did approve $2.3 billion in public works projects to create jobs.

In October, he formed the President's Emergency Committee for Employment. The committee came up with a list of inane recommendations (for example, the unemployed should spend less for food) and ran an equally inane advertising campaign to buck up the public's morale. The committee's director told a congressional committee, "I think that what we need is that everybody go back to work and have full pay for all jobs."

But stating the obvious didn't help much. Americans were willing to go to work, if they could find it. "I would be only too glad to dig ditches," a North Carolina man wrote federal officials in 1933, "to keep my family from going hungry."

Moving to the streets

Higher unemployment meant more people without rent money or mortgage payments, which meant more people became homeless. By the end of 1931, hundreds of thousands were on the street or living in temporary shelters.

In Philadelphia, there were as many as 1,300 evictions a month. Children in a daycare center played a game that involved moving toy furniture from one corner of the room to another. "We ain't got no money for the rent," a child explained to a teacher, "so we've moved into a new house. Then we got the constable on us, so we moving again."

In Chicago, Judge Samuel E. Heller presided over a landlord-tenants court. "I had an average of four hundred cases a day," he recalled several years later. "It was packed. People fainted, people cried 'where am I going?'"

Many homeowners were scarcely better off than renters. Deflation was at work in the housing market as well as elsewhere in the economy. A house that had sold for $5,000 in 1926 might be worth $3,200 in 1932. Banks were often eager to unload properties as fast as they could when the mortgage got behind, before the property's value declined further. By the end of 1933, it was estimated, as many as half of the home mortgages in the country were in default.

The homeless had few options, none of them attractive. For a dime, a single homeless man might get a bed for the night in a smelly and flea-ridden flophouse. If he didn't have a dime, he might seek a resting place near the municipal incinerator. It meant sleeping on garbage, but at least it was warm.

For a family, if there were no friends or relatives to go to, moving into abandoned buildings was an option, but it meant living with no electricity or running water. Some cities had shelters, but stays in them were limited.

Then there were *Hoovervilles:* collections of shacks and sheds made of everything from flattened tin cans to packing crates, derisively named after the president. Virtually every big and medium-sized city had one, perched on vacant land usually on the outskirts of town. In Oakland, California, the "community" was situated around and inside large abandoned concrete sewer pipes. In San Francisco, it was a field of abandoned trolley cars. St. Louis had the largest Hooverville, with distinct "neighborhoods." Charitable facilities that provided food — from soup kitchens to bread lines — were usually nearby.

Although the tenants were technically trespassing, most cities were pragmatic enough to tolerate them, mostly because no one had a better idea that was economically practical. (In Seattle, city officials twice burned down the city's Hooverville, and twice it was rebuilt.)

Local officials often did require that minimal health and safety regulations be met; for example, structures had to be built above-ground and have windows, and trash and human waste had to be disposed of properly. Some Hoovervilles established their own governments and adopted rules and regulations. Structures were even bought and sold.

In 1933, the Federal Transient Program began. The program took different forms in different areas. In small towns, the federal government contracted with local charities, hotels, and restaurants to provide food and lodging. About 300 camps were established in rural areas using surplus Army equipment. The program's facilities were efficiently maintained, and sometimes they provided work. By 1935, when it was phased out, the program had registered a million people and operated 600 centers.

In 1935, the Roosevelt administration shifted its focus to programs designed to keep families from becoming homeless in the first place. A sharp economic downturn in 1938 repopulated the nation's homeless "towns," but by the time the United States entered World War II in 1941, most of the Hoovervilles had been dismantled.

Going hungry

In mid-1933, Harry Hopkins, President Roosevelt's top man when it came to relief programs, sent a former reporter named Lorena Hickok to travel around the country and report to him what she found.

Hickok found hunger. In West Virginia, she was told there were children that had never tasted milk. In Kentucky, she was told that five babies had starved to death in the ten days before she arrived. In South Dakota, she found farmers eating soup made from spiny Russian thistle.

"We have been eating wild greens, such as Polk salad," a Kentucky coal miner wrote federal officials. "Violet tops, wild onions, forget-me-nots, wild lettuce and such weeds as cows eat, as a cow won't eat poison weeds."

That kind of desperate hunger in a nation that had fed itself and much of Europe, too, during World War I was hard to believe, so some chose not to believe it.

"Nobody is actually starving," President Hoover told reporters in 1932. "The hobos are actually better fed than they have ever been. One hobo in New York got ten meals in one day."

But there were people starving, and tens of thousands more suffering from nutrition-related diseases such as pellagra and rickets. The New York City Welfare Council reported 29 cases of starvation in that city alone in 1932, with 110 more dead from malnutrition.

The author Thomas Wolfe wrote of watching "the homeless men who prowled in the vicinity of restaurants, lifting the lids of garbage cans and searching around inside for morsels of rotten food."

In addition to grazing as the Kentucky miner's family did, there were reports of orderly lines at refuse dumps as people waited their turn to scavenge the garbage. A Chicago widow told a social worker she always removed her glasses before cooking meat she had found, to avoid seeing the maggots.

Some of the more well-to-do and perhaps well-intentioned citizens instructed their servants to give their leftovers to the poor, and Hoover's Secretary of War, Patrick Jay Hurley, even endorsed a suggestion for a federal program in which garbage from clubs, hotels, and restaurants would be collected in five-gallon containers and distributed to the needy by the Salvation Army. The idea was rejected.

Slightly less humiliating were the bread lines and soup lines that appeared in most cities and were sponsored by a combination of private donors and public agencies. Figure 4-1 depicts a typical bread line.

By the end of 1931, it was estimated that 85,000 meals a day were being served in New York City's 82 bread lines. The two biggest were at Times Square and sponsored by newspaper tycoon William Randolph Hearst. In Chicago, top gangster Al Capone sponsored the largest line.

An observer of a New York line wrote that "wretched men, many without overcoats or decent shoes, usually began to line up soon after six o'clock, in good weather or bad, rain or snow."

Photo by Underwood And Underwood/Time & Life Pictures/Getty Images

Figure 4-1: An aerial view of a New York City bread line in 1930, stretching the length of a block with tents set up for distribution.

Most disturbing was the impact hunger had on children. In October 1932, the New York City Health Department reported more than 20 percent of the children in the city's public schools were suffering from malnutrition. A survey by the American Friends Service Committee of mining regions in five states concluded the percentage of hungry children was sometimes as high as 90 percent. The committee said the children suffered from "drowsiness, lethargy and sleepiness," as well as mental disabilities. A Chicago principal told a congressional committee in 1932 that he instructed his teachers to ask an unruly child what he had had for breakfast before disciplining him, "which usually brings out the fact that he has had nothing at all."

A story widely reported in the 1930s concerned a West Virginia teacher who told an ill-looking child she should go home and eat something. The girl replied, "I can't. This is my sister's day to eat."

In 1933, Congress approved the Federal Emergency Relief Act, which was designed to pump federal aid for food, clothing, and other necessities through state and local governments. The act, which provided $500 million in aid, is covered in Chapter 13.

Marching on Washington

The lack of a coherent and forceful plan to combat the nation's deep troubles began to stir unpleasant thoughts of revolution in 1932.

Magazine and journal articles debated the chances of a mass insurrection. Chicago Mayor Anton Cermak told a House committee that the federal government could send relief to Chicago — or it could send troops to quell the violence that would follow if no relief came. A labor leader warned a Senate committee that if nothing was done, "and starvation is going to continue, the doors of revolt in this country are going to be thrown open."

In fact, there were sporadic incidents of violence and looting, much of it ignored by the newspapers for fear of encouraging copycat actions. But nothing occurred on a scale large enough to suggest an organized revolt until the "Bonus Army" reached Washington, D.C., in the summer of 1932.

The "Army" was a group of about 20,000 military veterans from around the country who wanted to accelerate the payment of bonuses they had been promised by Congress in 1924 for service during World War I. The bonuses were scheduled to be paid in 1945, but hard times had prompted the vets to seek immediate payment.

The veterans made camp around Washington, with the main settlement at a place called Anacostia Flats, across the Potomac River from the Capitol, and they waited. On June 17, the House voted to pay the bonuses, but the Senate rejected the idea. About half of the vets went home, but the rest stayed.

On July 28, Washington, D.C., police were ordered to evict the remaining veterans. A fight broke out, and two vets were shot and killed. President Hoover, who had refused to meet with the veterans (although he did offer them $100,000 in aid if they would disperse), ordered the army to clear them out.

Under the command of Chief of Staff General Douglas MacArthur and backed by six tanks, infantry and cavalry charged into veterans massed along Pennsylvania Avenue. Ignoring orders from Hoover to stay out of the main camp, MacArthur had the settlement burned. Two babies in the camp died from tear gas, a 7-year-old boy trying to rescue a pet rabbit was bayoneted in the leg, and hundreds were injured.

Administration officials tried to justify the attack. A War Department official called the vets "a mob of tramps and hoodlums, with a generous sprinkling of communist agitators." MacArthur insisted that if the vets had not been routed, "I believe the institutions of our government would have been severely threatened."

But newsreels, photos, and news accounts of the attack sickened many Americans.

"Soup is cheaper than tear gas bombs," New York Representative Fiorello La Guardia said in a telegram to Hoover, "and bread is better than bullets in maintaining law and order in these times of depression, unemployment and hunger."

Lessons Learned

Some lessons are learned the hard way, and two lessons from the Great Depression were learned in the hardest of ways.

It took the loss of the life savings of hundreds of thousands of Americans to win the creation of a national insurance program for bank deposits. And the hesitant and wrongly directed efforts of the Hoover Administration in response to the economic mess taught future administrations to move quicker — and in the opposite direction — when the U.S. economy was on the skids.

Safeguarding savings: The FDIC

Created by Congress in the wake of the 1933 banking industry crisis, the Federal Deposit Insurance Corporation is basically just what the name implies: a U.S. government corporation that insures deposits at banks and financial institutions that are members.

Starting with maximum coverage of $2,500 per customer per bank on January 1, 1934, the FDIC now insures up to $250,000 per investor per bank. (That amount is scheduled to decrease to $100,000 in January 2010.)

Keep in mind that the insurance amount is not per account, but per investor. For example, if you have $80,000 in a checking account (congratulations!), $100,000 in a savings account, and $100,000 in a certificate of deposit (CD) all at one bank, you'd have $280,000, which means $30,000 wouldn't be covered. But if you and your spouse are joint holders of those three accounts, then the total amount would be covered because each of you is entitled to up to $250,000 in coverage.

The FDIC is directed by a five-member board, appointed by the president and confirmed by the U.S. Senate. No more than three board members can be of the same political party. The corporation has about 4,500 employees and insures funds in about 8,500 institutions. Member banks pay insurance premiums and must meet minimum requirements for *liquidity* (availability of assets) and reserves.

The two most important things about the FDIC for most people to know are

✔ It does **not** cover stocks, bonds, mutual funds, or insurance annuities, even those that are purchased through an FDIC member bank.

✔ No one has ever lost a penny in an FDIC-insured account.

That's not to say that banks don't fail anymore. In fact, the longest the United States has gone without a bank failing since 1933 was from June 24, 2004, to February 2, 2007. From 1987 to 1989, slightly more than 200 banks per year failed, many of them in the Southwest, which suffered a sizeable slump in its energy industries. In July 2008, FDIC regulators took over the IndyMac Bank in Pasadena, California. With $32 billion in assets, it was the third-largest bank failure in U.S. history. The two bigger ones were in 1984 and 1988.

But it's probably safe to say that for all practical purposes, the U.S. government would have to fail before FDIC-insured deposits would be at great risk (which may or may not be of comfort to you).

Reacting to economic downturns

Since the Great Depression, the federal government's response to downturns in the economic cycle has generally taken one of, or some combination of, three forms: lowering interest rates to encourage more borrowing and private investment; increasing government spending, either through public works projects or tax cuts; and maintaining and expanding "safety net" programs such as welfare and unemployment insurance (see Chapter 5).

That's pretty much the opposite of what the Federal Reserve Board and the Hoover administration did in the months following the October 1929 stock market crash, when they raised interest rates and taxes and rejected the ideas of more government spending and direct relief programs.

Since the end of World War II, the trio of lower interest rates, government stimulus spending, and safety net programs has generally worked to minimize the impact of recessions, or at least helped shorten them. For example, after the 1987 stock market crash (which was actually bigger than 1929's when measured by the percentage of value lost), the Federal Reserve Board quickly lowered interest rates and increased liquidity in the financial system until it was clear there wasn't going to be a major economic meltdown.

In the face of the severe economic recession that began in late 2007, both the administrations of President George W. Bush and President Barack Obama employed combinations of tax cuts and public works spending, lowered interest rates, and expanded public assistance programs.

That's not to say that government tinkering hasn't sometimes caused problems. Some economists contend that periodic efforts to slow inflation by tightening the money supply have helped trigger recessions. As one economist put it in 1997, "None of the U.S. (economic) expansions of the past 40 years have died in bed of old age; every one was murdered by the Federal Reserve."

In general, however, the three-pronged approach of more government spending, lower interest rates, and provision of safety net programs has helped stave off an economic crisis like that of the 1930s.

Chapter 5

Coming Face to Face with Hard Times

The Great Depression deeply affected not only the U.S. economy but also the American psyche. The widely held belief that hard work and a responsible attitude would result in a comfortable and secure life (if not always wild success) was challenged by forces that seemed out of the control of everyone.

In this chapter, I show you how hard it was for some Americans to accept help, how hard it was for the federal government to give it (at least under Herbert Hoover), and how local governments and private sources tried to fill the gap. You also find out how people adapted to the times in their day-to-day lives, how traditional family relations and social institutions were affected, and how things got worse for those already at the bottom of the economy.

Looking for Relief

Since colonial times, Americans had had a high regard for standing on their own feet and a deep aversion to asking for help. In 1835, the French social scientist Alexis de Tocqueville noted how deeply ingrained the trait of individualism was in Americans. Individualism, he wrote, "is a mature and calm feeling, which disposes each member of the community to sever himself from the mass of his fellows, and to draw apart with his family and friends."

In October 1928, Republican presidential candidate Herbert Hoover gave a speech that extolled "the American system of rugged individualism" over the "European philosophy" of "paternalism and socialism." Hoover said "our country has become the land of opportunity to those born without inheritance, not merely because of the wealth of its resources and industry, but because of this freedom of initiative and enterprise."

When Hoover was confronted as president with the grim reality that millions of Americans needed help that was beyond their abilities to provide for themselves, his first impulse was to deflect the responsibility to state and local public and private agencies.

"The basis of successful relief in national distress is to mobilize and organize the infinite number of agencies of relief help in the community," Hoover said in February 1931. "This has been the American way of relieving distress among our people, and the country is successfully meeting its problem in the American way today."

He was partially right. The traditional way of handling hard times was to do so at the local level. Except for a few natural disasters, the federal government had steered clear of providing direct relief (that is, food, clothing, shelter, cash, and other necessities of daily life). But Hoover was wrong in contending that the country was "successfully meeting its problem."

Trying to help at the local level

The failure to provide enough help didn't result from lack of trying. In April 1931 in Portland, Oregon, voters approved a $2 million bond issue for relief programs. In Fort Wayne, Indiana, private fundraising drives raised $775,000. In Boston, city employees contributed one day's pay to a relief fund that collected $3 million.

Newspapers across the country called on their readers to find odd jobs or home repair chores for an out-of-work neighbor. The Moberly, Missouri, *Monitor-Index,* for example, announced on April 3, 1931, that the local Salvation Army was organizing a spring cleaning week: "A list of worthy unemployed is being compiled at the organization's headquarters, and residents will be asked to call on these unemployed for help in spring housecleaning, lawn raking, garden planting, cleaning basements and other spring improvements."

On the same day in Jefferson City, Missouri, a city alderman proposed temporarily raising the town's gasoline tax by two cents to finance some street repairs. The *Jefferson City Post-Tribune* reported that Alderman B.F. Reed "said the plan would result in the employment of forty or fifty men, which, he said is the principal object for the suggestion."

But local government and private relief efforts fell light-years short of meeting the need. In 1932, the total combined amount raised by charities and the municipal government in New York City reached $79 million. That was less than the city's army of unemployed had lost in wages in one month. In Chicago, it was estimated that lost wages were averaging $2 million a day, while relief funds were averaging only $100,000 daily.

"I am stating that the funds we have are altogether inadequate to meet the situation," Arthur T. Burns, the head of the Association of Community Chests and Councils, told a Senate committee in 1931.

Churches had suffered declining attendance — and leaner collection plates — throughout the 1920s, and most were in no position to extend substantial aid. States likewise were mostly broke in 1931, or close to it. With the exception of New York (where Governor Franklin D. Roosevelt had put together a competent relief agency), state relief programs were minimal.

The unemployment problem, meanwhile, was massive. By March 1933, about one of every four able-bodied, working-age Americans was jobless. Because most of them were men with families to support, that statistic meant that as many as 40 to 50 million people — from 30 to 40 percent of the entire U.S. population — had no regular source of income.

"We can no longer depend on passing the hat and rattling the tin cup," wrote William Allen White, the nationally known editor of the *Emporia* (Kansas) *Gazette,* in calling for federal intervention. "We have gone to the bottom of the barrel."

Getting the feds involved . . . slowly

Hoover remained stubbornly opposed to direct federal relief. His opposition wasn't based on a callous disregard for people's troubles. But he feared that federal relief programs would create a permanent underclass of Americans dependent on government handouts. He was also nervous about deciding questions such as who would get help first, how much help they would get, and for how long. And he was dubious about the federal government's ability to pay for it.

In February 1931, Hoover said that if the time ever came that local and state governments failed to have enough "resources with which to prevent hunger and suffering . . . I will ask the aid of every resource of the federal government." But, he added, he had "faith in the American people that such a day never come."

In March 1931, Hoover vetoed a bill that would have provided loans to needy veterans. "I regard the bill as unwise," he wrote in his veto message. "Of much greater importance is the whole tendency to open up the federal treasury to a thousand purposes . . . each of them breaks the barrier of self-reliance and self-support in our people."

But Congress overrode Hoover's veto, and the president grudgingly acquiesced to the idea of the federal government providing some help. Even then, however, it wasn't direct help. In early 1932, Hoover signed into law the establishment of the Reconstruction Finance Corporation. The RFC helped prop up banks and other businesses with federal loans, but it did little to help the jobless guy on the street.

As humorist Will Rogers put it, "the money was all appropriated for the top, in the hopes it would trickle down to the needy." But little trickling occurred, and jobless men waited for help.

Facing a reelection campaign and under increasing pressure from rival Democrats in Congress, Hoover finally agreed to expand the powers of the RFC so it could assist states in providing direct relief to people. But it was too little — only $30 million was spent by the end of 1932 — and too late for Hoover, who lost the presidential election to New York Governor Roosevelt.

In the early weeks of 1933, just prior to taking office, Roosevelt was absorbed by the nation's banking crisis (see Chapter 4 for details). But other administration officials brought the issue of relief to the front burner — even those who weren't known for their zeal for social issues.

"When we were campaigning," said FDR's crusty vice president, John Nance "Cactus Jack" Garner, "we sort of made promises that we would do something for the poorer kind of people, and I think we have to do something for them."

Roosevelt agreed. Less than three weeks after taking office in March, FDR asked Congress to create the office of Federal Emergency Relief Administration (FERA) and to give it $500 million to provide grants to states.

Some congressional Republicans were apoplectic at the idea. "I can hardly find parliamentary language to describe the statement that the states and cities cannot take care of conditions in which they find themselves, but must come to the federal government for aid," said Senator Simeon D. Fess of Ohio. Representative Robert Luce of Massachusetts declared, "[I]t is socialism. Whether it is communism I do not know."

Despite such bombastic indignation, the proposal easily passed both houses by the end of April 1933. How well it worked is covered in Chapter 13, along with other programs in Roosevelt's "New Deal."

The Arkansas "food riot"

On the cool and cloudy afternoon of January 3, 1931, Homer C. Coney decided he had been patient long enough.

Coney, a 46-year-old father of five, grew corn and cotton on 41 acres he rented near the central Arkansas town of England. A severe drought the previous summer had ruined Coney and other farmers in the area, and with no government aid on the horizon, his family was trying to make do on $12 a month from the Red Cross.

When a neighbor came by to beg, saying she and her two children hadn't eaten for two days, Coney loaded up his truck with other men and drove into England. They demanded food from Red Cross officials, who contended they lacked the necessary application forms to issue anything.

"Our children are crying for food and we are going to get it," one farmer said. "We're not beggars (but) we are not going to let our families starve!"

As the crowd swelled to several hundred, town merchants defused the situation by opening their stores and providing food and clothing. A part-time reporter for the Associated Press phoned in the story, dramatically — and erroneously — describing it as a "riot." But the exaggeration got the incident front-page play across the country and triggered an outpouring of small donations: $25 from a Winder, Georgia, manufacturing company; $5 from a man in Bridgeport, Connecticut; four pairs of socks and shoes from a couple in El Paso, Texas.

The story also caught the attention of arguably the best-liked man in America in 1931. Homespun humorist Will Rogers was a star of stage, screen, and radio, and he also wrote a nationally syndicated newspaper column. On January 7, he wrote, "it took a little band of 500 simple country people . . . to come to a country town store and demand food for their wives and children. They hit the hearts of the American people more than all your Senatorial pleas and government investigations. Paul Revere woke up Concord. These birds woke up America."

Rogers went to England, and then to the White House. After President Herbert Hoover turned down his appeal for direct aid to the region, Rogers organized a grueling 18-day, 50-show fundraising tour that raised more than $200,000. England pulled through.

In August, Rogers noted in another column that the farmers of England had sent 13 truckloads of food to struggling coal miners in Oklahoma.

"Say, you talk about a people and a place being appreciative of what was done for them when they was in trouble," Rogers wrote. "Now that's remembering, ain't it?"

Swallowing pride to keep from starving

Americans' allegiance to the tenets of individualism and self-reliance were never more evident than in the resistance of so many people to accept relief when it was offered.

"We lived on bread and water for three weeks before I could make myself do it (accept relief)," a New Orleans man told a federal investigator in 1933. An unemployed schoolteacher in Texas told another investigator, "If I can't make a living, I'm just no good I guess." In Pennsylvania, when an investigator asked a half-dozen unemployed miners what the government could do for them, one miner replied in broken English, "[W]ork! Give man work, that's all, no want relief if get work!"

Those who were less affected by the hard times, but who had been raised on the same ideal of self-reliance, sometimes reacted as if the country's problems were made worse by efforts to help the poor and unemployed.

"To give a gratuity to an individual is divesting men and women of their spirit, their self-reliance," said Patrick Jay Hurley, Hoover's Secretary of War, in June 1932. "It is striking at the very foundation of the system on which the nation is built."

Some of the down-and-out agreed. Frank Moorhead, a laid-off magazine editor, wrote in a 1931 article in *The Nation* that to keep up appearances, he set up an "office" in his home. There he would type randomly for hours, so neighbors would think he was working.

"I should like to find out at what stage of your poverty other people realize or sense it," he wrote. "I guess, after all, it's in the droop of the shoulders, the look in your eyes — furtive, expectant, resentful."

But for every Patrick Jay Hurley who seemed to consider poverty a moral defect, or every Frank Moorhead who stigmatized himself, there were others who saw the needy as neither more nor less than the products of very hard times.

"Three or four million heads of families don't turn into tramps or cheats overnight," wrote top Roosevelt aide Harry Hopkins in 1933. "An eighth or tenth of the earning population does not change its character, which has been generations in the moulding."

Changing with the Times

Many people who were out of a job, and who were unwilling or unable to get government help, created their own ways of making a buck.

Tapping the entrepreneurial spirit

Some enterprises were offshoots of people's normal occupations. Coal miners, for example, smuggled coal out of the mines in lunch buckets or dug it out of company land after dark and then sold it on the black market. These coal "bootleggers" even formed an organization called the Independent Anthracite Miners Association. The association's articles of incorporation stated that "we must dig the coal out of these mountains as a means of supplementing our measly income . . . in order to keep the wolf from our doorsteps."

Some people shined shoes: *The New York Times* reported counting 19 shoe shiners, ranging in age from 16 to 70, on one block of a Manhattan street in the summer of 1932. Other people sold things door to door: The Fuller Brush Company had so many salesmen — strictly on commission — that it was one of the relatively few firms in the 1930s to consistently make money.

Somewhat incongruously, given the hard times, people paid good money to watch other people do strange things. For example, boys climbed trees and tried to set endurance records for sitting in them, while passersby dropped coins in a box. Sometimes the tree sitters wore advertising for a local merchant. It apparently paid better than one would think. *The Literary Digest* reported in July 1933 that "the bank accounts of the numerous contestants . . . are not to be dismissed with a shrug." To read about other wacky things people did for money, see the nearby sidebar "Endurance for sale."

Hundreds of men wandered into old gold and silver mining regions in Colorado, Arizona, and California, looking as much for something to do as for precious metals. "We were more like scavengers," television journalist Eric Sevareid wrote in his 1946 memoir of being "on the bum" during the Great Depression. "The hope of finding gold, which almost none of us ever did, was more of an excuse to live in the hills, where life was cheap."

Endurance for sale

Americans in the 1930s had what *Time* magazine referred to as an "appetite for preposterous endurance." It was an appetite sated by the willingness of some people to walk, dance, rollerskate, or bicycle for days and weeks on end in hopes of winning some money.

While there were variations on the theme, the basic premise was that a promoter invited individuals, couples, or teams to compete in activities ranging from kissing to sitting in rocking chairs. The promoter sold tickets to people who wanted to watch, and the contestants who lasted the longest at the activity won cash prizes. Roller Derby winners could make $1,000 for first place. Marathon dancers might average $20 to $30 a day in tips, and free meals, for as long as they could stay on their feet.

In addition to prizes for lasting the longest, competitors could also earn money from the crowds for an especially good effort or for some extra form of entertainment, such as singing. And there were often very big crowds. A Roller Derby held in Chicago in late 1935 and early 1936 drew 10,000 people a day.

While they may sound like quaint versions of *American Idol,* the competitions could be brutal. Bicycle races were usually six days long with competitors hurtling around an oval wooden track hour after hour, occasionally at speeds approaching 30 mph. Roller Derbies, on similar tracks, covered 4,000 miles. And dance marathons could drag on for months. One critic labeled them "a macabre modern equivalent of a homicidal Roman gladiatorial spectacle."

Of course, not everyone was there for the spectacle. As a New York City reporter pointed out in 1933, a ticket to a six-day bicycle race cost $2.40, which was cheaper than most accommodations in the city: "It insures a gent some shelter, warmth, a bench and a certain amount of excitement if you like that sort of thing."

Making do with what you had

An optimist in the 1930s might have pointed out that if half the families in the United States were without income, it meant half did have some money coming in. And it's true that many American families didn't lose their homes, go on relief, or find themselves rooting through their neighbors' garbage cans for food.

Even so, the shaky economy, the unsettled political climate, and the shock of going from the seemingly shiny prosperity of the 1920s to the decidedly gloomy atmosphere of the 1930s all made for a general feeling of uncertainty.

In that atmosphere, even people with incomes economized. Many families planted gardens and did more canning and preserving food. They made more of their own clothes. Telephones were deemed less necessary: The number of phones in service nationally dropped from 20 million in 1930 to fewer than 17 million in 1933. Automobiles remained a vital part of American life, but fewer of the cars were new. In 1929, 4.4 million new cars were sold. In the 1930s, the annual number averaged 2.1 million. Book sales dropped 50 percent.

Getting sick was not an economically healthy thing to do. "You had to have money to be sick," the novelist John Steinbeck recalled. "Dentistry was out of the question, with the result that my teeth went badly to pieces."

Some people dealt with the drooping economy by creating their own economies. Barter systems — in which people traded goods and services with each other — sprang up around the country. Sometimes it was a straight swap: You fix my roof, and I'll give you some of my backyard rutabagas. In larger systems, *scrip* was used as a form of currency that could be exchanged for goods and services from anyone who was part of the system. A Washington state system used wooden nickels; a California system used seashells; an Oregon system used "rubber checks" — made of rubber.

At their peak in the early to mid-1930s, barter systems probably covered a million Americans in 30 states. A typical exchange, described in a 1939 paper by California social economist Clark Kerr (later chancellor of the University of California), worked like this: A music teacher owed $200 to a doctor. The barter cooperative she belonged to sent her three students, who paid her in scrip. She used the scrip to pay the doctor, who used it to get maid and stenographic services and new car tires from other members of the cooperative.

The systems worked on a limited basis but were no substitute for the real thing. As one observer put it, barter was "comparable to the relief a starving dog might get by eating his own tail."

Taking a Toll on the American Family

Toward the end of *The Grapes of Wrath,* John Steinbeck's 1939 novel about a family of migrant farmers during the Great Depression, the family's patriarch is talking to his wife.

"I ain't no good any more," Pa Joad says. "Funny! Woman takin' over the fambly. Woman sayin' we'll do this here, an' we'll go there. An' I don't even care."

Eroding men's self-worth

A lot of Depression-era men could empathize with Pa Joad. Many, if not most, men drew their self-esteem and authority as head of the household from the fact that they were nearly always the sole breadwinners in the family.

Having no job meant more than having no money. It meant a loss of purpose and a diminution of the man's role in the family. Mom did all the things that made the household function. Dad, if he was unemployed, was apt to sit around the kitchen table and sink deeper into depression.

That personal depression might deepen if Mom found a job, which was not an easy task. The percentage of the workforce made up of women increased only slightly from 1930 to 1940, from 24.3 percent to 25.1 percent. (In contrast, the percentage was 46.5 percent in 2008.) Women were often discriminated against in the workplace because of fears that they might usurp the rightful place of men. Many employers who hired single women, including school districts, would often fire them if they married working men and thus created two-income families. There was a federal rule against two people in the same family working for the government.

Women were most often hired because they would accept lower pay — a practice not only allowed by federal law but also practiced by the federal government in its relief and jobs programs. In projects run by the federal Works Progress Administration, for example, men were paid $5 a day and women $3.

Some families faced double whammies. A Eureka, California, woman who worked at the county court house was married to a surveyor who lost his job. Then she got pregnant and had to leave her position. "I'm happy of course," she wrote First Lady Eleanor Roosevelt in June 1934, seeking a government job for her husband, "but Tommy is nearly out of his head. He has tried every conceivable prospect, but you must know even pick and shovel jobs do not exist . . . A year is all I ask and after that I can go back to work and we can work out our own salvation. But to have this baby come to a home full of worry and despair, with no money for things it needs, it is not fair. It needs and deserves a happy start in life."

Despite the extra pressures imposed on families by the economic stresses of the period, divorce rates actually declined, dropping 20 percent between 1929 and 1933. But that wasn't necessarily good news. Men who saw themselves as failures because of unemployment often simply walked away and didn't come back, a much cheaper alternative than a formal divorce.

Sometimes, as Figure 5-1 shows, the one thing that kept couples together was having nothing else.

Figure 5-1: An evicted Los Angeles couple sits on the curb surrounded by their belongings in 1937.

With the future so uncertain, marriage rates declined in the 1930s for the first time in the United States since the early 19th century. And birth rates dropped as well, from 25.1 per 1,000 population in 1925 to 19.4 in 1940.

Even that number was too high for some women. For example, a Bakersfield, California, woman told federal investigator Lorena Hickok in 1933 that she worried about getting pregnant but couldn't afford contraceptives.

"I suppose you can say the easiest way would be not to do it," she said. "(But) you don't know what it's like when your husband is out of work. He's gloomy all the time and unhappy. You haven't any money for movies or anything to take his mind off his troubles. You must try all the time to keep him from going crazy. And many times — well, that is the only way."

Hitting children the hardest

The domestic disruptions caused by the Great Depression were perhaps hardest on children, who had no concept of the economic forces that had put life in such disarray.

Some families had no recourse but to commit their children to orphanages or similar institutions. A veteran social worker told a Senate Committee in 1933 that the number of children who had been given up by their parents had risen from 284,000 in mid-1930 to 400,000 in October 1932.

"It is the belief of those familiar with the facts that this increase . . . has been caused chiefly by the breaking up of family groups caught in the Depression and unable to care for their children because of inadequate relief or other conditions precipitated by unemployment," said Dr. Jacob Billikopf.

Newspapers routinely carried heart-wrenching stories of the crushing weight borne by some children:

- ✔ In January 1933, an 8-year-old boy in Big Spring, Texas, told a social worker who had come to his home that he felt it was wrong to go out and play when he should be tending to his father, who was ill with tuberculosis.

  "No school for this boy," wrote a reporter for the *Big Spring Herald* who had accompanied the social worker. "Only barely enough food. A chilly damp little room in which to live. No mother to care for him. Nothing in his days except to sit beside his father and watch him die."

- ✔ New York City columnist Gilbert Swan noted in February 1933 that those without shelter in the city sometimes went to the Central Park or Bronx zoo, where buildings were kept warm to protect the animals.

  "I happened by the other day when the animals were being fed," Swan wrote. "Two puny, rickety, haggard youngsters were tugging at the hands of a beaten-looking man. No words passed. The children looked blankly at the food, and their father. Obviously there was no bread for them."

- ✔ In Punxsutawney, Pennsylvania, in late 1933, a 15-year-old boy named Thomas Colbert was suffering from a chronic kidney disease. The illness had eaten the family's savings, and Alec Colbert, Thomas's father, had lost his job as a mechanic. The family had bought a small farm but lost it when they couldn't pay the mortgage. According to a November 21 headline in the *Indiana* (Pennsylvania) *Evening Gazette,* Thomas "Did Not Want to Be Any Trouble to (His) Parents." So he poisoned himself.

All I want for Christmas . . .

"Dear President Roosevelt,

Please help us my mother is sick three year and was in the hospital three month and she came out but she is not better and my Father is peralised and can not work and we are poor and the Cumunity fund gives us six dollars an we are six people four children three boy 15, 13, 12 and one gril 10, and to parents. We have no one to give us a Christmas presents, and if you want to buy a Christmas present please buy us a stove to do our cooking and to make good bread.

"Please excuse me for not writing it so well because the little girl 10 year old is writing. Merry Christmas."

— Letter to the president from Warren, Ohio, dated December 22, 1935

Scraping By at the Bottom of the Barrel

At just under 12 percent of the total population, minority groups were definitely in the minority in the United States of the Great Depression. The 1930 U.S. Census reported that 88.7 percent of the populace identified themselves as "white," followed by 9.7 percent "Negro," 1.2 percent "Mexican," and 0.3 percent American Indian. (By contrast, the U.S. population was 33 percent minority in 2008.)

But despite being a relatively small slice of the American pie, minority groups bore an inordinate amount of the Great Depression's burdens. What follows is a look at how the three largest minority groups fared during the 1930s.

African Americans

Most of the 11.9 million African Americans in the 1930s were already poor when the Great Depression began, so they didn't feel the jolt as sharply as the white community. But because they were poorer to begin with, they did feel it more deeply.

About 80 percent of African Americans still lived in the South during the decade, and half of those lived in or near small towns in rural areas. Only 10 to 12 percent of those who farmed owned their own land. Most were *tenant farmers* (farming on rented land) or *sharecroppers* (growing crops on borrowed money, which was repaid by giving up a percentage of the yield). And most were economically crippled even worse than they had been when the price of cotton dropped by more than half between 1929 and 1933.

Living conditions in the rural South ranged from bad to appalling. Fisk University sociologist Charles S. Johnson surveyed 916 black rural families in the mid-1930s. He reported that only 53 of the families had running water; 66 percent used "open privies," or pit toilets, and 10 percent had no toilet at all. Only 2 percent had electricity.

Lynchings, which had dropped to a post–Civil War low of 8 in 1932, climbed to 28 in 1933, 15 in 1934, and 20 in 1935. And if lynching wasn't uncommon, education for black children was: Some schools for African Americans opened only when the weather was bad and the students couldn't work.

About 400,000 African Americans left the rural South for Northern cities during the 1930s, but things were only marginally better there:

- ✔ In New York City's Harlem borough, the median annual income for black families in the mid-1930s was $1,300. In the white areas of the city, it was $1,750. Rents in Harlem, meanwhile, averaged $160 a year higher.

- ✔ In Cleveland, black families were twice as likely as white families to have annual incomes of less than $500 a year.

- ✔ In Chicago, African Americans made up just 4 percent of the city's population but 16 percent of its unemployed.

Employers, many of whom had not been shy about having discriminatory hiring practices before the economic plunge, now were even less likely to hire a black person with so many unemployed white people from which to choose. By the end of 1932, black unemployment was estimated at 50 percent.

One small bright spot amid the hard times for African Americans was that some white retailers became more polite to black customers. "You know, this depression has made the great Anglo Saxon easier to get along with," a black community leader wryly noted. "He smiles and is very friendly at his gas stations and stores."

But federal relief programs under FDR's administration were not always so friendly. Federal programs designed to help raise the price of cotton by paying landowners to plant fewer acres actually made things worse for black farm laborers or tenant farmers, because the landowners often pocketed all the subsidies while providing less work.

Some of the federal job programs indirectly allowed African Americans to be paid less than white workers by setting lower wage levels for job classifications that were dominated by black workers.

Still, the fact that they were included in federal programs at all made many black voters leave the party of hero Abraham Lincoln — and more to the point, Herbert Hoover — and join the party of FDR. More black voters had backed Hoover than supported FDR in 1932. In Roosevelt's reelection in 1936, however, 76 percent of African Americans voted for him.

The shift of African Americans from GOP allegiance to Democratic fealty continued through the rest of the 20th century and into the 21st, and black voters became one of the Democratic Party's most reliable voting blocs.

For his part, Roosevelt was very careful not to be seen as "pro-Negro," to avoid irritating Southern members of Congress on whom he was counting to help push through his economic recovery program.

In explaining why he could not back an anti-lynching bill in 1933, FDR told an executive of the National Association for the Advancement of Colored People, "If I come out for the anti-lynching bill now, they (Southern members of Congress) will block every bill I ask Congress to pass to keep America from collapsing. I just can't take that risk."

What FDR couldn't do because of politics, his wife Eleanor could because of her humanity. The First Lady was outspoken in her sympathies toward minorities and was roundly excoriated for it by racists around the country.

"We must all learn to work together, all of us, regardless of race or creed or color," Eleanor said in a 1934 speech on African Americans and education. "We go ahead together or we go down together."

Of course, then as now, not everyone felt the same way. U.S. Senator Theodore G. Bilbo of Mississippi, for example, actually proposed spending $1 billion in 1939 to deport all African Americans to the African country of Liberia.

But little by little, progress was made. In 1935, FDR issued an executive order specifically prohibiting discrimination on new federal public works projects. In 1937, he appointed the first black federal judge in U.S. history. And in 1939, the U.S. Justice Department created a Civil Rights section.

America's civil rights movement obviously had a long way to grow, but its roots may have taken hold during the Great Depression.

Latinos

The 1.4 million Latinos in the United States at the onset of the Great Depression shared some of the problems of African Americans — and had a few problems of their own.

The overwhelming majority of Latinos were from Mexico, which had been exempt from the U.S. immigration restrictions of the 1920s, mainly because growers in the southwestern United States needed a source of cheap labor.

Many Latinos moved among the fields of Texas, Arizona, California, and southern Colorado, although some moved to cities such as Detroit and Chicago for manufacturing jobs. A Latino community in Los Angeles had reached a population of 100,000 by 1930. There, as elsewhere, Latinos were subject to strict segregation both in housing and in public settings such as movie theaters.

When the U.S. economy hit the skids in late 1929, the Latino labor supply became part of a labor glut, and Latinos became convenient scapegoats. Texas Representative Martin Dies proclaimed that "the large alien population is the basic cause of unemployment."

A committee appointed by President Hoover recommended that the government toughen its immigration policies to reduce the labor supply, and in September 1930 Hoover agreed. The president invoked a provision in federal law that barred immigrants who were likely to become "burdens to taxpayers." That move all but closed the United States to immigration.

The feds also began clamping down on immigrants who were deemed to be in the United States illegally. About 80,000 Latinos were eventually rounded up by the Federal Bureau of Immigration (which in 1933 became the Immigration and Naturalization Service) and deported.

Latino farm laborers, meanwhile, faced a double dilemma. As the Great Depression deepened, wages dropped. Pay in Colorado beet fields dropped from $27 an acre in 1929 to $12.37 in 1932. Picking 100 pounds of cotton in Texas earned $1.28 in 1928; it earned 42 cents in 1931. At the same time, local government relief programs and charitable aid began to be restricted to "citizens only," which in most cases meant "whites only."

Although most federal relief programs under the Roosevelt administration were open to Latinos, the welcome mat had been all but pulled. In 1937, Congress closed a major federal jobs program to "aliens." The ban extended to private companies with government contracts. Not wanting to take a chance at losing a contract, the companies often fired everyone that might fit the "alien" description, whether or not they were U.S. citizens.

Faced with mounting hostility, many Latinos decided to leave. In Los Angeles, county officials even offered to pay their train fares. An observer described the departure of one train loaded with *repatriados,* or repatriated Latinos: "The loading process began at six o'clock in the morning. Repatriados arrived by the truckload — men, women, children — with dogs, cats and goats; half-open suit cases, rolls of bedding and lunch baskets." A punctilious official estimated the county saved $347,468.41 in relief aid for the $77,249.29 it spent on train fares.

Eventually, more than 300,000 Latinos, many of them U.S. citizens, left for Mexico. Some of those who stayed attempted to protect themselves by organizing their own unions, with mixed results. Those efforts are covered in Chapter 11.

Native Americans

In the mid-1880s, the federal government came up with the idea that the way to solve the country's "Indian problem" was to "assimilate" them. That meant, among other things, allotting parcels of land to individual Native Americans, shipping Indian children off to white-run boarding schools to "help" them lose their culture, and waiting for the Indians to forget about being Indians.

To help them along, Congress made all Native Americans U.S. citizens in 1924, whether they wanted to be or not. (Some states didn't want them to be; New Mexico and Arizona didn't let Indians vote until 1948.)

In 1928, a Congress-commissioned study reported that the assimilation idea was a dismal failure:

- ✔ Half of Native Americans had lost the land that had been allotted to them, either by selling it or losing it for nonpayment of property taxes. By 1925, the 138 million acres given to individual Indians was down to 48 million.

- ✔ A shocking 96 percent of Native Americans had annual incomes of less than $200.

✔ Infant mortality rates for Native Americans were twice the national average, and tuberculosis deaths were seven times the national average.

In 1934, the Roosevelt administration pushed a bill through Congress formally known as the Indian Reorganization Act (and informally known as the "Indian New Deal"). The act restored tribes' rights to own land collectively, reaffirmed their right to self-government, and encouraged them to preserve their cultural identities and traditions while expanding their business and education opportunities.

In the dozen years after the act's passage, tribes reclaimed a total of 4 million acres. But their overall economic lot did not improve, and when World War II began, the federal government lost interest in Native Americans again.

Lessons Learned

It took a descent into a swamp of joblessness, homelessness, and hunger in the Great Depression before a safety net of social services was woven that continues in place in the 21st century.

It also took the specter of economic disaster for women to break a longstanding tradition and enter the workplace.

Here's a look at how the Great Depression helped spur the federal government to take an active role in aiding people in need, and how women have fared in the workplace since the 1930s.

Weaving a social services safety net

A host of 21st-century social service programs have their roots in actions taken by the federal government in response to the Great Depression. They include the following:

✔ **Federal–State Unemployment Compensation:** Created as part of the Social Security Act of 1935, the program is administered by individual states under federal guidelines. It's financed by payroll taxes paid by employers. Almost anyone paid a salary or hourly wage is covered. Most states pay a maximum of 26 weeks of benefits. An estimated 8 million people collected $35 billion in benefits in the 2008 fiscal year.

✔ **Temporary Assistance for Needy Families (TANF):** Started in July 1997, this program is a successor to Aid to Families with Dependent Children (AFDC, 1960), which in turn was spawned by Aid to Dependent Children (ADC, 1935). The program is designed to give families up to 60 months of benefits, the levels of which vary from state to state. But it also requires recipients to work at least part-time. About 3.8 million families were participating in the program as of June 2008.

✔ **Housing Choice Voucher Program:** This program sprang from a 1937 law and is better known as "Section 8," after the part of the law that dealt with the program. Under it, low-income people pay a percentage (generally no more than 30 percent) of their income for rent. The federal government pays the rest.

✔ **Supplemental Nutrition Assistance Program:** Better known as the "food stamp" program, it provides assistance in buying food to low-income people. Until the late 1990s, recipients were issued booklets of coupons, or "stamps," to exchange for food. The coupons were phased out in favor of electronic debit cards. The program, which served about 31.5 million people in fall 2008, is the latest iteration of a program that ran from 1939 to 1943. It was revived in 1961 and became a permanent program in 1964.

Virtually all of these programs have been criticized, often with justification, for faults ranging from arbitrary eligibility rules to insufficient benefit levels. None of them have totally solved the problems they're designed to address. For example, the federal government estimated there were still 672,000 homeless people in the country in 2007, and that estimate is probably low.

But all in all, if you asked someone in a 1933 bread line, he'd almost certainly be glad to jump into a 21st-century social services safety net, holes and all.

Paying women what they're worth

World War II tossed out the window many of the traditional arguments about women going to work. Millions of women took jobs left vacant by men in uniform. One thing that didn't change, however, was the gender gap in wages: In 1944, women in war-production factories received an average of $31.21 a week, while men working in the same jobs were paid $54.65.

That gap remained relatively stable until the early 1960s, when Congress passed the Equal Pay Act, which made it illegal to pay men and women different wages for the same job. Between 1963 and 2008, the gender wage gap closed from women making 60 percent of what men received to 77 percent.

Even so, according to U.S. census numbers, the gap was still costing women from $400,000 to $2 million in lost wages over a lifetime. In 2009, several bills to strengthen and close loopholes in the 1963 law were pending in Congress.

In most recessions since World War II, women tended to lose their jobs at a lesser rate than men did. But in the recession that began in late 2007, the percentage of women becoming unemployed was actually higher than the percentage of men. Median wages for women also fell much farther (3 percent in 2007, compared to 0.5 percent for men), according to a report by the U.S. Senate Committee on Health, Education, Labor and Pensions.

Men or women still dominated certain jobs in the 2000s, just as they did in the 1930s. For example, 91 percent of registered nurses in 2007 were women, while 83 percent of industrial engineers were men. But gender barriers had come down in scores of occupations, and women filled jobs that few in the 1930s could have imagined them in, such as firefighter, airline pilot, and Secretary of State.

Chapter 6

Troubles on the Farm

*I*f one group of Americans was well-rehearsed for the onset of the Great Depression in late 1929, it was the 29 million people who lived on farms. That's because they had already been punched and pummeled by economic forces throughout the 1920s.

In this chapter, I show how the already-dreary situation for U.S. farmers got worse. I explain how some of them fought back and how the federal government came up with a plan to make farmers' lives better by paying them for not growing so much stuff. The chapter ends with Mother Nature walloping farmers with drought, dust, and bugs. It wasn't easy being a farmer in the Great Depression.

Farmers' Pre-Depression Depression

Americans had a long tradition of idealizing farmers and farm life. Thomas Jefferson referred to them as "the chosen people of God." The 19th-century orator and statesman Daniel Webster declared that farmers "are the foundation of civilization." And Theodore Roosevelt insisted that "everything possible should be done to better the economic condition of the farmer."

While such statements may have made farmers feel warm and fuzzy, the truth was that farming had always been a very tough way to make a living. It was heavily dependent on the uncontrollable variables of both nature and how much people were willing to pay for what they ate and wore.

Getting a boost from weather and WWI

But by the second decade of the 20th century, the stars seemed to align themselves in favor of U.S. farmers. Rainfall was reliable, and the weather generally cooperated. The outbreak of World War I in 1914 meant most European nations had to devote their attention and resources to fighting instead of farming. As a result, demand for U.S. exports of food and fiber soared.

The growth in demand came at the same time that technology was improving everything from irrigation systems to egg incubators. Particularly important were improvements in tractors that made them smaller and more maneuverable. The number of motorized farm vehicles tripled during and just after World War I.

The advent of tractors meant the demise of many horses and mules that had previously been used to supply power to farm machines. An estimated 9 million animals were destroyed in the decade following World War I, and 25 million acres that had been used to grow animal food were converted to grow people food.

The improved technology meant improved production, which, combined with higher prices, resulted in more profit. For example, in 1913 U.S. wheat farmers produced 751 million bushels on 52 million acres for a price of 79 cents a bushel. In 1919, the year after the war's end, wheat farmers produced 952 million bushels on 73.7 million acres for $2.16 a bushel. Gross income for all U.S. farm products rose from $7.9 billion in 1913 to $18 billion in 1919.

And as demand grew and prices rose, many farmers began acquiring more land so they could make even more money. Farm mortgage debt rose from $3.4 billion in 1910 to $6.7 billion in 1920 and more than $9 billion by 1925. It proved in most instances to be a classic case of overreaching.

Watching demand and prices fall

Two things happened to end the financial frolic on U.S. farms. The first was that World War I ended. Nations that had devoted most of their resources to the war began growing their own food and fibers again, reducing the demand for U.S. products.

The second was that farmers did precisely the wrong thing in the face of falling prices: They continued to overproduce, growing more crops and animals than there was a market for, either abroad or within the United States.

The result was that prices dropped precipitously. Wheat prices fell from a high of $2.16 a bushel in 1919 to 93 cents a bushel in 1923. Total farm income, which had reached $18 billion in 1919, was $6 billion a decade later. In 1929, the average per capita income of all Americans was $750. For farmers, it was $273.

And then things really got bad. As the entire country slipped into economic quicksand at the end of 1929, and being able to afford food became an everyday struggle for millions of people, demand — and prices — slipped sharply down:

- ✔ Chicken farmers in Missouri earned as little as 3 cents a dozen for eggs. Dairy farmers in Nebraska sold milk for as little as 2 cents a quart — when they could sell it at all.

- ✔ Corn was so cheap, an Iowa school district offered to trade a season ticket to high school basketball games for 600 pounds of ear corn, but only if the corn was delivered.

- ✔ In January 1933, an Iowa farmer reportedly sent five calves to the Chicago stockyards by rail. He got back a bill for $1.98: The sales price hadn't covered the cost of shipping and feeding them.

Total U.S. farm income, which had been at a lofty $18 billion in 1919, was $2 billion by 1932. Wheat prices, which had been $2.16 a bushel in 1919, dropped to 38 cents in 1932. The average per-acre value of farmland fell from $69.31 in 1920 to $29.68 in 1932. By the mid-1930s, only 16 percent of U.S. farm families were making more than $1,500 a year, which was the U.S. median family income. More than half of farm families were making less than $1,000 a year.

"We plan to live on our small income of $1 a week, besides $3.60 which we receive from the relief every week," a South Dakota farm wife wrote a farming magazine in February 1935. She added ominously, "If these plans don't work out, we won't need to make any more plans."

While prices and income dropped, however, mortgage payments and property taxes remained fixed. By 1933, 150,000 farms a year were being foreclosed, more than 17,000 a year in Iowa alone. By 1934, federal officials estimated that 30 percent of the farms in the northern and central states were owned by "creditors or government agencies which have been compelled to take over the property."

It wasn't just a lack of income that made life difficult for families, but also a lack of basic services and amenities. More than 1,300 rural counties had no general hospital. Nine of ten farm households had no indoor toilet, and eight of ten had no electricity. Hundreds of thousands of school-age children couldn't go to school because they were needed to work on the farm, they lacked clothes or shoes, or there was simply no school in their area.

Farm families in the Midwest burned cow manure for fuel, made soup out of the thorny Russian thistle tumbleweed, and watched their animals starve. On a visit to the Dakotas in 1933, federal investigator Lorena Hickok reported the area had become "the Siberia of the United States."

"A more hopeless place I never saw," she wrote. "Half the people — the farmers particularly — are scared half to death . . . the rest of the people are apathetic."

Sharecroppers: The worst of the worst-off

As bad as things were in the Midwest and Great Plains states, they were worse in the South. Drought conditions that plagued most U.S. farming regions at various times throughout the 1930s started in the South first, in 1930. That was just three years after devastating floods in the region had covered vast areas, wiping out entire crops.

In addition, the Southern farmer was much more likely than farmers elsewhere to be a tenant farmer or a sharecropper. About 75 percent of farmers outside the South owned the land they farmed. In the South, fewer than half did.

Tenant farmers ranked slightly above sharecroppers on the socio-economic pyramid. Tenant farmers were renters who often used their own equipment and kept the profits from their crops.

Sharecroppers were often virtual slaves, or at best medieval-style serfs. Landowners advanced money to the sharecroppers for seeds and supplies. The sharecroppers planted and reaped, then turned over a share of the crops to repay the debt, the rent on the land, and the use of equipment. Plus, landowners received a percentage of whatever amount was left. That left the sharecropper with not very much. A 1933 study of four Southern states found that the average annual income for working sharecroppers was $350 for white families and $294 for black families.

The sharecroppers' living conditions were for the most part horrendous. A January 1933 story in *The New York Times* about sharecroppers in Arkansas described them as living off lard, flour, and salt pork given to them by the Red Cross. Their homes were "shacks built of logs" and "dilapidated board houses."

"They have little furniture," the story related, "perhaps a bed, two or three chairs and a stove in one room, and a rickety table and stove in the kitchen. Many are less fortunate than this . . . a lawyer at Harrisburg told of visiting one family of five where all were living in one room, sleeping on the floor and with a fireplace of mud."

After touring some Southern states in 1934, Secretary of Agriculture Henry Wallace declared that "one third of the farmers of the United States live under conditions which are so much worse than the peasantry of Europe that the city people of the United States should be thoroughly embarrassed."

Fumbling federal efforts to help

A few efforts were made at the federal level in the 1920s to help the beleaguered farmer, none of them successful. Congress twice passed bills that would have authorized the federal government to buy excess crops at prices that reasonably reflected the farmers' cost of production, and then either store the crops until market prices rose or sell them to other countries for whatever they would pay. But President Calvin Coolidge vetoed both bills on the grounds that it was too expensive and that government should stay out of the market.

When Herbert Hoover succeeded Coolidge as president in 1929, one of his first efforts was to try to convince farmers to form *cooperatives* where they could coordinate crop production with each other. He also pushed a bill through Congress that created the Federal Farm Board, which was authorized to buy surplus crops and store them. But the cooperative thing never got going, and the Farm Board rather quickly ran out of money and storage space before it had much of an impact.

Farmers, meanwhile, were fed up with the Feds. At a January 1933 hearing of the U.S. Senate's Committee on Agriculture, the president of the Wisconsin Farmers' Union told senators, "I almost hate to express it, but I honestly believe that if some of them (farmers) could buy airplanes, they would come down here to Washington and blow you fellows up."

John Simpson, the president of the National Farmers Union, echoed the sentiment. "The biggest and finest crop of revolutions you ever saw is sprouting all over the country right now," he warned.

Fighting-Mad Farmers

As early as 1927, farmers in the Missouri River Valley in western Iowa and eastern Nebraska had talked about a strike. Following the veto by President Calvin Coolidge of a bill that would have had the federal government buy surplus crops, a group of farmers calling themselves the Corn Belt Committee drafted a resolution that stated in part, "if we cannot obtain justice by legislation, the time will have arrived when no other course remains than organized refusal to deliver the production of the farms at less than production costs."

What the committee wanted was "parity," which they defined as crop and livestock prices that covered the cost of production and transportation, plus a "reasonable" profit of 5.25 percent. But the architects of the idea received little support for the idea of a farmers' strike until 1932.

By then, the gap between "parity" prices and real-world prices was enormous. The parity price of corn was estimated at 92 cents a bushel; of hogs, $11.25; and of butterfat, 62 cents a pound. The real prices were 32 cents a bushel for corn, $3.85 for hogs, and 18 cents for a pound of butterfat. Meanwhile, the number of farms being foreclosed because farmers could not pay their mortgages or taxes was rising weekly.

Calling for a "holiday"

In May 1932, about 1,300 farmers met in Des Moines, Iowa, and formed the Farmers' Holiday Association. The "Holiday" part was borrowed from a practice banks used to avoid mass withdrawals: When a run on the bank began, the banker would declare a "holiday" and simply keep the doors locked until things cooled off.

What the farmers proposed to do was simple: refuse to deliver their crops and animals to market until they received fixed and fair prices, and prevent anyone else from delivering their products.

"Concede to the farmer production costs," the group's leader, Milo Reno, said in a radio address, "and he will pay his grocer, the grocer will pay the wholesaler, the wholesaler will pay the manufacturer, and the manufacturer will be able to meet his obligations at the bank. Restore the farmers' purchasing power, and you have re-established an endless chain of prosperity and happiness in the country."

The chances of a farmers' strike succeeding were pretty much zero from the start. For one thing, they were badly organized and never attracted a large enough following to have a major impact. Many farmers simply could not afford to withhold their crops, even if the prices they were paid were miniscule. Families and livestock had to be fed. In addition, many farmers were suspicious of anything that smacked of communism (and indeed, communists did try to gain a foothold in the association).

It was also extremely difficult to actually block all the possible ways to get to all the markets that existed. But that didn't stop the group from trying.

Facing the farmers in the road

The striking farmers used spiked logs and cables to block roads into towns that had agricultural markets. Cars were allowed to proceed; trucks with produce, grain, livestock, or dairy products were turned away, sometimes with a bit of force applied by club-wielding farmers. Local police, who were badly outnumbered (and sometimes sympathetic to the cause), couldn't do much, and so the strikers got bolder.

Lawyers for mortgage-holding companies were kidnapped, bankers bullied, and aggressive lawmen disarmed. After several strikers in Council Bluffs, Iowa, were arrested, a mob of 1,000 men marched into town and freed them. In Wisconsin, two cheese factories were bombed, and scores more closed temporarily in fear.

In late April 1933 in Le Mars, Iowa, a district court judge named Charles C. Bradley was dragged from his courthouse by a mob of 600 farmers. The judge was roughed up, and a rope was put around his neck. After he refused to promise to stop hearing foreclosure cases, the mob clapped a grease-filled hubcap on his head, removed his pants, and left him standing in the middle of the road.

The strikers even had a song: "Let's call a farmer's holiday/A holiday let's hold/We'll eat our wheat and ham and eggs/And let them eat their gold."

They also had a rationalization for their actions, which was that they were following American tradition. "They say blockading the road's illegal," a striker told a reporter for *Harper's Magazine*. "I says 'seems to me there was a tea party in Boston that was illegal too.'"

Holding "penny" auctions

The striking farmers had another tactic that was actually more effective than the roadblocks, at least in terms of actual results: They would sabotage foreclosure auctions. Sometimes doing so involved forcibly blocking the sheriff and auctioneer from starting the auction at all, and sometimes it meant bullying the mortgage holder into rethinking the foreclosure.

At one Iowa auction, farmers pushed their way through a police line, forced the mortgagor to forget about foreclosing, and then made the mortgagor and each of the cops kneel and kiss the American flag.

In slightly more subtle cases, the Holiday farmers would conduct "penny" auctions. Someone would bid a penny or other small amount for a piece of farm equipment being auctioned, and it was made clear that no one else was welcome to bid. After everything had been sold, the mortgage holder was prodded into accepting whatever pittance had been raised and relinquishing the deed, which was then turned over to the farm's owner.

For example, at an October 1932 foreclosure sale of a Nebraska widow's farm, 2,500 of her "neighbors" showed up. Her cows sold for 35 cents each, her disc plow for 25 cents, and her six horses for a total of $5.60. When it was over, everything had been sold for a bit over $100. The banker grudgingly turned over the $442 mortgage for the $100, and the widow was given back the farm and all its assets.

Catching Washington's attention

Just as the roadblocks failed to raise crop prices, the penny auctions didn't in themselves make a significant dent in foreclosure sales. But both kinds of actions did make a significant impression on the region's politicians and got the attention of people in Washington, D.C.

North Dakota Governor William "Wild Bill" Langer advised farmers during his 1932 election campaign to "shoot the banker if he comes on your farm. Treat him like a chicken thief." (Langer later imposed a short-lived embargo on North Dakota wheat, prohibiting wheat from being shipped out of the state until prices rose.) Iowa legislators passed a law in February 1933 that put a foreclosure moratorium on all mortgages that were not yet delinquent. Eight other states followed with similar laws.

The Holiday group also got the attention of the national media. In *The New Republic* in August 1932, journalist Donald R. Murphy wrote that the strike was "a significant symptom of the state of mind of a great conservative class which has borne depression for twelve years and which is finally ready to employ radical measures that seem to give it a chance to save itself from general bankruptcy."

After the election of Franklin D. Roosevelt in November 1932, the striking farmers took a wait-and-see stance and halted most of their road blocking and auction hijacking. Roosevelt and Congress quickly pushed through several bills designed to provide relief to farmers (covered in this chapter's next section).

Milo Reno

Depending on your point of view, Milo Reno was either a charismatic prophet or a demagogic rabble-rouser. Either way, he kept things lively in America's farm country during the Great Depression.

Reno was born in Iowa in 1866, the 12th of 13 children of a farm family. Pushed by his mother, he attended college in Iowa, where he studied theology. After a career as a farmer and part-time preacher, Reno joined the newly formed Iowa Farmers' Union in 1918. Within three years, he was union president and also ran two of the union's three insurance companies.

As founder, president, and chief instigator of the Farmers' Holiday Association, Reno was a tireless orator and organizer. Tall and thin-lipped, with a shock of bushy hair and a fondness for oversized cowboy hats, Reno became something of a media darling for several years during the 1930s. *Time* magazine described him as both "indefatigable" and "a bad weather bird" who showed up wherever there was dissension.

But as the Roosevelt administration's farm relief efforts took hold, Reno's fiery rhetoric became less interesting. He became a staunch FDR-hater and began championing the formation of a third major political party in time for the 1936 presidential race. Like the farmers' strike, the third-party idea failed to catch on. Reno died of a heart attack in 1936 at the age of 70.

The federal government's efforts weren't enough for some of the Holiday Association, including its president, Milo Reno. Reno wanted the government to guarantee set prices for farm products and set no limits on how much farmers could produce. "We were promised a new deal by which agriculture would receive the same consideration as others," Reno complained. "Instead, we have the same old stacked deck."

But others thought the Roosevelt plan was a fair start. "We don't care if Milo Reno does say that you shouldn't touch any of that (federal) money," the *Le Mars* (Iowa) *Sentinel* editorialized. "When you get a chance to get Uncle Sam's check for anywhere from $300 to $1,000 and even more, there's something wrong with you if you don't take it."

By the end of 1933, the farmers' strike was all but over. But it had served to shine the national spotlight on the plight of American farmers, and helped spur efforts to ease their burdens.

Paying Farmers Not to Farm

Within weeks of taking office in March 1933, President Roosevelt began pushing for a program to aid farmers. In May, FDR signed the Emergency Farm Mortgage Act, which provided $200 million for refinancing mortgages for farmers facing foreclosure.

He also signed the Agricultural Adjustment Act (AAA), which created the Agricultural Adjustment Administration, as well as doing some pretty interesting adjusting to U.S. agriculture. Previous efforts to deal with farm overproduction had centered on taking farm product surpluses off the market and storing them. Roosevelt favored a different approach: not growing or raising the surplus products in the first place.

That's exactly what the AAA did. Farmers who agreed to plant at least one-third fewer acres or raise at least one-third fewer animals were paid by the federal government for the ungrown or unraised products. The price was set at or near prices for the products that were actually grown or raised. Money to fund the program was raised by imposing a tax on food processors, which in turn slightly raised consumer prices. Other AAA elements came to include price supports for rice, fruit, peanuts, and milk. Another $2 billion was set aside for providing mortgage aid to farmers looking to refinance their loans.

A program run through the federal Commodity Credit Corporation further supplemented the act. The program allowed farmers to obtain loans from the federal government in return for agreeing to store part of their crops. If market prices rose, the farmer could reclaim his crops, sell them, and repay the loan. If prices didn't rise, the farmer could keep the loan and the Feds would keep the crop. By 1940, the federal government was storing more than $500 million worth of unwanted cotton, wheat, and corn.

Pumping money into the economy

In addition, the AAA authorized as much as $3 billion in new currency to be added to the U.S. monetary system. The idea was to "reflate" the economy because the more money there is in the system, the easier it generally is to get some of it. Prices can therefore be raised without putting goods and services out of the reach of consumers. By raising prices, farmers could more easily pay their mortgages and taxes, countering the *deflation* (drop in prices and consumption) that had plagued them for years.

An example: Farmer Jones got $2.19 a bushel for his wheat in 1919 and had mortgage payments of $50 a month. In 1932, wheat fell to 38 cents a bushel but the mortgage was still $50 a month. But with more money in the system, wheat prices rose to 69 cents in 1934, while the mortgage stayed at $50.

The act was certainly ambitious enough to draw plenty of criticism. Food processors hated it because of the tax it imposed on them. Mortgage lenders and people with lots of money hated the idea of more money being pumped into the economy because it meant the money they already had was less rare and, therefore, worth less.

Even some farmers were skeptical. "The way I figure it, we've got to pay this money back some day," an Iowa farmer told a touring reporter from the *Syracuse* (New York) *Herald* about a year after the act was in place. "The money I got for hogs and corn I didn't have to raise was a life-saver . . . but there is no reason to it I can see. The agents tell me I do not understand economics. Well, maybe I don't, but I wonder if they understand farming."

But like many of FDR's programs, most people were willing to give it a try and see if it would help the farmer. *BusinessWeek* magazine editorialized, "It might seem important to us to preserve in our country the one large class of property owners, the greatest body of entrepreneurs, the one stable and rooted element. It might seem worth a high cost — and it might be cheaper than to add them (farmers) to the breadlines of the cities."

Finding a glitch and a flaw in the AAA

The Agricultural Adjustment Act contained both a politically embarrassing glitch and a cruelly devastating flaw.

"[T]he slaughter of innocents"

The glitch was that FDR didn't get the bill from Congress and sign it until May 12, 1933. That turned out to be well after Southern farmers had planted their cotton crops and the spring litters of hogs had been born in the Midwest.

To reduce surpluses right away and get money to the farmers quickly, the farmers were persuaded to plow up 10 million acres of cotton and destroy 200,000 sows and 6 million piglets. All that potential clothing material and pork chops going to waste was a bit much to swallow for millions of hungry and ill-clothed Americans.

The noted defense and civil rights attorney Clarence Darrow proclaimed it a crime to "kill little pigs and throw them out on the prairies to decay while millions are hungry." Newspaper columnists labeled it "the slaughter of the innocents." Even Secretary of Agriculture Henry Wallace acknowledged it was "a shocking commentary on our civilization."

By October, an embarrassed government formed the Federal Surplus Relief Corporation, which diverted excess farm products to state and local relief agencies. Harder to fix, however, was the plight of the tenant farmer and sharecropper because of the AAA.

The greedy stiff the needy

The flaw was in the way the Agricultural Adjustment Act dealt with tenant farmers and sharecroppers, the farmers who most needed help. Because subsidies from the AAA were based on the amount of land a farmer owned, farmers who rented their land were left out in the cold. The act did call for landowners to share their federal loot with their tenant farmers and sharecroppers, but it relied on the landowner to pass on the money, and very few did.

Instead, many landowners either withdrew rental farmland from production or used the federal money to buy tractors and hire day laborers to work the fields. Either way, the tenant farmers and sharecroppers and their families were often out on their ears.

They found themselves with no place to go. Some tenant farmers (both white and black) in Arkansas organized a union in 1933 to try to get a share of the federal money. Beatings and whippings by goons hired by landowners ended that effort. Congress passed two bills, one to resettle displaced tenant farmers and the other to help them buy land. Neither worked very well. And the Roosevelt administration was hesitant to fix the problem for fear it would alienate Southern members of Congress whose votes were needed for New Deal programs to gain approval.

The result was that tens of thousands of the poorest farmers took to the road, many heading for the promise of a paradise in California. Whether that effort worked out for them is covered in Chapter 8.

Revamping the AAA

Coupled with a severe and persistent drought that decimated crops (which I cover in the next section) and reduced supplies, the Agricultural Adjustment Act did help raise farm prices and farm income. Wheat rose from 32 cents a bushel in 1932 to 69 cents in 1934, 92 cents in 1936, and $1.24 in 1937. Cotton, which had sold for about 6 cents a pound in 1932, averaged between 10 cents and 13 cents in the next four years. Gross farm income rose 50 percent between 1933 and 1936.

In 1936, however, the U.S. Supreme Court declared the act unconstitutional on the grounds that "Congress has no power to enforce its command on the farmer to the ends sought by" the act, and that the processing tax it contained was also illegal.

Roosevelt quickly countered the court's decision with the Soil Conservation and Domestic Allotment Act, which paid farmers to conserve soil by following the natural contours of the land *(contour farming)* rather than straight rows. It also provided funds for planting beans, clove, and other crops that renewed the soil. This time, the money came from the federal government's general operating budget and not a specific tax.

In 1937, another bill was approved that allowed the Secretary of Agriculture to set acreage limits for staple crops in order to stem surpluses. It had limited success, and farm surpluses continued until World War II came along.

Throughout the rest of the Great Depression, the Roosevelt administration continued to tinker with farm legislation. "(It) is in the nature of an experiment," Roosevelt told reporters. "We all recognize that. My position toward farm legislation is that we ought to do something to increase the value of farm products, and if the darn thing doesn't work, we can say so quite frankly, but at least try it."

Drought and Dust

On April 15, 1935, newspapers around the country carried a story written by Associated Press reporter Robert Geiger from a town called Guymon, Oklahoma.

It began: "Three little words — achingly familiar on a Western farmer's tongue — rule life today in the dust bowl of the continent: 'If it rains.' Ask any farmer, any merchant, any banker, and you hear them: 'If it rains.'"

Geiger used the term "dust bowl" to describe a specific geographic region: the western third of Kansas, southeastern Colorado, the Oklahoma panhandle, the northeastern two-thirds of the Texas panhandle, and northeastern New Mexico. But the phrase caught on. It was capitalized for emphasis and became the catchall term for what was the worst environmental and agricultural disaster in U.S. history.

The disaster began with the plow and the high price of wheat. For centuries, the Great Plains had been covered with hardy buffalo grass. The region had a semi-arid climate but was suitable for grazing animals. In the last part of the 19th century and first part of the 20th, however, people began ripping up the buffalo grass and replacing it with wheat.

In good years, with plenty of rain, the result was bumper crops. But in 1930, the rain stopped coming to much of the country's midsection. The next year saw a return to near normalcy, but in 1932 precipitation dropped precipitously. By 1934, the drought had spread to cover 75 percent of the country. At least 27 states were severely affected.

Peaks at the southern end of the Rocky Mountains received no snow in the winter of 1933–34. In parts of the Midwest, the top three feet of earth contained no detectable moisture. Between June 1933 and May 1934, almost no rain at all fell on the southern Great Plains.

The drought — which lasted in some areas through 1936 — was accompanied by blistering heat in the summers. On July 24, 1933, temperatures reached 117 degrees in Vinita, Oklahoma; 109 in Omaha, Nebraska; and 112 in Independence, Kansas. In 1936, parts of western Kansas had 60 straight days of temperatures of 100 degrees or more.

Roosevelt, the rainmaker

In August 1934, President Roosevelt toured drought-stricken areas of Minnesota and North Dakota. "It is a problem," Roosevelt understated to a crowd in Devils Lake, North Dakota. "I would not try to fool you by saying we know the solution of it . . . when I came out on the (train) platform this morning, I saw a rather dark cloud. I said to myself 'maybe it is going to rain.' Well it didn't. All I can say is, I hope to goodness it is going to rain, good and plenty."

And it did rain, although not "good and plenty." After the presidential train left, *The New York Times* reported, "the rain cut a path about 100 miles wide . . . with the heaviest fall in the cities the presidential train visited. In each case the showers came about seven hours after the (president) had departed."

But even Roosevelt couldn't be everywhere at once. Some communities in Kansas listened to pitches from salesmen with machines that could make it rain — they said. But, *The New York Times* reported, "thirty years ago, Kansas invested in rain-making machines which failed, and they are skittish of the new apparatuses."

In Mitchell, South Dakota, people turned to prayer. At 11 a.m. on July 10, 1936, with the temperature hovering at 104 degrees (the eighth straight day over 100), the town's 13 church towers began tolling their bells. Eleven thousand people fell to their knees and prayed for rain. It didn't work.

A plague of grasshoppers

One creature — make that billions of creatures — that loved the heat and aridity were grasshoppers. Encouraged to breed often by the dry conditions, grasshoppers proliferated across the northern Great Plains during the early and mid-1930s. In 1933, entomologists estimated grasshopper infestations covered 75 percent of South Dakota, with the insects laying as many as 5,000 to 10,000 eggs per square foot in some areas.

"The sun was shining brightly when we left home," a South Dakota woman wrote in 1933. "When we were about halfway, it just turned dark. It was grasshoppers, blocking the sun."

They came in such massive numbers that they stacked up four inches deep in streets, making cars skid as if they were on ice. It was reported that trains sometimes could not get traction on the track rails because they were covered with grasshoppers.

And they ate virtually everything: grain, vegetables, clothes left hanging out to dry, even the corks out of water jugs. A Nebraska woman in 1936 reported that her 5-year-old daughter left a doll outside, and the grasshoppers ate it.

To cope, farmers tried mixing bran, molasses, and arsenic and spreading it on the edges of fields. The grasshoppers ate it with enthusiasm, even consuming the abdomens of their poisoned comrades. The *Aberdeen* (South Dakota) *News* suggested farmers employ ring-necked pheasants, which were regarded by many farmers as a grain-eating pest in their own right, to gobble the grasshoppers. "Pheasants will utterly ignore grains as long as there is an abundance of insects," the paper advised.

Neither the poison nor the birds put much of a dent in the hordes of 'hoppers. It would take a return to more normal weather conditions to do that, and there wasn't much farmers could do about the weather.

Mountains of dust

On May 11, 1934, the captain of a German liner reported that the ship was late reaching port in New York City because of "a peculiar atmospheric cloudiness" it encountered while off the East Coast of the United States.

What the ship had run into was the middle of the United States, or at least part of it, in the form of dust. The dust — an estimated 300 million tons of it — had been picked up by strong northwest winds from the parched Great Plains and swept across the Mississippi River. It stretched from St. Paul, Minnesota, in the north to Nashville, Tennessee, in the south, reached heights of 15,000 feet, and was still so thick when it reached New York that pedestrians could not see the tops of the city's skyscrapers.

"The explanation of the dust cloud is simple," U.S. Weather Service meteorologist James H. Kimball told *The New York Times.* "The surface soil in the Upper Missouri and Mississippi valleys was fine and loose as a result of the drought. All that was needed was a persistent and direct wind."

From 1934 to 1938, big and small dust storms swirled through and out of the nation's midsection. They occurred most often in summer, although "brown snow storms" were not unheard of in winter. And while persistent, the winds were not always predictable.

"If the wind blew one way, here came the dark dust from Oklahoma," a Texas farmer contended in 1934. "Another way, and it was the gray dust from Kansas. Still another way, the brown dust from Colorado and New Mexico."

The statistics generated by the dust storms were stunning:

✔ Federal officials reported in late 1934 that the storms had wreaked havoc across 1,400 counties in 22 states.

✔ The 1934 *Yearbook on Agriculture* calculated that 225 million acres of farmland had either lost their topsoil or were in the process of losing it.

✔ The Department of Agriculture estimated that 19 million bushels of wheat were lost in one week to a dust storm in mid-1934.

Photographs of the storms, such as in Figure 6-1, inspired awe and dread in those who had never seen a dust storm in person. For those who encountered them all too frequently, it was an experience that was simultaneously familiar and terrifying.

Photo by Three Lions/Getty Images

Figure 6-1: A 1937 dust storm in Colorado caused total darkness that lasted for about a half hour.

A South Dakota observer described a 1933 storm this way: "By noon it was blacker than night, because one can see through night, and this was an opaque black. It was a wall of dust one's eyes could not penetrate, but it could penetrate the eyes, ears and nose. It could penetrate to the lungs until one coughed up black."

The dust was a killer. A 6-year-old boy walking home from school near Hays, Kansas, got lost in a dust storm, became tangled in a barbed wire fence, and suffocated. Six people died in a Colorado storm that lasted nearly a week. Infant mortality rates were sharply higher in Dust Bowl states.

Life's little chores became teeth-grinding labor. Dishes had to be washed before meals to get the dust off. Liquids had to be stored in jars, and holes punched in the lids for straws, to keep the dust out. Meat was fried at the highest temperatures possible so that hot air rising from it would keep the dust from settling.

"Wearing our shade hats, with handkerchiefs tied over our faces and Vaseline in our nostrils, we have been trying to rescue our home from the accumulations of wind-blown dust which penetrates wherever air can go," an Oklahoma woman wrote a friend in June 1935. "It is an almost hopeless task, for there is rarely a day when the dust clouds do not roll over."

Federal government efforts to help were substantial. In 1934, Roosevelt signed a bill that authorized him to establish grazing rights over 140 million acres of federal land, with oversight by the Department of Interior to ensure the land wasn't overgrazed. The government spent $85 million between 1934 and 1936 to buy ruined farmland and try to rehabilitate it. It also bought cattle in drought areas, destroyed those that were in such bad shape they couldn't be eaten, and distributed the meat from the rest to needy families.

And in 1935, Congress established the Soil Conservation Service (SCS) to teach and promote farming methods that preserved topsoil. The SCS encouraged farmers to form conservation districts to oversee soil conservation practices among themselves. Many of the districts continued to operate into the 21st century.

Combined, the programs resulted in an estimated 65 percent reduction in the amount of soil being blown by the winds. And in 1939, the rains came back.

Laughing away the Dust Bowl blues

To keep their spirits up, Dust Bowl residents tried to top each other with tall tales and tongue-in-cheek observations about the dust storms. "My uncle should be along soon," went one line, "because I just saw his farm go by." There was the story of the pilot who had to bail out over Amarillo: "It took him six hours to shovel his way back to earth." Or the fellow who was hit by a drop of water and fainted: "It took two buckets of dust to revive him." And then there was the Kansas woman who, when asked by a reporter how bad the latest storm had been, replied "Lady Godiva could have ridden through it without even her horse seeing her."

Lessons Learned

The Great Depression radically changed the relationship between the American farmer and the federal government. Here's a look at how government has redefined its role in agriculture since the 1930s, and how it handles surplus food and the poor.

The farmer and the Feds

Prior to the 1930s, the federal government rarely intervened in the agricultural economy. But since passage of the Agricultural Adjustment Act (AAA) in 1933, there have been at least a dozen major bills approved by Congress and signed by the president that deal with providing some form of financial aid to farmers.

Until the mid-1960s, major farm legislation was similar to 1933's AAA. The bills committed the federal government to guaranteeing prices on farm products and paid farmers not to plant or raise more than the market could buy. But in 1965, Congress began providing some direct income support to farmers that wasn't tied directly to how much they did or didn't grow. The idea was that surplus products could be sold to expanding markets in other countries. In 1977, "farm bills" began to include non-farm elements, such as nutrition assistance programs like food stamps.

 In 1996, the "Freedom to Farm" bill cut any remaining ties between federal payments to farmers and surplus production. One result was that surplus U.S. farm products began to swamp some world markets, undercutting farmers in other countries.

What's new on the farm?

When people talk about the "disappearing American farmer," they're not kidding. Consider this:

- ✔ **Fewer farm families:** About 24 percent of the U.S. population lived on farms in 1930. The number was 2 percent in 2008. The number of farms during that same period dropped from 6.8 million to 2.1 million.

- ✔ **Fewer farm workers:** About 21.5 percent of working Americans made their living on farms in 1930, producing 7.7 percent of the country's gross domestic product (GDP). In 2000, only 1.9 percent of the U.S. workforce worked on farms, producing 0.7 percent of the GDP.

- ✔ **Less reliance on farm income:** In 1930, about 30 percent of farm families had income from work off the farm. In 2002, 93 percent had off-farm income.

In 2008, Congress passed a $300 billion farm package, overriding the veto of President George W. Bush. The 673-page bill included $200 billion for nutritional assistance programs, $43 billion for subsidies to farmers, $30 billion for crop insurance programs, and $27 billion for conservation efforts.

While only about 25 percent of U.S. farms received subsidies in 2008, the program has been routinely criticized over the years for doling out taxpayer money to rich "farmers" that include foreign corporations and farm owners who rarely set foot on their farms. The 2008 bill, for example, "limited" subsidies to those who made less than $750,000 a year in farm income and less than $500,000 a year in non-farm income.

The definition of "farm relief" has come a long way since the Great Depression.

Feeding the poor

In 1933, the federal government suffered a public relations black eye when it convinced farmers to destroy 6 million piglets and 10 million acres of cotton to reduce surpluses. So the Roosevelt administration set up the Federal Surplus Relief Corporation, which eventually became the Federal Surplus Commodity Corporation, which eventually became the Surplus Marketing Administration, which eventually became the Emergency Food Assistance Program run by the U.S. Department of Agriculture.

Whatever it was called, the program's purpose was to take surplus farm products the government had bought from farmers and give them to people in need — through food banks, soup kitchens, and other distribution centers.

The system works okay when U.S. farmers have a surplus of commodities to sell. But when farmers have domestic and foreign markets for everything they produce, there is no surplus. In 2003, for example, the Feds provided $242 million in surplus commodities; in 2007 it was only $59 million.

In 2009, the program was expected to supply $92.6 million in surplus commodities. An additional $250 million for food assistance was included in the 2008 farm bill, along with a program that supplies monthly food boxes to needy Americans.

Chapter 7

Misery Loves Company: How the Rest of the World Fared

The United States didn't have a monopoly on suffering during the Great Depression. In fact, very few countries escaped hard times.

This chapter begins with an explanation of how post–World War I desires for revenge and debt repayment played important roles in bringing about the Great Depression, as well as what role the gold standard had in the whole mess. I then offer some snapshots of how various countries and continents fared during the period. Finally, I look at how the Great Depression was handled in countries run by some of history's nastiest people.

Tallying the Costs of War

In his memoirs, published in 1952, Herbert Hoover made it clear where he placed the blame for the calamitous gyrations of the world's economy in the 1920s and 1930s. In fact, blame was assigned in the very first sentence: "The primary cause of the Great Depression was the war of 1914–1918."

Hoover overstated World War I's impact as a cause of the Great Depression and understated the role that the United States — and its presidents — played in creating the mess. But he did have a point in that the war certainly changed America's role on the world stage.

For one thing, the war shifted the center of the world's economic system from Great Britain to the United States, which had become "the world's banker." The United States had loaned billions to the winning side during the war. After the war, it loaned billions more to the losing side, as well as continuing to funnel money to its wartime allies.

The United States was also the world's manufacturing leader. Improvements in technology and manufacturing techniques in the United States after the war resulted in American workers producing goods at twice the rate of their European counterparts. That made U.S. goods cheaper, which made them more sought after by the rest of the world, which hurt European manufacturing.

So when the U.S. economy sagged badly at the end of 1929, the rest of the world felt its pain. Or as the noted British economist John Maynard Keynes put it at the time: "When America sneezes, the world catches cold."

Paying reparations — or not

In addition to being a nightmarish waste of human life, World War I carried a hefty price tag: an estimated total of $186 billion. (That's about $2.7 *trillion* in 2008 dollars.) The United States, which didn't even get into the fighting until 1917, spent $22.6 billion, much of it in the form of loans to allied countries. Great Britain incurred $35.3 billion of the war's expense. Germany spent $37.7 billion — and wasn't done paying, even after the war ended.

Article 231 of the war-settling Treaty of Versailles declared flatly that Germany was responsible for "all the loss and damage" suffered by the countries that fought against it. Germany agreed — extremely grudgingly — to make a staggering $33 billion in *reparations* (payment of damages) to its former foes. France was to get 52 percent, Great Britain 22 percent, Italy 10 percent, Belgium 8 percent, and smaller countries the rest.

That was a hefty hunk of change to demand from a country whose economy had been eviscerated. Germany had lost 90 percent of its merchant fleet and 75 percent of its iron ore production. The democratically elected government put in place by Germans after the war responded to the pressure by printing money like it was, well, paper. The result was not just inflation, but super mega hyperinflation. In 1923 it took 1 *trillion* German marks to buy what one mark could buy in 1914. People literally used wheelbarrows to carry their money.

The United States, meanwhile, had a difference of opinion with its recent allies about the whole reparations idea. Three consecutive U.S. presidents — Woodrow Wilson, Calvin Coolidge, and Warren G. Harding — all offered to cancel part of the $12 billion owed the United States by European nations *if* the Europeans would give Germany a break on reparations payments. The European countries refused, suggesting that the United States should write off their debts anyway since U.S. military and civilian losses had been so much smaller than the Allies' losses.

In 1923, Germany defaulted on its reparations payments. In retaliation, France and Belgium invaded the Ruhr River region, which was the heart of Germany's coal and steel industries. German workers refused to labor under the foreigners, crippling the industries and exacerbating Germany's already feeble finances.

Trying temporary fixes: The Dawes and Young plans

To head off more trouble, Great Britain and the United States suggested an international committee be formed to find a compromise. The ten-member panel (two each from Belgium, France, Britain, Italy, and the United States) was headed by U.S. financier Charles G. Dawes. In August 1924, the Dawes committee offered a plan under which France and Belgium would vacate the Ruhr region, Germany would follow a repayment plan that called for smaller payments in the first few years, and international bankers would manage some of Germany's economy.

Dawes, who became U.S. vice president under Coolidge in 1925, was a co-recipient of the 1925 Nobel Peace Prize for his efforts. And the plan did help Germany get its inflation under control and its economy a little more stabilized.

But by 1929, German unemployment rates were soaring and the country was again having trouble making its reparations payments. Another international committee was formed, this one chaired by U.S. businessman Owen Young, who had served on the Dawes committee. The Young panel reduced German payments and removed foreign oversight of Germany's economy.

The real fly in the economic ointment applied by the two committees' plans was that they relied on a circular path of finances: The United States made large public and private loans to Germany, which then used the money to pay reparations to other countries, which then used the money to repay their debts to the United States — while borrowing another $7.8 billion from U.S. lenders between 1924 and 1929. As goofy as it was, the system worked for a while.

But as the 1920s ran toward their end, U.S. banks and investors became more interested in pouring money into the U.S. stock market than into Germany, and U.S. loans eventually stopped. When the loans stopped, Germany stopped making reparations, and European countries stopped making debt payments to the United States. And when the U.S. stock market crashed in late 1929, U.S. banks withdrew whatever they could get back from their investments in Europe, making matters worse for the affected countries.

In June 1931, President Hoover proposed a one-year moratorium on all the various debt repayments, which was somewhat grumpily agreed to by the European countries. But Hoover refused to cancel Europe's debts to the United States altogether. To do so would have been highly unpopular with U.S. taxpayers, who saw themselves paying higher taxes if the countries the United States had bailed out in World War I didn't pay their debts.

"You have no idea what the sentiment of the country at large is on the inter-governmental debts," Hoover wrote financier Thomas Lamont in explaining his refusal to forgive the debts.

Germany and Austria, meanwhile, had agreed in spring 1931 to form a "customs union" to foster free trade between the two countries. This situation alarmed France, which withdrew its large deposits from Austria's main bank. That withdrawal put banks in Austria, Germany, and other countries on the edge of collapse. In the ensuing economic downturn, German efforts to repay its war reparations stopped. All told, it had repaid only about one-eighth of what it had agreed to pay.

Making things worse with tariffs

Americans had always had a love-hate relationship with *tariffs* (fees imposed by a country on goods, food, or raw materials imported from other countries). That is, Americans who grew, manufactured, or mined things generally liked tariffs because the fees helped block foreign competition. American consumers, on the other hand, generally disliked tariffs because they tended to drive up prices. Farmers often opposed tariffs, too, because they drove up the prices of manufactured goods.

To help get the country out of a post–World War I slump, Congress in 1922 approved a set of tariff rates that were the highest in the nation's history. The tariffs effectively prevented other countries from selling much of anything to Americans, which hurt their economies. And that situation made it harder for them to pay war debts and other U.S. loans. In 1927, a world economic conference concluded that protective tariffs were bad things. An informal moratorium on tariffs was agreed upon, with hopes that tariffs in place would eventually be lowered.

But in 1929, a Republican-dominated Congress decided to make good on a 1928 campaign promise to "protect" U.S. industries and farmers. After a fierce fight that took 17 months, Congress narrowly approved a bill authored by Representative Willis Hawley of Oregon and Senator Reed Smoot of Utah. The Hawley-Smoot Act dramatically raised tariffs on more than 650 goods, products, and raw materials, from anvils (from 1.5 cents to 3 cents a pound) to wool rags (7.5 cents to 18 cents a pound).

The bill raised howls from critics who saw it for what it was: The beginning of a trade war. More than 1,000 economists signed a petition asking President Hoover to veto the bill. But despite his reservations that the bill went much too far, Hoover signed it into law. Almost before the ink was dry from the six ceremonial pens he used, other countries retaliated with steep tariffs of their own against U.S. products. Eventually, 33 nations put up trade barriers. That included Great Britain, which had for decades been a champion of free trade.

The tariff wars drastically slowed down international trade, which dropped from $36 billion in 1929 to $12 billion in 1932. As trade slowed and international investments dried up, nations' economies began creaking to a halt. By 1933, unemployment was 20 percent or higher in most European countries. The world's industrial productivity rate dropped by 40 percent from its level in the mid-1920s. Even non-industrial countries in Latin America and Africa were hurt because markets for their agricultural goods and raw materials dried up.

Kicking the Gold Habit

In the late 19th and early 20th centuries, much of the Western world adhered to a monetary system known as the *gold standard*. Basically, it meant a nation tied its currency to gold. Nations could then have a good idea what their currency was worth to other nations. For example, an ounce of gold could be worth $20 U.S. or 5 British pounds. That meant a British pound was worth $4 U.S.

The idea was for the system to facilitate international trade because everyone would know what everyone else's money was worth. The system would also help prevent inflation (see Chapter 2 for an explanation of inflation) because the money supply of each country would be tied to the amount of gold it had. And the system would help stabilize prices.

An example: The United States develops a more efficient way to make widgets and can thus sell them for less than British-made widgets. British companies that need widgets would then buy U.S. widgets, and gold-backed British money would flow to the United States. That would increase the U.S. money supply, and the resulting currency inflation would raise U.S. widget prices. Meanwhile, less gold in Britain would mean less currency, causing British widget prices to drop. In theory, British and U.S. widget prices would eventually even out.

But for the gold standard system to work, the countries involved had to adhere to a few rules (which were completely voluntary). They had to keep balanced budgets, where government spending was no greater than revenues from taxes. They had to export more than they imported, to keep their gold levels up. And they had to raise interest rates when their gold holdings sagged. Doing so would cause an overall drop in domestic spending, which would bring the currency back in line with gold reserves.

The war changes the rules

The gold standard was okay in normal times. But the advent of World War I meant combatant countries had to spend a lot of money in a hurry. They had to drop the gold standard and switch to *fiat currency,* which is basically money that has no real value other than as an agreed-upon medium of exchange. (We agree that an apple is worth a piece of paper that says "one dollar." You give me the apple; I give you the piece of paper.)

The advantage of fiat money is that you can put as much as you want into circulation, as long as the printing press holds out and everyone keeps agreeing the paper is worth goods and services. The disadvantage is that it can lead to inflation, where prices go up as the money supply goes up.

After the war, countries gradually began returning to the gold standard. Between 1924 and 1929, more than 40 nations went back to the system, including Britain in 1925, France in 1926, and Italy in 1927. (The United States never really left the gold standard system.)

But the gold standard was a very poor system to have when it came to fighting a major recession. Instead of the higher interest rates and tighter money supplies dictated by the gold standard, effectively fighting a recession calls for lower rates and expanded money supplies. Those tools make it easier for businesses to borrow and give consumers more to spend — and more confidence to spend it.

Some countries were quicker to pick up on this fact than others, and the ones that figured it out first generally started climbing out of the Great Depression first. Great Britain and Sweden bailed out of the gold standard in 1931 and soon began recovering. France didn't drop it until 1936 and was still staggering when World War II began three years later.

In the United States, President Hoover adhered to the economic medicine prescribed by classic gold standard theory — and nearly poisoned his patient. The U.S. money supply was tightened, interest rates were raised, and taxes increased. Things only got worse.

Goodbye, gold standard

When Franklin D. Roosevelt replaced Hoover in March 1933, the new president made it clear from the outset that he was far more concerned with curing the country's economic ills than abiding by international monetary traditions.

"Our international trade relations, though vastly important, are in point of time and necessity secondary to the establishment of a sound national economy," Roosevelt said in his inaugural address.

On his second day in office, FDR halted all exports of gold. In April, he issued an executive order banning private holdings of gold except as jewelry, and he took the country off the gold standard.

A "bombshell message"

In June 1933, representatives of 66 countries convened in London at an economic conference. They hoped to find a way to defeat the Great Depression through international cooperation and to put an end to tariff wars and currency manipulations that had led to a "beggar they neighbor" attitude among nations.

Roosevelt sent his Secretary of State, Cordell Hull, as the head of a U.S. delegation. American representatives huddled away from the main conference with British and French financial experts. The expectation among conference delegates was that the "Big Three" would come up with a plan to stabilize the world's currencies.

But on July 3, FDR stunned everyone, including Hull, by proclaiming via a telegraph (which came to be known as "the bombshell message") that the United States would not be a party to any plan to stabilize exchange rates or currencies, and also wouldn't be going back to the gold standard. In fact, Roosevelt said, the United States would be primarily concerned with cleaning up its own economic mess.

"I do not relish . . . continuance of the basic economic errors that underlie so much of the present worldwide depression," Roosevelt said bluntly. ". . . A sound internal economic system of a nation is a greater factor in its well-being than the price of its currency in changing terms of the currencies of other nations."

The message effectively ended the conference because without the "world's banker" taking part, a multinational economic plan wouldn't have much chance of succeeding. In April 1934, Roosevelt drove a further wedge between the United States and its World War I allies by signing a bill that prohibited U.S. banks from making loans to countries that were tardy in their war debt payments to the United States. Every country except Finland promptly quit paying anything. It was clear that countries would have to fight the Great Depression on their own.

Looking at the Great Depression around the World

In 1933, perhaps for the first time since the early explorers came and went, more people left the United States than immigrated to it. Part of the reason was due to tighter immigration policies that had been in place since the early 1920s. But part of it was due to the tough times the United States was going through. (Heck, if that's what people wanted to experience, they could stay home.)

The length and depth of the Great Depression varied from country to country. Here's a quick look at how some other nations fared, starting with the United States' neighbors to the north and south.

Canada

Many Canadians had traditionally gone south in tough times. But that tactic didn't work when times were just as tough in the United States. In 1924, more than 200,000 Canadians immigrated to the United States. In 1933, only 6,000 did.

The Canadian economy relied heavily on foreign trade in the 1920s. More than one-third of its gross domestic product (GDP) was derived from sales of its raw materials (such as lumber) and crops (such as wheat). So when foreign markets dried up, so did Canada's economy. Wheat prices dropped from $1.60 a bushel in 1929 to 38 cents in 1932. The country's GDP dropped 40 percent from 1929 to 1933.

Canadian industries had been "protected" by high tariffs. But there was no domestic market for what they produced. As a result, hundreds of thousands of workers were laid off, with unemployment rates reaching as high as 27 percent in 1933.

Canada's agricultural midsection shared several things in common with the U.S. Midwest in the Great Depression, all of them bad. Like their Yankee counterparts, Canadian farmers suffered through severe drought, scorching temperatures, smothering dust storms, and plagues of grasshoppers (see Chapter 6). In fact, the Canadians one-upped the Americans by also enduring hailstorms that were severe enough to kill horses and destroy entire crops.

Canada's political leadership during the Great Depression both mirrored and contrasted with the U.S. experience. When the hard times began, Liberal Party leader William Lyon Mackenzie King was prime minister. King lost the post to Conservative Party leader Richard D. Bennett in 1930. As staunch a conservative as Herbert Hoover, Bennett nonetheless pursued some remedies that were surprisingly liberal, such as minimum wage laws and unemployment insurance. But Canada's highest court struck down many of the reforms as unconstitutional (just as the U.S. Supreme Court did to some of Roosevelt's New Deal programs). Bennett was ousted in 1935, and Mackenzie King again assumed leadership.

Canada did have two things going for it that the United States didn't. One was a fairly stable banking system. While thousands of U.S. banks failed, dragging with them the savings of hundreds of thousands of people, not a single Canadian bank failed during the period. The other advantage was Canada's membership in the *British Commonwealth* (a loose confederation of autonomous nations with allegiance to the British crown). That association helped shield Canada from defaulting on its foreign debts and gave it open and tariff-free markets among other Commonwealth countries for its exports.

Mexico

There's an old Mexican saying that the country should be pitied because it is "so far from God, so near the United States."

But that wasn't completely the case in the Great Depression. True, the United States was Mexico's best customer, and when the U.S. economy tanked, Mexican exports were badly hurt, dropping 65 percent between 1929 and 1932. And true, Mexico had to absorb some 300,000 Latinos who were pushed out of the United States as unwanted labor during the 1930s (see Chapter 5).

But Mexico had a couple of things going for it that weren't hurt by its proximity to Uncle Sam. First, its export–import ratio stayed in the positive column (more going out than coming in) throughout the Great Depression (although the ratio did shrink considerably). Second, it had plenty of silver on hand.

Mexico had been on a bimetallic standard of both silver and gold. But as its money supply contracted and tax revenues shrank, the Mexican government, under President Pascual Ortiz Rubio, switched to a silver-only standard in July 1931. The country began minting silver pesos and issuing millions of silver-backed notes.

Mexico benefited further when the prices of silver and oil, both of which it exported, went up in 1934. In 1938, President Lázaro Cárdenas *nationalized* (that is, took government control of) the oil industry. The railroads had already been nationalized. Nationalization meant the Mexican government got the lion's share of the revenues from the railroads and oil production, which had heretofore gone to private, and mostly British or American, companies.

The result of these changes was that Mexico's gross domestic product actually grew during the Great Depression. The agricultural side of the Mexican economy did not fare as well as the industrial side. But all in all, Mexico's experience during the 1930s was less of a Great Depression and more of a Not-That-Bad Depression.

Great Britain

The British were already in a bit of a financial hole when what the Brits sometimes referred to as the "Great Slump" hit the world in late 1929. The pre-Depression doldrums were a result of Britain having gone back on the gold standard in 1925. The overvalued British pound made the country's exports expensive and therefore hard to sell.

The U.S. stock market crash and the subsequent drying up of U.S. loans and investment hit Britain hard. British exports were cut in half, and unemployment rose from 1 million in 1929 to 2.5 million in 1930 and 3 million in 1931 — about 24 percent of the workforce.

The pre–stock market crash government, led by the Labour Party, gave way to a coalition government dominated by the Conservative Party. The government cut wages of public sector workers and reduced payments to a financially shaky unemployment insurance system. The system was funded by employee contributions and covered relatively few people. The government also raised income taxes. The results were an increase in unemployment and a decrease in economic activity.

In 1931, Great Britain went off the gold standard and instituted a government-funded unemployment insurance system. The government also held down public sector spending, kept private-sector wages down, and in short did everything it could to keep the costs of manufactured goods for export down. That was important because Britain imported more than half its food and needed a healthy balance between what it sold and bought from abroad.

The cumulative effect of the British efforts was that its economy did not fall as far or crash as hard as the U.S. economy. By 1935, British unemployment was at a more reasonable 10 percent. In the last half of the decade, the country's economy was further boosted by heavy government spending on rebuilding Britain's military in anticipation of a showdown with Nazi Germany. That turned out to be a wise investment.

France

The French got to the world's Depression party a little late and stayed until it was almost over. Unlike other countries, France had been more wary about speculative investments in extravagant building projects — or the U.S. stock market. As a result, its monetary system was in better shape than those of other nations, and it held large gold reserves.

French unemployment rates were also low in the first years of the Great Depression, in part because it had lost so many work-aged men during World War I. But the global slump finally caught up with France in 1932. Tourism and the foreign sales of French products such as perfume slowed. Unemployment rates reached 15 percent in 1932. While not as steep as in other nations, the rate stayed at that level for several years. A series of strikes led to an agreement between labor and management to increase salaries and thus stimulate the economy. That step had only moderate success, and the French economy continued to sputter until World War II shifted its attention to other matters.

Latin America

Latin American countries were generally vulnerable to the fallout from the Great Depression and pretty powerless to do much about it. Many of the nations in Central and South America were heavily dependent on the export of crops (such as coffee) or raw materials (such as oil or iron ore). When international demand waned, the Latin American nations could do little with their own products because many of them lacked much in the way of manufacturing plants.

The other big problem many Latin American countries had was that their biggest trading partner and investor was the United States, and in the early 1930s, Uncle Sam wasn't buying much and didn't have anything to lend.

But a couple of things worked in the region's favor. It didn't have much absolute need for imported goods, and its unemployment problems were addressed by the fact that many out-of-work people in the cities simply returned to subsistence farming in the rural areas and were not dependent on government welfare or unemployment insurance programs.

Some countries were hit harder than others. In Brazil, which was run by a dictator named Getulio Vargas, the country's textile industry ramped up as its coffee industry sagged. Vargas was also chummy with fellow dictators in Germany and Italy, and he established coffee-for-machinery barter arrangements. In Chile, on the other hand, the country's main exports were iron ore and copper, the demand for which fell sharply. Chilean exports dropped 76 percent from 1929 to 1933 while its imports dropped more than 80 percent.

If there was a cheery note in the Great Depression for Latin American countries, it was that after World War II, the region found itself far less dependent on the United States for trade and investment, having gotten along without it during the 1930s.

Africa

Most of the African continent was still under colonial domination by European powers at the onset of the Great Depression. Private companies that held virtual monopolies often dominated the economies of African colonies.

Because of this situation, the companies — rather than the Africans themselves — bore the direct brunt of the Depression. In many cases, the companies responded to lower prices for their products by flooding the market, which served to drive prices down even more.

But while the companies and colonial governments felt the initial sting of the economic downturn, Africans weren't entirely spared. In some cases, colonial governments replaced lost sales revenues with various taxes on workers. In the Belgian Congo, failure to pay the taxes resulted in forced labor, which amounted to slavery. In other white-dominated colonies such as Rhodesia, Africans were forced to abide by labor "contracts" that had the same effect as serfdom.

Linking Depression and Despotism

In 1920, the British economist John Maynard Keynes morosely noted that the victorious nations of World War I had been so spiteful and selfish that the losers were sure to someday rise up and shake off the second-class status to which they had been relegated.

"Men will not always die quietly," Keynes wrote. "For starvation, which brings to some lethargy and a helpless despair, drives other temperaments to the nervous instability of hysteria, and to a mad despair. And these in their distress may overturn the remnants of organization, and submerge civilization itself."

The Great Depression was tailor-made for triggering the madness of which Keynes wrote. People weren't quite sure how the world got into this mess and were even less sure how to get out of it. But that fact didn't deter some individuals who were remarkable for their abilities of persuasion, their charisma, and their monstrous thirst for power at any cost.

In Japan, a collection of military officers seized control. In Italy, the power went to a former schoolteacher: Benito Mussolini. Germany was dominated by a failed painter from Austria: Adolph Hitler. And Russia was ruled by a seminary student–turned bank robber–turned revolutionary: Joseph Stalin. Following is a brief look at how these countries fared economically.

Military Japan

Japan was still relatively new to industrialization in the 1920s, and its leaders strove to adapt Western technology and industrial methods. But the country was heavily dependent on trade for importing fuel and raw materials, and it didn't have a wide variety of goods to export. In the late 1920s, its silk exports faced competition from artificial fabrics made in the West, and the value of Japanese exports dropped by 50 percent between 1929 and 1932. Bad rice harvests compounded Japan's economic troubles.

These economic troubles sparked sharp anti-Western feelings and led to fervent nationalism. They also helped the army gradually gain control of the government. With government assent, Japanese textile manufacturers began exploiting the workforce, paying starvation wages and requiring workers to live in barracks at the mills.

The army also successfully pressed for increased industrialization so more military equipment, weapons, and other supplies could be produced. By 1937, Japan had conquered much of China, and its military efforts helped pull the country through the Great Depression.

Mussolini's Italy

Benito Mussolini had come to power in Italy well before the onset of the Great Depression. After becoming prime minister in 1922, Mussolini quickly developed an almost completely undeserved reputation as a master planner who ran an efficient and economical government. In reality, "Il Duce" ("The Leader") was erratic and contradictory. But he was also lucky. Italy's unions and business leaders were relatively docile and rarely blinked at his economic efforts.

Those efforts included starting a "Battle for Land," which consisted of draining swampland to create farms, and coercing Italians to trade their gold coins and jewelry in return for a steel wristband that said "Gold for the Fatherland" on it. He also forced citizens to turn over foreign stocks and bonds to the national bank, and he nationalized about 75 percent of Italy's businesses.

When all was said and done, Mussolini didn't really screw up the Italian economy too much. The Great Depression didn't hit it all that hard. Of course the Italian economy wasn't all that big a deal to begin with. In fact, with only 2.8 percent of the world's manufacturing, Italy was the least economically important of Europe's big countries.

Hitler's Germany

In November 1923, a doughy little guy with a silly mustache jumped on a table in a Munich beer hall and proclaimed "the Nationalist Revolution." Adolf Hitler was promptly arrested and served a year in prison, long enough to put together his plans for when he got out. Using what a 1933 *Time* magazine article called the "Sheer gift of gab, lung power and personal magnetism," Hitler rose to prominence at the head of the National Socialist, or Nazi, Party. By early 1933, the Nazis controlled the German Parliament, and Hitler had been named chancellor. Later, he became known simply as *Der Führer* (The Leader).

When Hitler came to power, the German economy was in shambles. Unemployment was nearing 30 percent. But the Nazis quickly developed a mass jobs-creation program fueled by huge governmental investments in public works projects that ranged from highways to affordable automobiles called "the People's Cars," or "Volkswagens." Inflation was managed by rationing consumer goods, discouraging discretionary spending, and implementing wage and price controls.

As the decade moved along, Germany also began re-arming itself, spending huge amounts to create an industrial infrastructure that could churn out war machinery. By 1939, German unemployment was nearly invisible, and the country's gross domestic product was 50 percent higher than it had been in 1929. Hitler had led the creation of a war machine, a part of which can be seen in Figure 7-1. Germany was ready for a world war.

Photo by Hulton Archive/Getty Images

Figure 7-1: Adolf Hitler on his way to a Nazi Party rally in Nuremberg, circa 1935.

Stalin's Soviet Union

It's safe to say that no world leader in the 1930s committed more crimes against humanity in the name of economic progress than Joseph Stalin. It's probably also safe to say that no leader pulled the wool over the eyes of the world better than Stalin.

Stalin, who came to power in the mid-1920s, was pushing to turn the Soviet Union away from an agriculture-based economy to an industrial economy well before the onset of the Great Depression. He also wanted to make the country as economically self-sufficient as possible. And he was largely successful in both efforts. In 1926, about 80 percent of the Soviet populace lived on farms. By 1939, about 50 percent did. Because the country didn't rely on international trade, it weathered the Great Depression without severe upheaval.

At least that's what it looked like to the outside world. Americans were effusive in their praise of what seemed to be an efficient economic system. The esteemed newspaper editor William Allen White called the Soviet Union "the most interesting place on the planet." Humorist Will Rogers observed that "those rascals in Russia . . . have got mighty good ideas. Just think of everybody in a country going to work."

In fact, a lot of jobless Americans thought it was a great idea. In 1931, a New York City–based Soviet trade agency named Amtorg announced that it had 6,000 jobs for skilled workers in the USSR. More than 100,000 Americans applied, and about 10,000 eventually went.

What they found when they got there was a nightmare. Stalin's method of getting people to move off farms to factories, or to build canals and roads, was to totally disregard their right to live. It's estimated that as many as 14 million people died in Stalin's "collectivization" of farms, which meant turning them from modest enterprises into massive agricultural factories. The food supplies for entire villages were seized and transferred elsewhere, leaving the villagers to starve. By 1934, another 500,000 Soviet citizens were in *gulags,* or prison camps, where they were used as slave laborers.

Many of the Americans who immigrated to Stalin's Soviet Union were not allowed to leave. A New Jersey mechanical engineer who did come back to the United States told a magazine reporter that "The people are in rags. There is depression everywhere . . . how anything fine or good can come from such squalor and misery is more than I can understand."

Lessons Learned

Two of the lessons learned from the Great Depression are these:

- ✓ In an economic crisis, international cooperation is better than competition.
- ✓ Rigid currency systems aren't a good idea in tough times.

Here is a look at two organizations that seek to foster international economic cooperation, and a brief recounting of what happened to the gold standard after the Great Depression.

The World Bank

In July 1944, representatives of 45 nations met in the town of Breton Woods, New Hampshire, to build a framework to help countries get along, economically speaking, after World War II ended. One idea to bear fruit was the creation of a World Bank.

With more than 180 countries as members, the World Bank keeps tabs on global economic issues and provides advice — and money — to developing countries. The bank is headquartered in Washington, D.C., and is run by a board of 24 directors. The voting power of each country is determined by its deposits in the bank. At the start of the 21st century, the United States controlled about 17 percent of the votes, more than twice as many as runner-up Japan.

The World Bank is organized into five institutions:

- ✓ **International Bank for Reconstruction and Development (IBRD):** It provides loans, at market interest rates, to middle-income developing countries.
- ✓ **International Development Association (IDA):** It provides interest-free loans to low-income developing countries.
- ✓ **International Finance Corporation (IFC):** It provides loans and loan guarantees to private sector business deals within developing countries.
- ✓ **Multilateral Investment Guarantee Agency (MIGA):** It provides loan insurance against loss from noncommercial risks such as political coups or civil wars within developing countries.
- ✓ **International Centre for Settlement of Investment Disputes (ICSID):** It arbitrates arguments among investors and developing countries.

The World Bank has been criticized for requiring borrowing nations to adopt government structural reforms that hurt education and social service programs, and for rules that prohibited the bank from canceling or restructuring debts. But it was also highly praised for its efforts in helping communist nations switch to a free market system in the 1980s and 1990s.

The International Monetary Fund and the end of the gold standard

Like the World Bank, the International Monetary Fund (IMF) was born at the 1944 Breton Woods conference. The idea was to establish an organization that would monitor the world's monetary system and try to head off the fiscal feuding that had marked the Great Depression.

Countries that joined the IMF agreed to keep their currencies tied to the U.S. dollar, which would be tied to gold, at $35 an ounce. That meant, for example, that eight Mexican pesos would be worth one U.S. dollar, and therefore eight Mexican pesos were worth 1/35th of an ounce of gold. Currency exchange rates could be adjusted only when trade balances got severely out of whack, and only with IMF approval. The idea was to create some stability among the world's currencies and prevent countries from devaluing their currency so their goods would be cheaper and thus more attractive than competing countries' goods in global markets.

But by the end of the 1960s, the system was putting too great a strain on the U.S. economy. The expenses of the Vietnam War and the sweeping "Great Society" social service programs under President Lyndon B. Johnson meant the United States needed to put more money into circulation than the IMF system would allow. So in August 1971, President Richard M. Nixon ended the convertibility of U.S. dollars into gold.

The result was that nations' currencies were free to float against each other. That change turned out to be a pretty good thing because it gave countries more flexibility when it came to dealing with economic crises such as the oil embargoes in the mid 1970s.

Since 1971, the IMF has focused on monitoring its 185 member countries' economic situations, giving them advice and lending money when necessary. The IMF differs from the World Bank in that the bank focuses on long-term help for developing nations, while the IMF concentrates on currency and financial sector situations.

Part III
Living Through the Great Depression

The 5th Wave   By Rich Tennant

"No, seriously. I sold my soul to the company store."

In this part . . .

Beyond all the facts and figures and economic data of the Great Depression are the people who lived through it. How they did so is every bit as instructive as all the numbers — and much more interesting.

This part starts with the story of Americans on the road, some trying to escape a life in ruins, others looking for a better life just over the next state line. Then it covers some of the period's true characters, from machine gun–toting desperadoes to homegrown Nazis and communists.

The part continues with a look at how Americans coped with the doom and gloom by going to the movies or pursuing other diversions. It ends with the story of organized labor during the Great Depression, perhaps the only part of the economy that did pretty well during the era.

Chapter 8

On the Road

*W*hen faced with the hard times and uncertainty of the Great Depression, most Americans hunkered down at or near home. The best course for them seemed to be to wait things out in familiar surroundings. But hundreds of thousands of others decided that maybe, just maybe, things would be better someplace else.

This chapter looks at who hit the road during the 1930s, with the focus on two of the largest groups that did so. The first group was the young: people under the age of 21 who saw no future for themselves at home. The second group was the families who fled the drought-stricken farms of southwestern states for the promise of a new start in California.

The "Wandering Population"

As the Great Depression's impact deepened in 1932, it became clear that local government and private organizations were not going to be able to handle the huge numbers of people who needed help. The ranks of the unemployed had swelled to the point of bursting. Only about a quarter of those who needed aid were getting it, and most of that relief was in the form of just enough food to survive. Many people began to think that life elsewhere couldn't possibly be as bad as it was at home. So they went to see.

By the end of 1932, an estimated 2 million Americans were on the road. Up to 25 percent of them were believed to be under the age of 21.

"The Depression," reported *Fortune* magazine in September 1932, "along with its misery, (has) produced its social curiosities, not the least of which is the wandering population it spilled upon the roads. Means of locomotion vary, but the objective is always the same — somewhere else. There were the hitchhikers whose thumbs jerked onward along the American pike, and the number of spavined Fords dragging destitute families from town to town in search of a solvent relative or a generous friend."

Riding the rails

As *Fortune* noted, many people hitchhiked or piled what possessions they could squeeze into the family car or truck and drove off. But many took to the railroads that crisscrossed the country — not inside passenger coaches as paying customers, but hidden away in boxcars filled with human cargo.

In 1927, the Southern Pacific Railroad reported evicting 78,099 trespassers from trains or railroad yards. By 1932, the number was 683,457. In just one month during that year, the railroad reported, it evicted 80,000 transients from boxcars in California alone. An average of 700 "train hoppers" per day passed through Kansas City, Missouri.

But hopping a freight train was a tricky and dangerous business: In 1932, the Interstate Commerce Commission reported, 5,962 trespassers were killed on and around trains, 1,508 of them under the age of 21.

Some of the transients had been riding the rails well before the Great Depression started, as part of the "invisible poor" during the seemingly opulent decade of the Roaring Twenties. But the overwhelming numbers of people riding the rails or hitchhiking around the country were those who had no other particular place to be. They were dispossessed farmers and laid-off factory workers.

The writer Thomas Wolfe described them as "the flotsam of the general ruin of the time — honest, decent middle-aged men with faces seamed by toil and want, and young men, many of them teens, with their unkempt hair. These were wanderers from town to town, the riders of freight trains, the thumbers of rides on highways, the uprooted, unwanted male population of America."

Not all of the wanderers were men. The estimates of the number of women on the road or riding the rails varied from about 15,000 to more than 100,000. Women often dressed like men, both because it was more practical for travel and also to keep a lower profile and thus reduce the risk of assault. Other women wanderers viewed the risks of assault as part of the life. "You have to put up on the road with certain things," a young woman told a social worker in 1937, "and you got to give in when forced."

Some women got by as prostitutes, risking rape, pregnancy, and disease for as little as a dime a customer. "So one day a guy says to me 'get wise, sister, get wise,'" a teenage transient told Thomas Minehan, a University of Minnesota sociologist who traveled the rails doing interviews in 1932 and 1933. "So I got wise."

"Waiting for nothing"

Many of the nation's new transients were high school and college graduates who had both careers and senses of self-worth that were snuffed out by their new lives.

"It is the first couple of weeks at tramping that hurt a man the most," a 25-year-old mechanical draftsman told *The Forum* magazine in early 1932. "Added to the uneasiness of any animal in a strange environment is the human feeling of depravity from his beggar's status. One talks badly, goes hungry for unnecessarily long periods of time . . . goes blocks out of his way to avoid policemen."

Thomas Kromer, an unemployed teacher, wrote an account of his life on the road called *Waiting For Nothing.* In it, he describes a typical meal at a homeless shelter: "They shove this stew before us. It is awful. It smells bad. The room is full of the stench of this rotten stew. What am I going to do? What can I do? I am a hungry man. Food is food to a hungry man, whether it is rotten or not. I've got to eat."

Once someone was on the road, it was hard to get off. Few employers were willing to give a job to a stranger who looked like a bum. "Believe me sir," a transient told a federal investigator, "three days in a box car, in zero weather, without water, sleep or food would make anybody look like a thug. But give me three days of heat, food, soap and water, a razor and a bed, and I will look just as I am — a graduate of the University of Chicago."

Being run off or arrested

Vagrancy became a national problem. Local relief agencies couldn't cover the needs of their own residents, let alone tens of thousands of transients. States were similarly overwhelmed. So local and state authorities devised other methods of handling unwelcome visitors. For example,

✔ Signs outside the city limits of Tucson, Arizona, read, "Warning to Transients. Relief Funds for local residents only. Transients, do not apply."

✔ In Atlanta, Georgia, transients were arrested and sentenced to 30 days in jail, and then they were rented out as forced labor to the state highway department or even private companies.

✔ The Los Angeles Chamber of Commerce seriously suggested establishing concentration camps for transients. The L.A. police chief came up with an alternative: blockading the entire state from "undesirable elements." See "The bums blockade" sidebar for details.

In 1932, Congress considered making vagrancy a federal crime, but the body's saner members prevailed, and the proposal was dropped. In 1933, the Roosevelt administration established the Federal Transient Program. By January 1934, 40 states had federally funded transient aid programs operating. But in most cases, the sheer numbers of applicants overwhelmed the program, and it was closed in late 1935. The transient problem continued until the United States entered World War II in late 1941.

The bums blockade

With its hospitable year-round climate, California was a magnet for transients during the Great Depression. The state held just 4.7 percent of the entire U.S. population, but by June 1934 was hosting 14 percent of the country's transients. So in February 1936, Los Angeles Police Chief James Edgar "Two Guns" Davis decided to stem the flow of transients by sending 126 of his officers to entry points around the state. There they stopped anyone who looked "undesirable." (The first man stopped was a 62-year-old Chicago native who had been riding freights for four days in freezing weather.) If they had no money and no job, they were offered a choice of turning around or being arrested and serving six months in jail, where, Davis said, they would find only "beans and abuse."

A federal court judge warned Davis the blockades were unconstitutional. The sheriff of one county chased the LAPD out of his jurisdiction. The department became the butt of national jokes. (A sign reading "Los Angeles City Limits" was put up just outside Reno, Nevada.) But Davis refused to recall his men, and hundreds of transients were refused entrance (much to the consternation of officials in the neighboring states of Arizona, Nevada, and Oregon, who were left as hosts for the blocked transients).

In early April 1936, a Hollywood film director, who had been refused entrance to the state by deputies because of his unkempt appearance, sued Davis. After it was revealed that the chief's top aide had threatened to bomb the director's house if he didn't drop the suit, Davis finally recalled his officers. The chief abruptly retired in 1938 after a corruption probe threatened his pension. And the transients kept coming.

The "Boxcar Children"

In early April 1934, a 15-year-old boy stood before a judge in Salt Lake City and told his story. The boy's name was Robert Cozad. Up until about a year before his appearance in court, Cozad had worked on a farm near Muscatine, Iowa. When he lost the job, he told the judge, he began "riding the brakes," or hopping freight trains to look for work.

"I tried to get home last winter from San Diego, where a police officer let me work in a gymnasium and sleep there," Cozad said. "But out of St. Louis, I almost froze to death, so I beat it back to California. I started three days ago to try again to get home. I was in a boxcar out of Las Vegas with about 30 men, and a brakeman found me shivering. Today I was arrested. I told them I was not quite 16 and expected to be on the next freight out of Salt Lake."

Instead of catching a freight, Cozad (who eventually went home, served in World War II, and died in 1990 at the age of 72) was put on a work detail at a nearby federal flood control project.

There were a lot of kids like Robert Cozad during the Great Depression. They were variously referred to in the newspapers as "the boxcar children," "the wandering youth," or "the wild boys." Some were on the road for the adventure. But most were there for the same reasons their older counterparts on the road were there: hard times. In his 1934 book *Boy and Girl Tramps of America,* sociologist Thomas Minehan said 83 percent of the 466 homeless youths he interviewed gave "hard times at home" as their answer for being on the road.

"He didn't exactly kick me out, but he gave me plenty of hints," a 17-year-old boy named Joe told Minehan about how his father helped put him on the road. "He hasn't worked steady in the last three years. There's seven of us at home, and I'm the oldest . . . I thought I'd stay until Christmas. I got the kids a duck for Christmas, but I ain't saying how I got it. Then, before the old man could start giving any more hints, I scrams."

In 1932, the National Children's Bureau estimated that as many as 250,000 youths under the age of 21 were on their own and homeless. Others put the number as high as 1 million. Testifying before a congressional committee in 1933, the chief special agent of the Southern Pacific Railroad Company estimated that "75 percent of the 1932 (rail) trespassers ranged in age from 16 to 25 years." Sociologist Minehan reported that the youths he came in contact with in his study were as young as 11 and had been on their own for an average of 14 months.

"The migratory youth is a product of these times which have upset a whole world," a *Detroit News* reporter wrote, somewhat melodramatically, in 1933. "His elders, his friends, his teachers, his parents have failed to understand a perplexed youth. They have driven him from his home into the physical and moral hazards of transiency."

Locking up the schools

One of the reasons so many kids were on the road and in the streets was because a traditional anchor of childhood — the classroom — was locked up.

Money to pay teachers and heat classrooms simply dried up. Many, if not most, public schools in the United States ended their 1933–34 school year in January 1934. Five thousand of them were closed for the entire year. There were 25,000 fewer U.S. schoolteachers in 1934 than in 1930. Forty percent of the 10 million high school–age kids in 1935 were not in school.

Not everyone thought this situation was a tragedy. Automaker Henry Ford opined that "it's the best education in the world for these boys, this traveling around. They get more experience in a few weeks than they would in years at school."

If Ford was right, it was fortuitous that they were getting some experience at something: A 1934 survey of 200,000 Pennsylvania youths looking for jobs found that 71 percent had never been employed. Without experience, they weren't likely to be employed during times as bad as the Great Depression.

Giving boys a purpose: The CCC

One federal program that was almost certainly the nearest and dearest to President Franklin D. Roosevelt's heart was the Civilian Conservation Corps (CCC). The program, which put needy young males to work restoring and improving federal lands, married two of Roosevelt's keen interests: conservation, and giving young people a purpose in life.

"It is my belief that what is being accomplished will conserve our natural resources, create future national wealth and prove of moral and spiritual value not only to those of you who are taking part, but to the rest of the country as well," the president said in a July 1933 message in the CCC's official newspaper. "It's my honest conviction that what you are doing in the way of constructive service will bring to you, personally and individually, returns the value of which it is difficult to estimate."

So eager was Roosevelt to get the program started that the first boy was enrolled 35 days after FDR took office in March 1933. By July, 1,300 camps housed 274,000 boys on federal lands throughout the country.

To qualify, applicants had to be between the ages of 18 and 25. (Later, the range was expanded to 17 to 28.) They had to be male, single, jobless, and at least 60 inches tall. They had to weigh at least 107 pounds, have "at least three working teeth," and be in good physical condition. Enlistments were for six-month terms that could be extended to as long as two years (or longer if the young man was promoted). The "soil soldiers," as they were called, got $30 a month, at least $22 of which had to be sent home.

The CCC was a multi-jurisdictional affair. The camps were built and maintained by the U.S. Army, while the work details were run by the U.S. Forest Service and supervised by "local experienced men," known as LEMs. The LEMs were paid $45 a month.

Liberals didn't like the army's involvement, fearing the program would amount to forced military training. They also didn't like the low pay. Conservatives thought it a bad idea to give thousands of members of the lower classes military training, for fear they might use it someday against the government.

The program did have its troubles. One camp commander in Oklahoma was killed by one of his charges. Another was arrested for providing members with prostitutes and liquor. Despite rules that specifically prohibited it, most camps were strictly segregated, and in the end, only 7 percent of the CCC members were African American. Moreover, as a relief project it was fairly insignificant because it helped relatively few individuals and families. But it did have some triumphs too.

Leaving their mark on the land

The work done by the CCC was varied in scope and impressive in quantity. Members built 47,000 bridges and 318,000 check dams to fight erosion. They fought fires and floods, marked thousands of miles of trails, constructed amphitheaters and boathouses, and planted more than 1 billion trees. They planted hatchery fish, drained bogs, and restored farmland. Many CCC projects can still be seen in state and national parks around the country.

At its peak in September 1935, the CCC had 502,000 members in 2,514 camps. By the time it closed in 1942 (because of World War II), 2.9 million boys and young men had been through the program.

"We built something, and I knew I had helped," one CCC member recalled. "It was something you could take pride in, and there wasn't a lot of pride available in those days."

The Real-Life Grapes of Wrath

In March 1939, Viking Press published a novel by California author John Steinbeck called *The Grapes of Wrath*. The book told the story of the Joads, a 1930s Oklahoma family run off their land by foreclosure. Loading up family members from three generations, the Joads headed west in a sedan turned into a truck, to what they hoped would be a new start in California. Along the way, they encountered all sorts of hardship, including having both grandparents die. When they got to California, they were met mostly with hostility, prejudice, and exploitation. The story doesn't end on an upbeat note.

The novel electrified the country. By the end of its first year in publication, it had sold 430,000 copies. The book, wrote First Lady Eleanor Roosevelt in her syndicated newspaper column, "made you dread sometimes to begin the next chapter, and yet you cannot lay the book down or even skip a page."

Not everyone loved the novel, which won a Pulitzer Prize and helped Steinbeck eventually win a Nobel Prize for literature. California farm owners screamed that it was an unfair vilification of them. Oklahoma officials weren't happy that it made their state look like hell on earth. *Time* magazine called it "a so-so book" infected with "exaggerations, propaganda and phony pathos."

"So-so" or not, by the end of 1940 the story of the fictional Joads had been made into a hit movie and helped trigger a congressional investigation into the plight of real-life migrant farm families.

There were certainly plenty of real-life migrant families, mostly from what was then referred to as "the Southwest" or "Cotton Belt": Oklahoma, Texas, Missouri, and Arkansas. Most of the migrant families from those states ended up in adjacent states. But hundreds of thousands followed the route of the Joads, moving west. Many headed to Oregon and Washington, seeking jobs on mammoth federal dam-building projects. Far more went to California. In one 14-month span between June 1935 and September 1936, 86,000 people from the southwestern states entered California, part of 350,000 migrants who came from all over the country to the state between 1935 and 1940.

Telling the rest of the story

Steinbeck's saga didn't tell the whole story of the exodus, however. For one thing, more than half of the Cotton Belt migrants weren't even farmers or farm laborers. About 40 percent were blue-collar workers, and another 16 percent were managers, proprietors, or other white-collar workers. Many of them had relatives who had been living in California for years and offered them a place to live and sometimes even jobs when they got there. They settled in metropolitan regions, particularly around Los Angeles. Between 1935 and 1940, census figures showed about 100,000 people from the Cotton Belt settled in and around Los Angeles.

Even those who were farmers seemed to have good reasons to go to California. One reason was better wages. In 1935, the average daily wage of a California farm worker was $2.95, with some form of housing included. In Oklahoma, it was $1.35, with no housing. "People think they are just a'flyin' if they can get $3 a day," one arrival from Arkansas told a University of California researcher.

Trouble was, there were a lot more workers than work. A billboard on U.S. Route 66 outside Tulsa, Oklahoma, told the tale: "NO JOBS in California/ IF YOU are looking for work — KEEP OUT/ 6 Men for Every Job/ No State Relief Available for Non-Residents."

But there was cotton in California. The crop, which had barely existed in California before the 1920s, was booming in the 1930s. Cotton acreage grew from 170,000 acres to more than 600,000 acres from 1927 to 1937. In the Cotton Belt, meanwhile, a federal program designed to help farmers get back on their feet was actually driving many of them off the land.

Contributing to the great migration: The AAA

In 1933, the federal government instituted the Agricultural Adjustment Act (which I cover in more detail in Chapter 6). Basically, the act was designed to reduce overproduction, and therefore raise farm prices, by paying subsidies to farmers in return for less being planted. Landowners who rented part of their property were supposed to share the subsidies with their renters, but there was almost no government oversight to see that they did. "I did everything the government told me to," boasted one Oklahoma landowner, "except keep my renters."

Instead, many landowners used the federal money to buy tractors and/or hire day laborers while evicting their tenants. "I bought tractors on the money the government give me and got shed of my renters," a landowner said. "They got their choice — California or WPA," a government relief program.

Coupled with the loss of as many as 20 percent of the Cotton Belt's small farms to foreclosure notices, the unintended consequence of the federal program was enough to push tens of thousands of farmers and their families to choose California.

Heading west

Although the Joads' trip in *The Grapes of Wrath* took on aspects of a forced death march, the trip from the southwestern states to "the Golden State" wasn't that arduous for most people. The most favored route was U.S. Route 66, which ran from Chicago through Missouri, Oklahoma, Texas, and the deserts of New Mexico and Arizona to the Pacific Ocean at Santa Monica. Some people took buses or trains, or paid $10 for a ride with another family going west.

Gasoline cost 10 cents a gallon; a car or truck in reasonably good shape could make the trip in three or four days. (Of course, as Figure 8-1 shows, not all vehicles were up to the task.) Most people camped along the road. Studies showed that the average family of four or five had $40 in cash and a net worth of about $200, including the vehicle they were riding in.

Still, there were poignant stories to rival those of Steinbeck's protagonists. One woman with six children was stopped at the California border and told she had to buy a $3 auto license. Tearfully, she told the police officer that she had only $3.40, adding "that's food for my babies." He gave her the license, and she was allowed into California.

Photo by Dorothea Lange/MPI/Getty Images

Figure 8-1: An emigrant family near Tracy, California, in 1937.

Life in California

Despite its "promised land" image in many of the decade's movies, California was not an economic oasis that escaped the cold hands of the Great Depression. Unemployment in the state reached as high as 29 percent in early 1933, and local government and private relief agencies faced uphill battles in providing food and temporary shelter for the needy.

But the state did recover quicker than most of the states in the Midwest and East, and even in the middle of the decade, wages were generally higher in California. Meat packers, for example, were paid 68 cents an hour in California in 1935, compared to 46 cents in Oklahoma or Texas. Machine shop workers earned 67 cents, compared to 60 cents in Texas or Oklahoma.

The prospect of better wages and the presence of friends and family already living in the state were what drew many of the Southwesterners to California. Many of them moved to new communities on the outskirts of metropolitan areas. A typical newspaper ad offered small lots for "$20 down, and $10 a month," and promised neighborhoods with "Good schools, churches, fine water" (and assurances to the almost exclusively white newcomers that the new communities were "race restricted"). Assimilating in the urban areas was a fairly smooth process for the newcomers. But for those Southwesterners who gravitated to California's vast Central Valley, it was a different story.

Fitting in where they weren't wanted

The Central Valley of California is really two valleys that run right into each other. To the north is the Sacramento Valley; to the south the San Joaquin Valley. The San Joaquin Valley is cotton country, and that's where most of the Southwesterners went when they arrived in California.

Unlike most of the country at the time, California agriculture was dominated by huge enterprises that were more crop factories than family farms. In 1939, *Fortune* magazine reported that fewer than 10 percent of California farms produced half of the state's crops, while the small farms that made up 41 percent of the total number of farms produced less than 6 percent of the crops.

The large farms had always been dependent on seasonal workers to get the crops in, and waves of migrants had filled the role: first Chinese, then Japanese, then Mexicans and Filipinos. At the outset of the Great Depression, 300,000 Mexicans and Mexican-Americans had been forced or coerced into leaving the United States because they were thought to be taking up jobs that could be filled by whites. (See Chapter 5 for more on the Latino exodus.)

The Southwesterners seemed to be the perfect replacements. But there was a big difference between the newcomers and the migrant workers who had come before. In most cases, California's migrant workers had been male adults and youths who moved from place to place as different crops came to harvest.

With few exceptions, however, the Southwesterners tended to stay put. That caused problems, as a 1937 report from San Joaquin Valley health officials pointed out: "Growers have lost their fluid Mexican workers, who miraculously appeared on harvest day and silently slipped away after the work is done . . . the large families of the Southwesterners harvest the cotton (but) when the cotton is harvested, the family hangs on, swelling our emergency relief rolls."

The region was not equipped to permanently house migrant workers who didn't migrate after the crops were in. So the new-comers set up squalid settlements of tents and patched-together shacks alongside roads or stagnant drainage canals that simultane-ously became drinking water supplies and sewage systems.

Maladies such as hookworm, pellagra, and rickets were common in the camps. In one season in just one county, 50 babies died of dysentery and enteritis. "Even in mid-day, the interior of the shack is dark," reported a social worker touring a migrant labor camp. "The noxious odors are strong with dampness, rot, stale atmosphere. Some shacks contain nothing but a bedroll."

As excited as they may have been about California's higher wages, the migrants soon found out the higher pay couldn't compensate for long stretches of unemployment. In 1938, the average migrant family was living on $650 a year, less than half the national family average of $1,500. The migrants found they had two choices: pack up the family and move to another camp, following the crops, or wait it out where they were. Most chose to wait it out, wanting to put down roots.

Feeling the sting of discrimination

The appalling living conditions weren't the Cotton Belt migrants' only problem. Many Valley residents regarded the newcomers as second-class citizens. The migrants were referred to disparagingly as *Okies* or *Arkies* and discriminated against just as other minorities were discriminated against. Some movie theaters had signs that directed "Okies and Negroes" to the balcony. Cafés posted placards reading "No dogs or Okies."

A University of California anthropologist studying the social effects of the large-scale farming system reported that longtime residents thought of the newcomers as "ignorant and uneducated, dirty of habit if not of mind, slothful, unambitious and dependent . . . not rarely is he (the Southwesterner) accused of being dishonest." The state's leading farm journal accused the newcomers of being "clay" in the hands of communist agitators, of spreading disease, and of fostering "unmorality (sic) in the schools."

The newcomers were also distrusted because of the roles they played — both real and exaggerated — in the series of bitter and sometimes violent farm strikes California suffered during the decade (more on those in Chapter 11).

While the claims of spreading disease and fostering "unmorality" were spurious, the Californians did have a legitimate beef about one thing: Taking care of the newcomers cost a lot of tax money. Between 1935 and 1940, taxes in five San Joaquin Valley counties doubled, while taxes in the rest of the state went up 50 percent. Much of that extra tax revenue went to pay for aid to the Southwesterners: Relief cases in the Valley went up 344 percent between 1937 and 1939, while they increased in the state as a whole by 77 percent.

In 1938, California business and agriculture leaders filed a petition with Congress, signed by 100,000 residents. The petition asked the federal government to lure the migrants back to their home states by promising them relief payments there, and by threatening to cut off relief if they stayed in California. "If they come to this state," declared one California legislator, "let them starve or stay away."

Putting down roots

But most of the Southwesterners stayed, despite state laws passed in 1939 and 1940 that increased the minimum residency to qualify for relief payments from one year to three years and then to five years.

"I would like to know who Californians think they are when they put themselves on a pedestal," one defiant Oklahoma woman wrote to the *Fresno Bee*. "Oklahoma is a full-fledged state within these United States, and as this is a free country, we have every moral and legal right to be here."

Toward the end of the decade, 13 federal migrant camps with showers, toilets, kitchen facilities, and communal halls were established in California, along with six mobile camps that could be moved as different crops reached harvest season.

Permanent settlements on the outskirts of Central Valley towns gradually replaced the tent camps. Dubbed "Little Oklahomas," the communities featured lots that could be had for $125 ($10 down and $5 a month). It often took the owner several years to complete construction of a permanent dwelling, but it got done. A 1940 *Time* magazine story noted that in Salinas, California, "Little Oklahoma has become East Salinas," with "new stucco or brightly painted five-room frame houses crowding out vestiges of the old tar-paper shacks."

And as with so many aspects of the Great Depression, the great migration of Southwesterners to California would be overshadowed by the oncoming world war. The war brought tens of thousands of new war production jobs to California and tens of thousands more newcomers. By 1945, the "Okies" were Californians.

Lessons Learned

While the Civilian Conservation Corps lasted only nine years, its impact lasted far longer, and it has become the ancestor of programs that match young people and public service. Sadly, another lesson of the Great Depression — the need to improve the shoddy treatment of migrant farm workers — has yet to be fully learned. Here's a look at two programs that could be said to be the children of the CCC, and a brief look at the status of migrant workers in 21st-century America.

Working to serve

The concept of a volunteer organization to help developing nations had been kicking around Congress throughout the 1950s. But it became a reality after John F. Kennedy won the presidency and established the Peace Corps in 1961.

The Peace Corps is an independent federal agency. Foreign governments in developing countries ask for help in specific areas, such as teaching English, or engineering, agricultural, or business skills, and the Peace Corps sends volunteers. From 1961 through 2008, the Peace Corps sent about 200,000 volunteers to 139 countries.

The volunteers, who in early 2009 were 60 percent female, 94 percent unmarried, 94 percent college graduates, and an average of 27 years old, sign up for stints that are usually 27 months but can last a maximum of five years. Volunteers are given allowances to cover the cost of living in the country to which they are assigned, a round-trip air ticket, medical and dental insurance, and a $6,075 "transition award" when they return.

The domestic version of the Peace Corps is AmeriCorps. President Bill Clinton and Congress created this agency in 1993. There are three subdivisions of AmeriCorps:

- **AmeriCorps State and National:** This division provides grants to public agencies and nonprofit and religious groups, which use the money to recruit and train workers to help meet community education, environmental, health, and public safety needs.

- **AmeriCorps VISTA (Volunteers In Service To America):** VISTA was originally begun in 1965 and became part of AmeriCorps in 1993. It functions like AmeriCorps State and National, except that it focuses on problems in low-income communities.

✔ **AmeriCorps NCCC (National Civilian Community Corps):** NCCC consists of teams of 10 to 12 members located at four centers around the United States. They essentially function as AmeriCorps' emergency teams, responding to specific requests for help in the geographic region they cover.

AmeriCorps members receive living allowances during their one-year assignment and end-of-stint education grants that in 2009 were $4,725.

Losing ground in the fields

As the United States got deeper into World War II and more men were called to military service, a shortage of farm labor developed. So in 1942, the U.S. and Mexican governments reached an agreement that allowed Mexican workers — called *braceros* — to enter the United States. Thousands of Mexicans, some of whom had been pushed out of the United States during the Great Depression, entered the country, most of them taking jobs in farm fields in the West and Southeast. Many of the jobs in the West had been held by the "Okies": migrants from the southwestern United States in the 1930s.

The bracero program ended in 1964, in part because advances in mechanized farming had reduced the need for workers, and in part because criticisms were leveled at both governments for the harsh treatment and brutal living conditions endured by the workers.

But hundreds of thousands of migrant workers, in the country both legally and illegally, continued to labor in the fields under deplorable situations. Landowners sometimes tried to insulate themselves from responsibility for the workers by hiring them through a farm labor contractor, who acted as a middleman.

In 1983, Congress passed the Migrant and Seasonal Agricultural Workers Protection Act (MSPA). The act requires labor contractors to register with the U.S. Department of Labor and sets standards for pay, working conditions, transportation, and housing.

But abuses have continued. In 2008, a congressional committee heard testimony that *pineros,* migrant workers who labor in reforestation and clearing timber, were often ripped off by their employers or not equipped with safety gear. Another committee was told about tomato field workers in Florida who were beaten and kept in virtual slavery.

A 2008 study by the U.S. Department of Agriculture reported there were about 1 million migrant farm workers in the United States, down from about 3 million in 1953. The study found that migrants were 10 times as likely as nonmigrants to have homes with no stove and 17 times as likely to live in overcrowded conditions. It found that, adjusted for inflation, farm worker hourly wages had risen 76 cents from 1975 to 2006, about 2 percent per year, to $9.87.

"While critical to many agricultural sectors," the study concluded, "hired farm workers remain among the most economically disadvantaged working groups in the United States. This relative position within the U.S. occupational structure has changed little over time."

Chapter 9

Demagogues and Desperadoes

● ●

In This Chapter

▶ Criticizing the status quo — and FDR

▶ Making political noise from the left (communists) and right (Nazis)

▶ Fighting crime while admiring criminals

▶ Lessons learned

● ●

Many historians still marvel at how Americans kept their political cool during the Great Depression. After all, there was plenty to be confused and angry about. People in other countries, faced with similar situations, either embraced new dictators or continued to put up with old ones. But Americans embraced neither revolution nor rule by despots.

Because they didn't embrace radical extremes, however, doesn't mean Americans didn't think about them. This chapter takes a look at some of the leading leader wannabes of the 1930s, as well as efforts to influence the political process from both the left and right of the ideological spectrum. It also examines how Americans who were frustrated and wanted to strike out at "the man" did so vicariously through the bloody exploits of the Great Depression outlaws.

The Soapbox Supermen

By the beginning of 1934, the Great Depression was more than four years old, and people were getting more than a little tired of it. The enthusiasm and optimism generated by the election of Franklin D. Roosevelt in November 1932 had largely worn off.

Lorena Hickok, one of a group of investigators sent out by the Roosevelt administration to take the pulse of the country, wrote back to Washington, D.C., in April 1934 that the country's pulse was a bit feeble.

"I've been out on this trip now a little more than two weeks," Hickok wrote. "In all that time I've hardly met a single person who seemed confident and cheerful . . . nobody seems to think anymore that this thing is going to work."

Hickok also noted that she was hearing more talk about the possible need for not only a new government, but a new kind of government. "If I were 20 years younger and weighed 75 pounds less," she joked, "I think I'd start out to be the Joan of Arc of the Fascist movement in the United States."

Despite Hickok's gloomy analysis, Americans made it clear in the 1934 congressional elections that if they were growing restless under Roosevelt, they didn't think it was time to give the Republicans another chance. The GOP lost 14 seats in the House of Representatives and 10 in the Senate. Yet Roosevelt's real political problems were to come not from Republicans but from an elderly doctor in California, a Roman Catholic priest in Michigan, and a bombastic U.S. senator from Louisiana. Here's a look at the trio of trouble.

Francis E. Townsend

Francis Townsend said his idea came to him after watching two elderly women look for something to eat in garbage cans behind his Long Beach, California, home. Townsend was a 66-year-old physician/real estate salesman in the fall of 1933. His idea was to provide financial security for older people.

The Townsend plan, which he called the Old Age Revolving Pension Plan, was simple — and simplistic. Under it, everyone over the age of 60 would be guaranteed a pension of $200 a month, provided they spent the entire amount each month in order to stimulate the economy. The funds would come from a tax on all wholesale and retail sales. Economists pointed out that the plan would take half of the nation's wealth to provide security for only 8 percent of the population.

A lot of people ignored the economists. By 1935, 5,000 "Townsend Clubs" had sprung up around the country. By the beginning of 1936, a staggering 20 million Americans — one-fifth of the entire adult population — had signed petitions urging congressional passage of his plan.

Charles E. Coughlin

Charles Coughlin was a man of the cloth, but he may have been born for radio. His voice had such an entrancing quality, author Wallace Stegner wrote, "that anyone turning past it on the radio dial almost automatically returned to hear it again."

Born in Canada in 1891, Coughlin was a Roman Catholic priest with a small parish in the Detroit suburb of Royal Oak when he began a radio program in 1926. A staunch anti-communist and ardent nationalist, Coughlin's program became so popular that by 1930, he was on 17 CBS-owned stations. It later became so controversial that by 1932, CBS dropped him.

 Undeterred, Coughlin started his own network. His "Golden Hour of the Little Flower" show was soon broadcasting to an estimated audience of 30 million people each week over 60 stations, and raking in $20,000 a week in contributions. (In 2008, the audience of Rush Limbaugh, the nation's most popular radio personality at the time, was estimated at about 14 million.) Coughlin reported getting 80,000 letters a week — more mail than FDR — and *Fortune* magazine dubbed him "just about the biggest thing that ever happened to radio."

Coughlin was initially an ardent booster of Roosevelt, saying the country's choice was "Roosevelt or Ruin" and that FDR's package of proposals, dubbed the *New Deal,* was also "Christ's Deal." But the "radio priest" eventually differed sharply with the president over several issues. A virulent anti-Semite, Coughlin began referring to the New Deal as the "Jew Deal." By the end of 1934, he had formed a quasi-political party called the National Union for Social Justice, which claimed 7.5 million members.

Huey P. Long

Huey Long was a one-time traveling shortening salesman whom Roosevelt regarded as "one of the two most dangerous men in America" (the other being Army Chief of Staff Douglas MacArthur).

Long was born in a log cabin in 1893, the seventh of nine children. By the age of 21, he had finished law school, and after paying his dues in lower elective offices, he was elected governor of Louisiana in 1928. He was called "Da Kingfish" by his friends (after a popular radio character), and Long had a *lot* of friends. As governor, Long built hundreds of miles of new roads, eased taxes on the poor, imposed new taxes on oil companies and other businesses, and supplied textbooks and buses to the state's schools.

"I'm for the poor man," he told reporters, "all poor men. Black and white, they all gotta have a chance. 'Every man a king,' that's my motto."

But Long was also a virtual dictator. Through coercion or bribery, he controlled almost every judge in the state, most of the legislators, and the police. Critics were beaten, kidnapped, jailed, or blackmailed into silence. Long was so powerful that he had himself elected a Democratic U.S. senator from Louisiana while also holding on, for a time, to the governor's office.

Like Coughlin, Long started out a Roosevelt supporter and turned into a leading Roosevelt basher. Like Townsend, Long had a grandiose plan for curing the country's ills. Under his Share Our Wealth Plan, Long proposed to limit the amount of money an individual could have or could make in a single year. The money confiscated from those who had more than the limits (which varied from $1.5 million to $5 million in cumulative wealth and from $600,000 to $1.8 million in annual income) would be redistributed so that every American family would have $5,000 worth of annual salaries and amenities like a car and a homestead.

Like Townsend's plan, it was mathematically goofy. Economists pointed out that taking all the money from the rich and giving it to the poor would amount to about $400 per family, not $5,000. It was a fact lost on lots of people. Long developed a national following and became a force in Washington, D.C., as well as Louisiana.

Heading for a showdown with FDR

In May 1935, Long, Townsend, and Coughlin began talking about forming a third political party to run against Roosevelt in the 1936 presidential election campaign, with Long as the candidate. "I'll tell you here and now," Long said in the summer of 1935, "FDR will not be the next president of the United States. If the Democrats nominate Roosevelt and the Republicans nominate (former President Herbert) Hoover, Huey Long will be your next president."

Roosevelt was acutely aware of the threat from the troika of demagogues. "I am fighting communism, Huey Longism, Coughlinism, Townsendism," FDR told a reporter. "I want to save our system" from "crackpot ideas." Roosevelt also knew that Long didn't actually think he could win in 1936 but would run to pull enough votes away from Roosevelt to keep the president from winning.

"Long plans to be a candidate of the Hitler type," FDR wrote in a letter to the U.S. ambassador to Germany. "He hopes to defeat the Democratic Party and put in a reactionary Republican. That would bring the country to such a state by 1940 that Long thinks he could be made dictator."

But the best-laid plans of Long, Coughlin, and Townsend went awry on the evening of September 8, 1935. Coming out of a legislative session in the Louisiana Capitol, Long was shot by a man whose family reputation had been smeared by the senator. Long died two days later. (His bodyguards pumped 61 bullets into the assassin.)

Without a bonafide candidate, the hopes of Coughlin and Townsend were dashed, although they tried anyway. A North Dakota congressman named William "Liberty Bill" Lemke was recruited, and he ran on the Union Party ticket. Coughlin vowed to quit radio if Lemke didn't get at least 9 million votes in the election.

As strange as it sounds now, the Roosevelt camp had reason for concern about the election, if not Lemke. Several polls predicted that the Republican candidate, Kansas Governor Alf Landon, would win easily. But the pollsters asked the wrong voters, neglecting to include people at the bottom of the economic ladder or African Americans, who traditionally had voted Republican but switched in huge numbers to FDR's Democratic Party.

Roosevelt won a smashing victory, gathering 27.7 million votes to Landon's 16.7 million and Lemke's 880,000. FDR carried every state but Maine and Vermont. "I knew I should have gone to Maine and Vermont," Roosevelt quipped after the returns were in.

Coughlin, who died in 1979, did not give up his radio show until 1942, but he never again attained the popularity or influence he once had. Townsend, who was briefly jailed for refusing to testify before a congressional committee, faded from the public eye and died in 1960 at the age of 93. As their influence decreased, however, there remained considerable noise during the 1930s from the left and the right of the political spectrum.

Fascists, Nazis, and Reds

It's a truism of American politics that Americans don't mind radical change — as long as it's done in moderation. The veracity of that idea, however, was sorely tested in the Great Depression. The desperate times had people thinking that maybe something desperate needed to be done.

"Never before or since have I heard so much open and bitter cynicism about democracy and the American system," said six-time Socialist presidential candidate Norman Thomas.

Some Americans thought the president should seize power. "What we need now is martial law," magazine publisher Bernarr Macfadden told readers of *Liberty Magazine.* "This is no time for civil law. The president should have dictatorial powers . . . the Constitution should not interfere with the remedies which are essential to get us out of this appalling depression."

Hatching the "Business Plot"

If a former Marine Corps major general was to be believed, at least one group of business leaders thought power should be seized from the president. In November 1934, retired Major General Smedley Butler told a congressional committee that a man named Gerald MacGuire had approached him in mid-1933. MacGuire was heir to the Singer Sewing machine fortune and one of Wall Street's richest investors.

Butler said MacGuire wanted him to participate in a fascist coup of the government. The plan, according to Butler, was to install Butler in a cabinet-level post as "secretary of general affairs." Roosevelt would remain as a puppet, but a group of business leaders would actually run things. Butler said he was promised an army of 500,000 veterans and $30 million in financial backing.

MacGuire vehemently denied the whole thing, which came to be known as the "Business Plot," and there was little corroborative evidence. Nonetheless, the committee concluded that "there is no question that these attempts were discussed, were planned, and might have been placed in execution when and if the financial backers deemed it expedient." But for reasons never made entirely clear, nothing came of the allegations or the committee's investigation.

Defending the wealthy

Some of the folks suspected of being in back of the "Business Plot" put together an organization in August 1934 that they called the American Liberty League. The members included business giants such as DuPont, General Foods, General Motors, and Standard Oil, and politicians from both parties — including Al Smith, the 1928 Democratic presidential candidate-turned-Roosevelt hater. The organization's purpose was to "defend and uphold the

Constitution" and "foster the right to work, earn, save and acquire property." Left unstated but obvious to everyone was that the League's purpose was to defeat Roosevelt's bid for a second term in 1936 and to portray the administration's depression-fighting programs as at best socialist and at worst communist.

The wealthy had good reason to be nervous. In his annual message to Congress in January 1936, FDR called for "unceasing warfare" to be waged on "our resplendent economic autocracy." The Liberty League hit back at a New York luncheon of 2,000 people later in the month — a gathering *The New York Times* called "the greatest collection of millionaires ever gathered under one roof."

"The New Deal smells of the stench of Communistic Russia," Smith told the crowd. "There can be only one Capitol, Washington or Moscow. There can be only one atmosphere of government, the clean fresh air of free America, or the foul breath of Communist Russia."

Actually, that sort of rhetoric and the League's opposition probably ended up helping Roosevelt, because the enemy of the rich had to be the friend of the poor — and there were a lot more poor people than rich people during the Great Depression.

Trying to get a footing as communists

While Roosevelt's enemies were trying unsuccessfully to paint his administration with a communist brush, the real communists were struggling mightily to establish themselves in Depression-era America.

Under a Soviet strategy called "the Popular Front," American communists tried to enhance their image as ordinary Americans who just happened to believe the government model the United States should follow was that of the Soviet Union. They joined churches and formed book clubs, dining clubs, and theater groups. They ingratiated themselves with Hollywood celebrities by sponsoring anti-Nazi or pro-Spanish Republic groups. The communist newspaper *The Daily Worker* even began running a large sports section.

But outside of a few intellectuals and a few labor unions, the communists made no significant inroads during the 1930s. And after Soviet leader Joseph Stalin signed an alliance with Germany's Adolf Hitler in August 1939 (just before Germany invaded Poland and started World War II), the communists lost what little credibility they may have had.

Shilling for Der Führer

Another group trying to make a mark in Depression-era America came from the right. After Hitler rose to power in Germany in 1933, some Germans and German-Americans formed groups to support the new German leader and his National Socialist, or Nazi, Party.

The first of these groups called itself the "Friends of New Germany" and had the blessing of Hitler's government. The group, which never grew larger than 5,000 to 10,000 members, mainly held rallies to rhetorically rough up communists and Jews, and soon was more of an embarrassment to Germany than an asset. In October 1935, German Nazi officials ordered the organization to disband.

In less than a year, another group sprung up, calling itself the "German-American *Bund*" (meaning "organization"). A fellow named Fritz Kuhn, who had fought for Germany in World War I but had become a naturalized U.S. citizen, headed the group. Kuhn's group held rallies, set up recreational camps for youths and families, and simultaneously extolled the joys of Hitler's Germany and the "evil conspiracies" being concocted by Jews.

The Bund began attracting the attention of U.S. federal agents when reports surfaced that Kuhn had a force of 200,000 men ready to take up arms. In reality, the group never had more than perhaps 7,500 members, and Kuhn was a first-class chowderhead. Hitler's government was so unimpressed that it ordered the group to stop displaying Nazi symbols or emblems, and the German ambassador to the United States referred to Kuhn as "stupid, noisy and absurd."

The Bund held its largest rally at New York's Madison Square Garden in February 1939. The rally attracted a crowd of about 22,000. But after the rally, Kuhn was arrested for embezzling money from his group. After the Japanese attack on the U.S. Naval base at Pearl Harbor on December 7, 1941, the Bund was formally dissolved and some of its other officers were arrested for attempting to avoid the draft or engaging in subversive activities.

Sticking with the Constitution

In the end, none of the extremist efforts made much headway with Americans, despite the anger, fear, and uncertainty generated by the Great Depression.

That fact was underscored by two surveys conducted by pollster Elmer Roper in late 1939 for *Fortune* magazine. The surveys found that 67 percent believed it was government's responsibility to provide for people in need, while less than 10 percent believed it was time to change the entire U.S. Constitution.

Most importantly, almost two-thirds believed "the future holds opportunity for advancement," and 76 percent believed their children faced a better future than their own.

Robin Hoods and Dirty Rats

The 1930s saw the resurrection of an American archetype: the outlaw. Instead of the 19th-century six-guns, horses, and "head 'em off at the pass" motif, the Great Depression version was machine guns, Fords, and "come and get me coppers!"

Although violent crime rates actually decreased during the decade (compared with the previous decade), bank robberies, kidnappings, daring jailbreaks, and desperate shootouts between cops and killers became front-page news on an almost daily basis. Perhaps people wanted to hit back at whoever had caused the Great Depression, and they got a vicarious kick out of the brash behavior of criminals.

Whatever the reason for the public's fascination with bad guys and bad girls, it was certainly aided and abetted by the mass media. Hollywood studios quickly figured out that gangster films were the single most popular genre among moviegoers. The studios churned out 50 such movies in 1931 alone.

In the early years of the Great Depression, criminals were often depicted as tragic figures that went bad because of a tough break somewhere along the line. They were also often portrayed as committing crimes against even more insidious criminals, such as corrupt politicians, bankers, or businessmen (which a lot of people may have wanted to do themselves).

In a 1932 piece about actor James Cagney's role as a gangster in *Public Enemy,* New York essayist Lincoln Kirstein wrote that "when Cagney gets down off a truck, or deals at cards, or curses, or slaps his girl . . . he is, for the time, being the American hero, whom ordinary men and boys recognize as themselves."

Newspapers sensationalized crooks by giving or playing up catchy nicknames such as George "Baby Face" Nelson, Arthur "Pretty Boy" Floyd, George "Machine Gun" Kelly, and Alvin "Creepy" Karpis. They installed various criminals as the nation's "Public Enemy No. 1," even though there was no such official list.

And there was no such thing as too much crime news. For example, the day after bad guy John Dillinger (whose wanted poster can be seen in Figure 9-1) was gunned down outside a Chicago movie theater (where he had been watching — what else? — a gangster movie), the *Fresno Bee* carried five front-page stories on crime. Three were related to Dillinger, one described a Texas prison break by pals of Clyde Barrow (of Bonnie and Clyde), and another told of the manhunt for Baby Face Nelson.

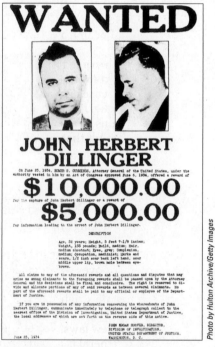

Figure 9-1: A 1934 FBI wanted poster for John Dillinger, offering a reward of $10,000 for his capture.

The papers — and other media — also shamelessly played up the Robin Hood angle. The papers reported how Bonnie and Clyde sometimes burned mortgage notes when they robbed a bank. The iconic 1930s troubadour Woody Guthrie wrote a song about Pretty Boy Floyd that included the lyrics: "There's many a starving farmer/The same old story told/ How the outlaw paid their mortgage/ and saved their little home."

A popular tale was how bad man Dillinger (see the sidebar on him later in the chapter) once asked a farmer during a bank robbery if the $50 in the farmer's hand was his or the bank's. When the fellow said it was his, according to the story, Dillinger told him to keep it. "He robs those who became rich robbing poor people," an admirer wrote to an Indianapolis newspaper. "I am for Johnnie."

Thirsting for justice

However much Americans liked reading about or watching criminals on the silver screen, however, most people didn't really like the idea of criminals going unpunished. Seemingly everyone had a cure for a crime wave that, according to statistics, didn't really exist. The cures ranged from public hangings to reinstating whipping as a punishment to establishing a "Devil's Island" prison for hard-core bad guys (which actually came about in 1933 when San Francisco Bay's Alcatraz Island became a federal prison).

New York passed a law that made it a crime to be someone "who bears an evil reputation" and "consorts with thieves and criminals or frequents unlawful resorts." Most cases under the law were thrown out as unconstitutionally vague. But that didn't stop the New York commissioner of corrections, Walter N. Thayer, from calling for a National Public Enemies Act that would allow the jailing of any "individual with a known record who consorts with known criminals and has no visible means of support."

"Any city can be cleared of known criminals in 48 hours," Thayer asserted, "if the hands of the police are unshackled and if the powers that be will assure them of backing and support."

But the powers that be wouldn't assure them of federal backing and support, at least not while Herbert Hoover was president. Hoover balked at more federal involvement in fighting crime because it would cost money and intrude on state's rights. In a 1930 speech, Hoover said, "Every state has ample laws . . . what is needed is the enforcement of those laws, and not new laws. Any suggestion of increasing federal criminal laws in general is a (bad) reflection on the sovereignty and the standing of state government."

Left unsaid by Hoover, at least publicly, was that he had little faith in the federal Division of Investigation (which formally became the Federal Bureau of Investigation in 1935). Federal investigators were not allowed to carry firearms, could not make arrests, and had such a reputation for corruption that they were sneeringly referred to as "the Department of Easy Virtue."

After Roosevelt replaced Hoover in the White House in 1933, however, the federal government took a new approach. In April 1934, Attorney General Homer Cummings announced a 12-bill crime-fighting package that included making federal crimes of bank robbery, interstate flight to avoid prosecutions, and transporting stolen goods. These statutes would thwart criminals who committed a robbery in one state and then fled to another state where they had committed no crime. The bill also allowed federal agents to carry weapons and make arrests, and it outlawed machine guns. The laws finally gave FBI director John Edgar Hoover the tools he had been waiting for since he took over the bureau in 1924.

In signing the package on May 18, 1934, Roosevelt issued a bit of a scolding to the media and the public: "Law enforcement and gangster extermination cannot be completely effective so long as a substantial part of the public looks with tolerance upon known criminals . . . or applauds efforts to romanticize crime."

Emphasizing the good guys

Hollywood heeded Roosevelt's advice to quit glamorizing the bad guys. In true Hollywood fashion, in fact, it went overboard. The Motion Picture Producers Association prohibited its members from making films about John Dillinger, stating that the decision was "based on a belief . . . that such a picture could be detrimental to the best public interests."

A new censorship code, established at the end of 1934, effectively banned gangster movies by prohibiting a long list of things from being shown on the screen. Those included giving the lead role to a bad-guy character; showing cops being killed; depicting the crimes of arson, kidnapping, or revenge murders; "flaunting firearms"; displaying machine guns or other illegal weapons; and ending the movie without the bad guy being killed or sent to prison.

Stripped of their most popular genre, some enterprising filmmakers got around the ban by making pictures about the good guys — specifically the FBI. Eight such movies were made in 1935. The most successful was called *'G' Men,* a nickname for federal agents, or "government men." The film starred James Cagney, who played a young agent in pretty much the same way he played a young criminal four years earlier in *Public Enemy.*

The FBI officially kept all the Hollywood adulation at arm's length in order to head off charges that it had encouraged the films. But the bureau's director, J. Edgar Hoover, ate it up. Hoover, who looked and often acted like a dyspeptic owl, had a flair for publicity and an intense sense of duty. He played up the seriousness of crime in the period by collecting often inflated and at best unreliable crime statistics from local jurisdictions. "The criminal in America is on the march," he solemnly warned in 1934.

As law enforcement hunted down and killed or captured the most high-profile criminals, Hoover made sure the bureau received ample credit, no matter what its real role had been. As FBI director until his death in 1972, Hoover would become one of the most powerful Americans of the 20th century. He would often use his powers unethically and possibly illegally. But in the 1930s, he was a hero.

"Pick a small boy these days and ask him who of all the people in the world he wants to be like," the *New York World-Telegram* reported in 1936, "and ten to one he will reply 'J. Edgar Hoover.'"

John Dillinger

"John Dillinger, ace bad man of the world, got his last night — two slugs through his heart and one through his head. He was tough and he was shrewd, but he wasn't as tough or as shrewd as the federals, who never close a case until the end."

Thus began the July 23, 1934, International News Service story that capped the criminal career of the 1930s' number-one "public enemy." Born in 1903, Dillinger got his start in crime by robbing a grocery store in 1924. His lack of experience showed, and he was quickly caught and served nine years in prison.

Dillinger made up for lost time when he was released in 1933 by beginning a 14-month crime spree that saw him kill ten men, engineer three jail breaks (once with a "gun" carved from a bar of soap), escape from two gun battles with police, and grab more than $265,000 ($4.4 million in 2008 dollars) from various banks.

Dillinger became a folk hero, vaulting athletically over bank counters and seeming never to lose his cool. After being captured in January 1934, Dillinger posed for pictures with law enforcement officials and then promptly escaped from an "escape-proof" jail — in the sheriff's new car. During the break, he took two hostages, and when he released them, Dillinger gave them each $4 for their troubles.

His demise came when a mysterious "woman in red" told FBI agents he would be attending a movie at a Chicago theater. Two dozen agents and police ambushed him as he left the theater and gunned him down. Or, as another newspaper story put it the next day:

"A stiffening corpse in the county morgue and a muddied pool of blood in the filth of an alley was all that was left today of John Dillinger, arch criminal of modern times. Dillinger died as he had lived — in a hail of bullets and a welter of blood."

Lessons Learned

The correlation between hard economic times and increased crime rates would seem to be a no-brainer. But as the experiences of the Great Depression show, that's not necessarily so.

Almost every recessionary period in the United States since the 1950s has been accompanied by a rise in crime rates, particularly property crimes such as robbery and burglary. The factors that contribute to the increases include

- ✔ The obvious effects of falling wages and greater unemployment rates creating a bigger pool of people that may be driven to commit a crime.

- ✔ Greater use of alcohol and drugs as an escape, which could lead to lowered inhibitions to commit a crime, or make economic situations more desperate.

- ✔ More vacant stores and houses, which can invite more crime since there may be fewer potential witnesses.

- ✔ Smaller police budgets that translate to less law enforcement.

But in the Great Depression of the 1930s, crime rates went up in the first part of the decade and then steadily declined through the rest. Sociologists and criminologists theorize that the rise in crime during the first two or three years was due to a combination of two things. One was the onset of hard economic times.

The other, and more important, factor was Prohibition: the nationwide ban on liquor sales that spurred a massive illegal black market and sparked widespread violence as various criminal organizations vied for control of the trade. When Prohibition ended in 1933, crime rates began dropping even though hard times continued.

But researchers have suggested that another factor besides the end of Prohibition may have contributed to the drop: the creation of programs that put people to work (such as the Work Progress Administration and the Civilian Conservation Corps) and social safety net services.

A 2007 study by economists from the University of California, Brigham Young University, and the University of Arizona concluded that "relief spending during the 1930s lowered property crime in a statistically and economically significant way."

Put another way, if you give people money, or a way to earn it, they are less likely to steal it.

Chapter 10

Having Fun in Spite of It All

*W*hile the tentacles of the stagnant national economy touched all but the wealthiest Americans during the 1930s, that didn't mean the sun never shone and everyone moped around waiting for World War II to start and get things moving again. The economic conditions meant less work, but that also meant more leisure time.

This chapter covers what people did with that leisure time, from listening to a *lot* of radio to going to *lots* of movies. It covers the heyday of comic strips and their offspring, as well as how people entertained their ears. I take a look at the return of legal drinking with the end of Prohibition in late 1933, and the chapter concludes with the pastime of driving around the country.

More Time to Play

In 1936, a federal committee formed by President Franklin D. Roosevelt to study the country's resources reported that in the previous year, Americans had spent $17 billion on food, $9.5 billion on housing, $5.25 billion on clothing, $3.8 billion on automobiles, and $1.6 billion on recreation.

That last figure on recreation spending may seem surprisingly high, given that people were still in the midst of the most pro-longed economic calamity in U.S. history. But people had more time on their hands for recreation — and recreation spending — precisely *because* the economy was sailing stormy seas.

Cutting down the workweek

Prior to the Great Depression, a typical U.S. workweek generally
included at least a half-day's work on Saturday, and very often a
full day. That meant there were no such things as weekends, at
least not in the modern sense of the term.

But when hard times hit, many companies reduced their hours of
operation or split jobs among workers so that fewer would have to
be laid off. In 1933, the Roosevelt administration urged employers
to adopt a maximum 40-hours-per-person workweek as part of the
National Industrial Recovery Act's efforts to create more jobs.

By the time the U.S. Supreme Court overturned the act as
unconstitutional in 1935 (see Chapter 13 for details), the five-day
workweek had become a well-established fact for many businesses
and industries. (In 1938, Congress approved the Fair Labor
Standards Act, which mandated a 40-hour-maximum workweek.
The act took effect in 1940.) And fewer hours working meant more
leisure time for millions of Americans.

Finding uses for free time

Because most people were watching every dime, they often looked
for things to do at home, whether it was hobbies such as gardening
or playing games such as contract bridge. (Both activities were
very big in the 1930s.) Other pastimes, like bowling or miniature
golf (also big in the decade), cost a little money.

But whether they were free or for a fee, there seemed to be no
shortage of things to do, even with a depression going on. In 1935, for
example, the new things to do included seeing the first feature-length
Technicolor movie *(Becky Sharp),* playing a new board game called
Monopoly, attending a Major League Baseball game at night (at least
in Cincinnati), and drinking beer out of a can. And if you were of a
mind to just stay home and relax, there was always the radio.

When Radio Was King

With the exception of the automobile, probably nothing had a
greater impact on American life in the first half of the 20th century
than radio. Born in the early 1920s, the medium grew up in the
Great Depression and became a member of most American
families — especially when radios got cheaper. Manufacturers
began encasing radios in plastic shells rather than wood, and they
rewired the sets so they didn't require large transformers. Those
changes made them lighter and less expensive.

In 1930, half of U.S. households had radios. By the middle of the decade, that number was up to 60 percent of households, which was twice as many as had telephones. By 1939, 86 percent of households had radios, as did 20 percent of motor vehicles, and Americans were listening to the radio an average of 4.5 hours a day.

A survey by the National Recreation Association in 1937 found that Americans' favorite pastime was listening to the radio, and social workers reported radios were often the last possession destitute people would part with when selling off their household items.

What Americans listened to varied. There were comedy shows, often hosted by comics who had made the leap to radio from vaudeville or the movies. There were vivid dramas, which in at least one case proved too vivid. That was in October 1938, when Orson Welles and the Mercury Theatre presented a version of *The War of the Worlds* that was so realistic it caused a panic among thousands of people who thought Earth had been invaded by Martians.

"You know, Orson," President Roosevelt told Welles a few days after the broadcast, "you and I are the two best actors in America."

People also could listen to real-life drama as it unfolded, such as the farewell address of the terminally ill baseball star Lou Gehrig, the abdication of the British throne by King Edward VIII so he could marry an American divorcee, and the German invasion of Poland.

Influencing America on the public airwaves

Radio exerted enormous influence on the country, turning America, as a 1933 study put it, "into a vast auditorium, into all corners of which a single voice can carry with dramatic ease and clarity." Radio gave people a commonality of experience that jumped across family and neighborhood and even regional boundaries. It sold people things and told people things, and much of what was said over the airwaves was believed.

"When (people) say 'the radio,' they don't mean a cabinet, an electric phenomenon, or a man in a studio," wrote essayist E.B. White. "They refer to a pervading and somewhat godlike presence, which has come into their lives and homes."

All this influence was being exerted over public property. In 1927, Congress declared that the airwaves belonged to the public and that the federal government had the responsibility to regulate who could broadcast and on what frequency. In 1934, the Federal Communications Commission (FCC) replaced what had been called the Federal Radio Commission and became the country's supervising agency for nonprint mass media.

In the 1930s, the radio segment of the U.S. mass media was basically four major networks with which three-fourths of the country's 600 to 800 radio stations were affiliated. The presence of four coast-to-coast networks (the Columbia Broadcasting Service, the Mutual Radio Network, and two controlled by the National Broadcasting Company, NBC "Red" and NBC "Blue") gave U.S. businesses national avenues on which to advertise — and they jumped at the opportunity.

Between 1928 and 1934, radio advertising increased 316 percent, even as newspaper ads were dropping 30 percent and magazine ads 45 percent. By 1938, according to an FCC survey, one-third of radio time was devoted to commercials; one-third to music; and the rest to news, sports, religious shows, talk shows, comedies, and dramas — many of which were aimed at women and called "soap operas" because their sponsors often sold cleaning products.

Most shows had a single sponsor, and the show's star often was the product's primary pitchman. That situation resulted in products and characters or celebrities sometimes becoming fixed together in the public's mind, such as Ovaltine drink mix with Little Orphan Annie, Pepsodent toothpaste with "Amos 'n Andy," and Jell-O dessert mix with Jack Benny.

Radio ads were generally short and snappy, often with clever and annoyingly hard-to-forget jingles, and sometimes they made audaciously ludicrous claims:

- ✔ Cigarettes could ease digestion.
- ✔ Business careers could be ruined by not shaving closely enough.
- ✔ Mouthwashes could kill "up to 86.7 percent of germs" (though apparently never more than that).

Many ads also featured *tie-ins,* in which listeners were invited to write in for free samples or other "gifts." That allowed advertisers to measure how well their message was getting across.

Politicking over the air

Early on, politicians figured out the potential of radio to influence the public. In 1928, 20 percent of the Republican Party's presidential campaign budget was for radio ads — the party's single largest expense. In 1932, the GOP bought 42.5 hours of airtime for political messages and speeches, while the Democratic Party bought 51.5 hours.

In 1936, Republicans set aside $1 million for radio advertising, and an adviser wrote to GOP presidential candidate Alf Landon that "the handling of Republican publicity should be on the same basis as the handling of any other article that wants to be merchandised to the public." (It didn't help much; Landon was crushed by Roosevelt.)

Political parties weren't the only ones to recognize the potential and power of radio. Individuals such as Father Charles Coughlin and Louisiana politician Huey Long (covered in Chapter 9) used the radio as a pulpit from which to bash their opponents and extol the magnificence of their own ideas. But the most successful exponent of political persuasion over the radio was Franklin D. Roosevelt.

On Sunday, March 12, 1933 — eight days after taking over the Office of the President — Roosevelt sat before the fireplace in the Diplomatic Reception Room of the White House and addressed the nation over all of the radio networks.

It was the first of what would be 30 "fireside chats" during his 12-plus years as president. (The "fireside chats" name was suggested by a radio executive.) In all of them, FDR would speak as though he were just talking with neighbors over coffee and pie, never patronizing his audience even when explaining complex issues.

As humorist Will Rogers put it after the first fireside chat on the country's banking problems: "Our president took such a dry subject as banking (and) made everybody understand it — even the bankers."

The chats were also an important political tool for Roosevelt. They allowed him to put his agenda before the country without filters, which was particularly helpful because most of the country's major newspapers and newspaper chains opposed both the president and the New Deal and routinely editorialized against them.

"Shhhhh! 'Amos 'n Andy' is on!"

Nowhere was radio's influence more evident during the Great Depression than from 7:00 to 7:15 (EST) every evening except Sunday. Movie theaters would stop their films and pipe in the NBC Red network; department stores would crank up their radios; the number of phone calls around the country would drop by 50 percent. And millions of Americans — including President Roosevelt — would drop whatever they were doing and listen to two white actors pretend to be two persistently optimistic black men who ran a one-cab taxi company and repeatedly failed at get-rich-quick schemes.

At its peak in the mid-1930s, "Amos 'n Andy" drew an audience estimated at 40 million — about one-third of all Americans. It was the equivalent of a Super Bowl TV audience, only it tuned in six nights a week, week in and week out. The show was so popular that the network eventually began rebroadcasting each segment at 11:30 p.m. (EST) so people on the West Coast could hear it in prime time.

"Amos 'n Andy" was far more than a radio show. It made people smile during a period where there wasn't a lot to smile about, and it served as a unifying force by giving perfect strangers something in common to discuss. Its impact was reflected in a comment by the noted British playwright George Bernard Shaw during a 1933 tour of the United States. "There are three things which I shall never forget about America," Shaw said, "Niagara Falls, the Rocky Mountains, and 'Amos 'n Andy.'"

Not everyone was smitten by the show. The *Pittsburgh Courier,* the country's most influential African American newspaper, gathered 740,000 signatures on a petition to have "Amos 'n Andy" pulled off the air for what the petition said were offensive racial stereotyping and propagation of racist attitudes toward African Americans. But the protests fell on deaf ears. "Amos 'n Andy" continued in various forms on the radio until 1960.

Trading Real Life for Reel Life

If radio had a rival in the Great Depression, it was movies. Radio had the advantages of being free and readily accessible. But movies offered pictures to go along with the sound. And the darkened environment of the theater afforded customers at least the façade of anonymity and a place for many people to dream of other lives.

"Each day, millions of men, women and children sit in the windowless temples of the screen to commune with their vicarious friends and lovers," observed writer Leo Rosten.

The relative newness of *talking pictures* (movies with sound, which debuted in late 1927) helped the movie industry keep the Great Depression at bay for a short time. But by 1933, ticket sales had slumped from 80 million a week in 1930 to 60 million. The cumulative value of stock of the five major studios — RKO, Paramount, Warner Brothers, Metro-Goldwyn-Mayer, and 20th Century Fox — fell from about $1 billion in 1929 to less than $200 million in 1933.

Filling the seats

To combat declining ticket sales, theater owners cut their prices from 50 cents to 25 cents for adults and 10 cents for kids. (That's $3.93 and $1.57 in 2008 dollars.) Owners also looked for extras they could add to their product. The extras included cartoons, abbreviated films called *shorts,* newsreels, or a combination of these. Gradually, the *double feature* became standard. It usually teamed an "A" picture with recognizable stars and big production values with a "B" picture featuring secondary actors and bargain-basement production values.

Theater managers also added nonscreen extras. Popcorn, candy, and soda, once thought to be a nuisance because of the cleanup involved, became theater necessities when owners realized they could make more off food concessions than off admission tickets.

In the winter of 1932–33, a Colorado theater manager came up with something he called "Bank Nights" to stimulate attendance on the slowest nights at the box office, usually Mondays and Tuesdays. Patrons wrote their names in a book in the lobby, alongside a number. Tickets with corresponding numbers were put in drum, a ticket was drawn at intermission, and some lucky patron won a cash prize, usually around $150 (about $2,400 in 2008 dollars).

Variations on the game featured prizes that ranged from china to livestock. By the end of 1937, it was estimated that 5,000 theaters were hosting weekly promotions like Bank Night, giving away prizes totaling $1 million.

The extra screen features, the snacks, and the promotions, combined with films that were generally better made than those of an earlier decade, got people going to the movies again, as reflected in the Figure 10-1 photo.

By 1938, the average family spent $25 a year on movie admissions, and there were 1,700 movie theaters at which to spend it. That was double the number of hotels in the country and triple the number of department stores.

Photo by John Kobal Foundation/Getty Images

Figure 10-1: People flock to the Astor Theatre in New York to see the movie *A Free Soul.*

Weekly movie ticket sales reached 86.5 million by the end of the 1930s. That was the equivalent of two-thirds of the country going to the movies every week. In contrast, *combined* ticket sales for the United States and Canada in 2007 equaled about 26.9 million tickets a week, the equivalent of less than 8 percent of the two countries' populations going to a weekly movie.

Keeping it clean

Sensitive to criticism in the early 1930s that it was portraying too much sex and violence on the screen, Hollywood voluntarily began to censor itself, particularly when it came to sex. In 1934, the Motion Picture Producers and Distributors of America began requiring films to have a "certificate of approval" from an industry-created censorship board that had been created in 1930.

The board established a fairly rigid code of do's and don'ts:

- Married couples had to have twin beds.

- Gangsters couldn't be shown living the high life, even if they were gunned down later on.

- Words such as *sex, God,* and *hell* were forbidden.

(Producer David O. Selznick had to get special permission so that Clark Gable could utter the famous line "Frankly, my dear, I don't give a damn" at the end of *Gone with the Wind.*)

Producing the stuff of dreams

Film historians and movie buffs often refer to the 1930s as "Hollywood's Golden Age." It was certainly one of the film industry's most prolific periods. As many as 5,000 films were made during the decade, spurring one critic to call it "Fairyland on a production line."

The quantity of films produced assured there would be a wide variety of genres. Gangster films were an early favorite in the decade (see Chapter 9). Lavish musicals, such as *42nd Street* and *Footlight Parade,* brought sparkle to the screen, even if they were black and white. There were film biographies *(The Story of Louis Pasteur, Voltaire),* horror films *(Dracula, Frankenstein,* and *King Kong),* and adventure flicks *(Robin Hood, The Lives of a Bengal Lancer).* And late in the decade, there were epic Technicolor films like *Gone with the Wind* and *The Wizard of Oz.*

Not everyone was enamored with the influence of movies on the American public during the period. In a 1936 *Harper's Magazine* article, critic Ruth Suckow complained that films too often sugar-coated life and resulted in too much hero worship of actors. "(Movies) have come to represent certain national ideals, reduced to the lowest common denominator," she wrote. "For that is what the screen does — it reduces while it magnifies, grinds down what it exalts into the typical."

But others have contended that movies during the period gave people not only an avenue of escape but also feelings of hope.

"American movie audiences, escaping from the realities of the Depression outside the movie theater, withdrew inside to see human grit triumph over suffering and human kindness triumph over financial, political and moral chicanery," wrote film historian Gerald Mast. "If the optimism of Hollywood films provided the audiences with the tranquilizer it needed, it also strengthened the audience's belief that eventually good people would make bad times better."

That optimism was reflected in a 1933 film song that became something of an anthem for Americans, not only when facing the grimness of the Great Depression but also in the succeeding decade when facing totalitarian countries in World War II. The song was "Who's Afraid of the Big Bad Wolf?" from Walt Disney's *The Three Little Pigs.*

More Fun for the Eyes and Ears

While radio and movies dominated the leisure time of most Americans during the Great Depression, they were by no means the only pastimes to occupy the senses. Light reading, of things such as comics, comic books, and magazines, was also popular. And Americans found other ways to listen to music besides on the radio.

Reading comic strips and their offspring

Comic strips had been a part of U.S. newspapers since the late 19th century, but they really came into their own in the late 1920s and early 1930s. Unlike their 21st-century counterparts, one comic strip could take up an entire page of a Sunday comics section, and the story lines tended to be more drawn out and convoluted. Newspapers were happy to provide the space because the strips were consistently at or near the top of best-read features in subscriber surveys.

Modern comic readers would find many familiar names in the comic strips that populated newspapers of the 1930s, such as Mickey Mouse, Donald Duck, Dick Tracy, Tarzan, Blondie, and Little Orphan Annie. A few less familiar figures emerged in that period as well: Flash Gordon, Secret Agent X-9, Buck Rogers, L'il Abner, Mandrake the Magician, and Terry and the Pirates.

Comic strips had the same appeal during the Great Depression as radio, movies, and other leisure-time activities, serving as respites from reality for adults and opening new worlds of imagination for children.

Critics took a less kindly view. In a 1937 article in the *Saturday Review,* Lowell Thompson complained that comics were too violent and full of cruel humor. "A tolerant contempt for the average man," he wrote, "has ousted a spread-eagle faith in democracy."

But Thompson was decidedly in the minority. Comics were so popular that they often spun off into other media, such as radio shows, feature films, and movie serials. A kid could listen to Flash Gordon on the radio Saturday morning, watch him at the movies Saturday afternoon, and read about him in the Sunday comics.

Leapin' lizards!

In 1924, a cartoonist name Harold Gray created a comic strip featuring the adventures of a small girl named Little Orphan Annie. The redheaded kid had a dog named Sandy, a favorite saying ("Leapin' lizards"), and eventually a foster father named Oliver "Daddy" Warbucks.

The strip was fabulously successful (it was reported to be President Herbert Hoover's favorite). By 1934, Gray was reportedly making $100,000 a year from the strip and another $50,000-plus from a radio show featuring the characters.

At first aimed at children as a humorous strip, and then at older audiences as an adventure comic, "Annie" also served as a vehicle for Gray's conservative/libertarian political views. "Daddy" Warbucks was an unabashed champion of capitalism and a powerful tycoon who was not above meting out justice on bad guys without all the trouble of a court trial.

Gray hated President Roosevelt and Roosevelt's New Deal policies. How much? In 1944, despondent at FDR having won a fourth presidential term, Gray killed off Daddy Warbucks with a mysterious disease, implying there was no longer room in the country for capitalists. After FDR himself died in April 1945, Gray resurrected Warbucks a few months later. Asked why, Gray smirked that "the situation changed last April."

The comics also spawned new forms of reading material during the period. There were comic books, the first modern version of which was born in 1933. Called *Famous Funnies,* it was a collection of comic strip reprints that was given away as a promotion by a cleaning products company.

The comic strips also gave birth to *Big Little Books*. These were squat cubes of cardboard and paper, measuring about 4 inches by 4 inches and containing several hundred pages of big print and pictures. They were designed for kids and included most of the major comic strip characters, as well as adventure stories.

A slightly more sophisticated version of the comic book was the *pulp* magazine, so called because of the cheap wood pulp paper on which it was printed. The pulps featured fewer pictures and more words than comic books and usually focused on a specific genre, such as Westerns, detective stories, or horror. And they sometimes featured writers who were destined for greatness in other literary forms, such as playwright Tennessee Williams and novelist Sinclair Lewis.

Swinging to a new sound

At the beginning of the Great Depression, popular music was dominated by what has been referred to as the "country club" sound: Full orchestras, with carefully balanced horn and string sections, produced music to soothe — or stupefy — an audience. Such music filled radio airtime okay, but it didn't sell records, particularly in an economy without a lot of disposable income. In fact, the uninspired music and the rapid rise of radio combined with the hard times to almost kill off the record industry. Between 1927 and 1932, record sales fell from 104 million per year to 6 million. The entire music industry went from a $50-million-a-year concern to a $250,000-a-year basket case.

That changed on August 21, 1935. A 25-year-old clarinet player and bandleader named Benny Goodman was performing with his orchestra at the Palomar Ballroom in Los Angeles. Bored and depressed because the group's cross-country tour had been a flop, Goodman decided to "swing" in the last set, playing up-tempo and improvised stuff the musicians usually saved for after-hours jams.

The crowd went nuts for the new sound, which was really a derivation of jazz that black musicians had been playing for years.

"A good swing band, smashing away at full speed, with the trumpeters and clarinetists rising in turn . . . and the drummers going into long drawn-out rhythmical frenzies could reduce its less inhibited auditors to sheer emotional vibration," wrote historian Frederick Lewis Allen.

Some thought the music was a health hazard. A psychologist told *The New York Times* that swing music was "dangerously hypnotic" because it was "cunningly devised to a faster tempo" than the average adult's pulse rate of 72 beats per minute.

Despite such worries, swing music swept the country, and Goodman's band was soon joined by groups headed by Tommy and Jimmy Dorsey, Glenn Miller, Bob Crosby, Duke Ellington, Count Basie, Harry James, and Artie Shaw.

Record sales rebounded to 35 million in 1938, and records were the best-selling Christmas gift that year. In addition to the popularity of the swing sound, several other factors came into play:

> ✔ **Radio-phonograph consoles:** These items featured both a radio and a phonograph and became popular because they offered listeners an option when they wanted to hear a specific song.

✔ **Radio commercials:** As radio ads became more numerous, they became more irritating for people who wanted to listen to uninterrupted music. The consoles allowed an easy way to switch to records.

✔ **Jukeboxes:** By the end of the 1930s, an estimated 325,000 bars, cafés, and other spots had record machines in which customers could drop a nickel and hear their favorite tune. The "jukes" used a lot of records.

Drinking and Driving

On January 16, 1920, the Eighteenth Amendment to the U.S. Constitution took effect. Popularly known as *Prohibition,* the amendment made it illegal to make or sell alcoholic beverages in the United States. But it didn't take long to see that the idea of making America a better place by banning booze was a flop.

There is some statistical evidence that Americans drank less after Prohibition than they did before it began. But Prohibition also fostered illegal activity on the part of otherwise law-abiding citizens; gave criminals a monopoly on a lucrative industry; and added to a general disrespect for law and order.

By the third year of the Great Depression, two more pragmatic arguments against Prohibition had been added:

✔ A legal liquor industry would mean new, legitimate jobs.

✔ A legal liquor industry presented an opportunity for governments to raise revenues through taxes on alcoholic drinks.

In the 1932 presidential race, the repeal of Prohibition was not much of an issue. Democratic candidate Franklin D. Roosevelt favored repeal, while Republican candidate Herbert Hoover favored at least letting the states decide. But Prohibition was still a controversial enough issue that it dominated as many local and state races that year as the hard economic times did.

Bringing back legal booze

In February 1933, Congress submitted the question of repeal to conventions called in each state. While waiting for the necessary three-fourths of the states to vote for repeal, new President Roosevelt signed a law in his first month in office that allowed the sale of two types of liquor: beer with an alcoholic content of up to 3.2 percent, and light-alcohol wines. "I think this would be a good time for a beer," FDR grinned after signing the measure.

At 3:33 p.m. (Mountain Time) on December 5, 1933, Utah became the 36th state to ratify the Twenty-First Amendment, thus repealing Prohibition. Nationwide, people celebrated with a drink or two.

Well, not quite everywhere. Legal alcohol was in short supply, leaving much of the country's liquor in the hands of bootleggers. "Liquor has been sold illegally for 13 years," New Jersey Governor A. Harry Moore observed, "and it will not hurt if this is done for a few days more."

Drinking also did not become legal everywhere. The amendment allowed states and counties to decide for themselves if they wanted to allow the sale of alcoholic beverages. Fifteen states made selling liquor an exclusive state government monopoly. But only eight states chose to stay dry altogether, leaving 40 states where people in the Great Depression had something else to spend their recreation dollars on.

Touring America

"We are," noted humorist Will Rogers in 1931, "the first nation in the history of the world to go to the poor house in an automobile."

As was customary with Rogers' witticisms, this one had a large chunk of truth in it. Even in the depths of the Great Depression, Americans never lost their love for the automobile. At the beginning of the depression in 1929, there were 26.8 million registered vehicles in the country. In 1941, there were 38.9 million, a 45 percent increase during hard times. In 1937, half of U.S. families owned cars, and a New York City auto show that same year featured an impressive 200 models of cars, trucks, and even a few car-trucks.

Researchers looking at the spending and social habits of Muncie, Indiana, residents found that car ownership "was one of the most depression-proof elements of the city's life . . . far less vulnerable, apparently, than marriages, divorces, new babies, clothing, jewelry and most other measurable things, both large and small."

One reason it was easy to stay in love with cars is that cars were becoming easier to love. Improvements in suspension, brakes, and tires made cars safer, more comfortable, and more reliable in the 1930s than a decade earlier. At 5 to 10 cents a gallon (79 cents to $1.58 in 2008 currency), gasoline was still relatively cheap. And more and more cars were equipped with amenities such as radios.

Sunday drives to the beach or into the countryside were favorite pastimes: "Give Americans a one-piece bathing suit, a hamburger, and five gallons of gasoline," Rogers observed "and they are just as tickled as a movie star with a new divorce."

While foreign travel by Americans dropped, "touring" trips around the United States became popular in the 1930s, especially to national parks and monuments, which saw a 400 percent increase in visitors between 1935 and 1939. Gas stations and lunch rooms sprouted alongside the nation's highways, along with motor hotels — *motels* — which were hybrids of urban hotels and rural motor camps.

Coupled with the forests of billboards that sprang up, the mass of roadside conveniences transformed U.S. highways, in the words of one critic, "into the ugliest spots on earth." Maybe. But at least this type of travel was affordable.

Lessons Learned

The Great Depression changed the way many Americans looked at work and its relation to life. The long-held ideal that hard work guaranteed success was a bit hard to swallow for the guy who had worked diligently for 20 years, only to find himself suddenly unemployed — and unemployable — when times got hard.

That, in turn, changed how he felt about leisure time. There was less guilt about enjoying one's self and more enthusiasm in finding ways to do it. Oh, and Americans managed to maintain their love for the automobile throughout the 1930s.

Here's a look at how leisure time stacked up in the early 21st century — and how the country's love affair with cars became more of a love–hate relationship.

Changing how we spend leisure time

"We work," the Greek philosopher Aristotle wrote, "to have leisure." In the United States of the 21st century, Aristotle's observation may be more accurately worded, "We work to have leisure by ourselves."

In the 21st century, leisure time takes a much different form than it did in the Great Depression. In the 1930s, hours away from work were more compartmentalized. For the most part, people worked from a set time to a set time on set days. That meant it was fairly easy to schedule social activities with friends and family.

 In contrast, studies have found that modern leisure time tends to be more fragmented. In a 2008 Harris poll, people estimated they had lost four hours of weekly leisure time from the year before, while at the same time estimating they were working only one hour longer per week. Researchers theorized the difference was "gray hours," where people weren't physically at work but were checking on things at work via home computers, cellular phones, or personal digital assistants (PDAs).

The proliferation of wireless communication devices makes it simultaneously easier and harder to be away from work. It also makes it more likely that Americans will use their leisure time in smaller chunks. That means leisure time is becoming more individualized and less communal. A 2006 survey, for example, found that 75 percent of respondents would rather watch a movie at home than at a theater, mostly because they were "too busy" to go to the theater.

The privatization of leisure time was also reflected in a 2007 study of leisure time use by the U.S. Bureau of Labor Statistics. The survey found that the average American enjoys just under five hours per day of leisure time and spends 2.6 hours watching television, compared to 38 minutes socializing or talking with others.

Spending time in traffic

The traffic engineer Henry Barnes once said, "Traffic is the mother-in-law in the otherwise perfect romance between Americans and their automobiles."

The "mother-in-law" is much harder to ignore these days than it was in the 1930s. There were 247.3 million motor vehicles registered in the country in 2007. That translates to about 1.3 Americans for each vehicle, compared to 3.3 people per registered vehicle in 1940.

More vehicles means more traffic, and more traffic means significant losses of time and money, as reported by a 2005 study:

- ✔ **Drivers snarled in traffic** burned 2.9 billion gallons of wasted fuel, enough to fill 58 supertankers.

- ✔ **Traffic jams** consumed 4.2 billion hours of time.

- ✔ **The wasted time** and fuel carried a price tag of $78 billion, a 420 percent increase from 1982 figures.

The study concluded that drivers in urban areas waste the equivalent of one week per year in traffic. That's a fair chunk of leisure time!

Chapter 11

Labor Rising: Unions in the Great Depression

*L*abor unions embarked on a roller coaster ride of highs and lows from just before World War I to just before the onset of the Great Depression. They were nearer the bottom than the top when the economic hard times hit. The 1930s proved to be even more chaotic than the 1920s for organized labor, but this time the decade ended with U.S. workers higher than they had ever been.

This chapter examines labor's story from the entry of the United States into the world war in 1917 to the beginning of the Roosevelt administration in 1933. I then take a look at what Roosevelt did, and didn't do, for labor and how the labor movement split itself in two. The chapter ends by recounting some of the biggest — and bloodiest — strikes in U.S. history. Put on a hardhat and grab a picket sign; it's going to be a bumpy ride.

Disorganized Labor

Even before the United States entered World War I in April 1917, organized labor had pledged to be a good patriot. In March that year, 79 unions promised "full labor support" once the country was in the war, as long as basic union rights were protected. The federal government, in turn, agreed to enforce union standards in all government contracts.

Despite the mutual pledges of cooperation, however, 4,450 strikes occurred by the end of 1917, involving 1 million workers. The cause of most of the disputes was that wages were not keeping pace with rising wartime prices.

So government officials and union representatives conferred again and agreed in April 1918 that a new agency was needed to try to head off strikes. The government established the National War Labor Board, which served as an arbiter in labor–business disputes. The government also promised that in its contracts with companies it would insist on eight-hour workdays (as much as possible), on the recognition of workers' right to organize, and on equal pay for equal work for the increasing number of women entering the workforce.

Even without the government guarantees, organized labor had reason to smile during the war. As the large number of workers entering the military made the civilian labor market tighter, wages rose, and so did union membership — from about 3 million in 1916 to 4.1 million in 1919 and 5 million in 1920.

But as prices continued to rise even after the war ended, wages again lost ground. The result was more than 3,500 strikes in 1919. A multi-union strike in Seattle virtually paralyzed the city for four days. In Boston, most of the city's police force walked out. Steelworkers and coal miners also staged widespread strikes.

The steel strikes were broken by the companies using replacement workers (sneeringly referred to as *scabs*), and by companies' propaganda that alleged the strikers were part of a communist conspiracy to overthrow capitalism. The coal strikes were stopped when a federal court issued an injunction against the strikers for engaging in work stoppages that threatened national security.

Losing ground in good and bad times

In 1920, the country ran into a post-war recession. By the time it ended in 1922, 5 million people were out of work. As usual when unemployment is high, union membership sagged, dropping from 5 million in 1920 to 3.5 million in 1923.

But a curious thing happened when the country began to prosper again: Union membership continued to sag. One reason was that technological and organizational improvements had greatly increased the productivity of the average worker. That meant fewer workers were needed to produce the same amount of goods. That, in turn, resulted in unemployment rates staying fairly high during the decade of the 1920s, even when the economy improved.

Another reason union membership stalled was that many employers insisted on *open shops,* which meant that workers did not have to join a union and that no union had exclusive rights to deal with management on behalf of workers. Some companies also insisted on what were called *yellow dog contracts,* which new workers were forced to sign. The contracts forbade the workers from joining a union, thus reducing their rights to those of a "yellow dog."

Employers also co-opted unions by embracing the idea of *welfare capitalism.* The term referred to the practice of companies offering benefits to workers (often in lieu of pay raises) that ranged from company-sponsored social clubs to profit-sharing programs. Workers could buy company stock at a discount, or they received it as a bonus for good work. By 1926, some 600 companies had established *employee representation plans,* which in effect were company unions operated by the personnel department that provided at least the veneer of someone looking out for the workers' welfare.

"The assertion may be boldly made that the decreasing membership in most of the unions, and the great difficulty they are experiencing in holding their members together, is due to the fact that the employers — the so-called 'soulless corporations' — are doing more for the welfare of workers than the unions themselves," boasted an official of the National Association of Manufacturers.

Exposing management's dark side

Of course not every company or every industry took a paternal interest in its workers. Many companies relied on spies placed among workers to help the firms weed out union organizers. Some companies conspired with corrupt union leaders to pad the leaders' pockets, in return for the union bosses ensuring rank-and-file members didn't resort to job actions such as slowdowns or strikes.

Working conditions were often appalling. Steel mill workers averaged workweeks of 69 hours. One Pittsburgh steel mill safety manager admitted in 1928 that the mill "had a lot of equipment that is out of date, lacks the new safety devices and is liable to break down at any time, causing serious accidents." But, he added, management wouldn't replace it because it still worked.

That kind of attitude led to huge numbers of worker casualties. In one year, the steel industry averaged 63 injuries a day, four of them resulting in death or permanent injury. It was common for steelworkers' clothes to catch on fire; if they survived, they had to pay to replace them.

Some companies made no pretense of having benevolent feelings toward their employees. When a congressional committee asked Pittsburgh Coal Company chairman Richard B. Mellon why the company kept machine guns mounted at its coal pits, he replied, "you cannot run the mines without them."

Sinking with the economy

By 1929, union membership had sunk to 3.4 million, lower than at any time since 1917. While corporate profits had grown by 62 percent in the decade, wages had risen only 8 percent. That meant workers were ill prepared for the economic Armageddon that followed the October 1929 stock market crash.

In fact, they appeared shell-shocked. As unemployment rose and paychecks shrank, U.S. workers grew decidedly less militant. Companies pledged not to cut wages and then ignored their pledges. The fringe benefits of "welfare capitalism" were rescinded. Still, there were few strikes. Organized labor made little attempt to pressure the federal government into launching recovery programs, nor did it strenuously object when companies unilaterally cut wages.

"Today labor stands patient and hopeful," noted the Cleveland *Plain Dealer.* "Never before has there been a period of depression so free from labor strife . . . in the face of enormous hardship, labor has showed its good citizenship and sturdy American stamina."

By early 1933, the 110-union American Federation of Labor (AFL) was losing 7,000 members a week, and overall union membership dipped below 3 million. What was left of organized labor looked to Washington, D.C., to see what a new president could do for them.

A New Deal for Workers

During the 1932 presidential contest between incumbent Republican Herbert Hoover and Democratic challenger Franklin D. Roosevelt, most labor groups, including the American Federation of Labor, officially stayed neutral.

That didn't stop most rank-and-file workers from wholeheartedly embracing Roosevelt. The wealthy Roosevelt promised not to forget "the forgotten man at the bottom of the economic pyramid." He campaigned for direct government relief to struggling families and stated his support for an unemployment insurance program. All that warmed the hearts of working people.

"I am a long ways from you in distance, yet my faith is in you," a South Carolina textile mill worker wrote Roosevelt. "My heart is with you and I am for you, sink or swim."

The feeling wasn't necessarily mutual on FDR's part. He was more interested in improving workers' economic status than their workplace status, and his feelings were more paternal than fraternal when it came to unions. That reality may have been reflected by the fact that his Secretary of Labor, Frances Perkins, was a social worker by training, not a union activist or official.

Even so, Roosevelt enjoyed strong labor support throughout the Great Depression. In his reelection campaign in 1936, labor groups formed a political action committee called the Non-Partisan League to help. Unions contributed nearly $800,000 to his campaign, about $500,000 of which came from the United Mine Workers (UMW).

The UMW was headed by labor's leading figure in the 1930s, John L. Lewis. After Lewis and Roosevelt had a falling out over remarks FDR made about a 1937 steel strike, Lewis withdrew his support of the president and endorsed FDR's GOP rival, Wendell Willkie, in 1940. Even with Lewis's defection, however, Roosevelt won third and fourth terms with strong labor backing.

In return, Roosevelt backed several key pieces of pro-labor legislation during the Great Depression, although not all with the same enthusiasm.

Section 7(a): Supporting the right to unionize

In June 1933, Congress passed the National Industrial Recovery Act (NIRA). Among the bill's provisions (the rest of which are covered in Chapter 13) was Section 7(a). This section contained three key provisions having to do with labor:

- ✔ Employees had the right to organize and to bargain as a group without employer interference.

- ✔ No new employee could be made to join a "company union" or be prohibited from joining any union he or she chose.

- ✔ Companies would agree to minimum wages, maximum workweeks, and other workplace conditions, to be established by the industry to which they belonged and approved by the president. While industries worked on their own codes, they were asked to agree to a minimum wage of 40 cents per hour and a 40-hour maximum workweek, as well as the abolition of child labor under the age of 16.

"In my inaugural," Roosevelt said after signing the bill, "I laid down the simple proposition that nobody is going to starve in this country. It seems to me to be equally plain that no business which depends on paying less than living wages has any right to continue."

Union leaders were ecstatic with the NIRA. Union recruiters worked overtime to sign up new members. John L. Lewis, the United Mine Workers president, had sound trucks blare "the president wants you to unionize . . . it is your patriotic duty to unionize." People did. The AFL claimed to have added 1.5 million workers, the United Mine Workers 300,000, and the International Ladies Garment Workers Union 150,000.

The joy was short-lived. Some employers coerced workers into joining company unions and declined to negotiate with other unions. With what *Time* magazine said were 7,000 different industries drawing up codes and more than 10,000 pages of federal regulations, the program's framework became a hopeless snarl. Employers thought it went too far; labor decided it didn't go far enough. A National Labor Relations Board was created in 1934 and charged with settling disputes. But it lacked the authority to enforce its decisions, and in 1935 the U.S. Supreme Court made the issue moot by overturning the NIRA for being unconstitutional.

The Wagner Act: Giving unions real strength

While the NIRA had proved to be a mess, its rejection by the Supreme Court left labor without any meaningful legal protections. That situation changed within six weeks of the court's decision, however, when Congress passed the National Labor Relations Act and Roosevelt signed it into law on July 5, 1935.

Better known as the *Wagner Act* (after its chief author, Senator Robert Wagner of New York), the measure guaranteed the rights of workers to form their own union. It specifically prohibited employers from interfering in any way with worker organizing, and it required companies to bargain exclusively with whatever union workers voted to join.

Most importantly, it created a new National Labor Relations Board (NLRB) to monitor union elections, hear complaints about unfair labor practices, and issue "cease and desist" orders that could be appealed to a federal court.

"By preventing practices which tend to destroy the independence of labor, it seeks for every worker within its scope, that freedom of choice and action which is justly his," said Roosevelt, who was not a big fan of the bill until he saw how popular it was with Congress and the public.

One thing the act did *not* do was set any standards for wages or hours. Nor did it require employers to sign a contract with a union.

Still, the measure was a huge triumph for labor, perhaps the biggest in U.S. history. For more than a century, the labor movement in the United States had struggled against a host of obstacles that blocked its right to organize in a meaningful manner. Now it had that right. The measure also firmly established the role of the federal government in relations between labor and management.

Many legal experts expected the Supreme Court would overturn the Wagner Act as it had the National Industrial Recovery Act. As a result, many employers ignored the law. The National Labor Relations Board conducted only 76 elections between 1935 and 1937. But the court upheld the act in April 1937, and between 1937 and 1940, the NLRB supervised 3,310 elections.

The Fair Labor Standards Act: Raising wages, cutting hours

Two issues that weren't settled by the Wagner Act were establishing a federal minimum wage and setting a limit on how many hours an employee could be required to work without extra compensation.

One reason for these omissions was that starting in 1918, the Supreme Court had rejected several minimum wage laws as unconstitutional. Another was that some labor groups feared that adopting a minimum wage would give employers an excuse to use it as a maximum wage too. Southern lawmakers were afraid that a minimum wage law would remove the region's only attraction for industry: its low wages. And conservative members of Congress thought the idea was the next big step on the way to socialism.

But Roosevelt had made the issue part of his 1936 reelection campaign and was determined to push a bill through. When Congress failed to act in the summer of 1937 (even after the Supreme Court had made an about-face and had found a state minimum wage law constitutional), FDR summoned lawmakers into special session in late 1937.

A bill — the Fair Labor Standards Act — was finally approved in June 1938, but not before it endured 72 amendments or proposed amendments, most of them aimed at narrowing how many industries would be affected by the bill. One congressman joked that if the measure passed, the Secretary of Labor should be required to report within 90 days "whether anyone is covered by the bill."

In fact, the final version of the bill applied to industries that covered only about 20 percent of the workforce. It set an initial minimum hourly wage of 25 cents (which was to move to 40 cents in 1940), and workweeks were limited to 44 hours (decreasing to 40 hours in 1940). Extra hours required pay at time-and-a-half rates.

Just as importantly, the bill set 14 as the minimum age for workers outside school hours and 16 during school hours. Children had been shamefully exploited during the Great Depression. A 1938 survey of 449 children by the Department of Labor's Children's Bureau found that nearly 25 percent of them worked 60 hours or more per week for a median wage of just over $4 a week.

"It is the most far-reaching, the most far-sighted program for the benefit of workers ever adopted here or in any other country," Roosevelt said the night before he signed the bill. "Without question it starts us toward a better standard of living and increases purchasing power to buy the products of farm and factory."

Even though the bill didn't cover everyone, the 12 million people who were making less than 40 cents an hour were grateful. And it served as the base for future changes in wages, hours, and child-labor laws.

Forming New Kinds of Unions

The American Federation of Labor (AFL) was established in the 1880s to serve as an association of autonomous unions, mostly representing skilled workers such as carpenters and machinists. The AFL's goals were both mercenary and pragmatic: to get as much money, job security, and decent working conditions as possible for its members.

Under the cautious leadership of a former cigar maker named Samuel Gompers and (after Gompers's death in 1924) a former coal miner named William Green, the AFL had focused its recruiting and organizing efforts almost exclusively on skilled workers. Part of the reason for this focus was discriminatory. Skilled workers tended to be white and second- or third-generation Americans. Many unskilled workers were minorities or immigrants.

What the AFL either failed or refused to recognize, however, was that as technology changed the workplace, it also changed the worker. More and more jobs were filled by unskilled men who performed specific — and often mind-numbingly repetitious — tasks on assembly lines and were as interchangeable to their employers as the parts they assembled.

The strength of a union in the new workplace was in numbers of members. But the AFL not only declined to pursue that large number of unskilled workers, it also insisted on compartmentalizing its members into small bargaining groups. If it took 19 men doing different tasks to make a car tire, for example, the AFL wanted 19 unions to represent them.

And despite being the leading labor force at the onset of the Great Depression, AFL leaders were more diffident and accommodating than aggressive when it came to making labor's voice heard. One AFL leader, however, was about to disturb the peace.

Setting up the CIO

The head of the United Mine Workers, John L. Lewis, was big, bushy-browed, and bombastic. A former miner who had once managed an opera house, Lewis had a theatrical manner that either amused or outraged his associates.

Once, when explaining why he seemed always to be in the spotlight, Lewis said, "He who tooteth not his own horn, the same shall not be tooted." When asked if he were worried about using known communists to help recruit union members, Lewis replied rhetorically, "Who gets the duck, the dog or the hunter?"

Unlike most other union leaders, Lewis saw great value for the labor movement in organizing unskilled workers. He also argued that it was better to have a few very large unions than a lot of small ones.

In October 1935, at an AFL convention in Atlantic City, Lewis became embroiled in a series of confrontations with federation leaders over the question of organizing unskilled workers. In one instance, he socked the leader of the carpenters union in the jaw after the man called Lewis a "bastard." ("Good for you," a disaffected carpenter telegraphed Lewis. "Now sock him again.")

With a few other union leaders, Lewis ultimately decided to take on the task of organizing the unskilled. The leaders created the Committee on Industrial Organization, later renamed the Congress of Industrial Organizations, or CIO, and divorced themselves from the AFL. "They have smote me hip and thigh," the colorful Lewis said of the split, "and right merrily did I return the blows."

Fighting in the ranks

From its beginning, the Congress of Industrial Organizations worked to expand the ranks of organized labor. It launched recruiting drives in industries such as tobacco, textiles, and laundries whose workforces were dominated by women and minorities. It established civil rights units within its local unions, and it even allowed in communists. "So what if he's a Red," snapped one union leader of a new member. "He's our Red."

The CIO was also more aggressive than the AFL in its negotiating tactics. It launched major offensives in the automobile and steel industries that involved violent confrontations, as I explain in the next section. And it was more politically active than the AFL, contributing money and campaign workers to local, state, and national contests.

 The competition between the two groups was both good and bad for labor. On the one hand, it helped swell union membership as the groups vied for members. By the end of 1937, the CIO claimed 3.7 million members, while the AFL claimed 3.4 million. Combined, that was more than twice as many unionists as there had been in 1933. On the other hand, the deep rivalry between the two groups and their leaders (the AFL's Green despised the CIO's Lewis, and vice versa) prevented labor from speaking with one voice.

The two groups quarreled about the best way to establish federal minimum wage and workweek laws. Complaining that the National Labor Relations Board favored the CIO, the AFL worked with conservative members of Congress to try to weaken the board. The AFL also accused its rival of being too cozy with communists.

When the country slipped into a new and deep recession in the fall of 1937, the AFL was better equipped to handle it. Its unions were older and more established, and its members were better able and more willing to pay dues because many of them worked in specialized jobs that paid better wages and were more recession-proof. By the end of the decade, the AFL had reasserted itself as labor's dominant organization. But the CIO's existence also forced the AFL to widen its umbrella and begin admitting unskilled and semi-skilled workers. In 1955, the AFL and CIO merged into a united federation.

Considering the workers no one wanted

One labor group that drew no interest from either the AFL or the CIO during the Great Depression was the farm workers of the South and Southwest. They had been specifically excluded from the protection of federal labor laws governing the minimum wage, number of hours worked, and union organizing rights.

That lack of federal protection made forming farm worker unions not only difficult but also dangerous. "Only fanatics are willing to live in shacks or tents and get their heads broken in the interest of migratory workers," summed up one labor leader.

Many of the farm workers were Mexicans or first- or second-generation Mexican Americans. The AFL had spent time and money trying to have them banned because they allegedly filled jobs that should have been filled by white Americans.

Still, some unionizing efforts were made, particularly in California, which was the nation's second-biggest farm state (trailing only Iowa in the value of its crop production). California farms were often giant "food factories" owned by companies such as Standard Oil, Shell Oil, and the Southern Pacific Railroad. There was often a glut of labor, and it was not unusual for a grower to promise one wage, only to reduce it when the workers reached the fields or orchards.

In 1930, communists helped workers form the Agricultural Workers Industrial League, which struck the fields of California's Imperial Valley. In 1931, workers walked out of Santa Clara Valley canneries after pay rates were cut by 20 percent. In 1932, there was a pea-picker strike. In 1933, it was strawberries; in 1936, lettuce.

In almost every case, tactics that ranged from the use of replacement workers to shootings and beatings by police or hired thugs defeated the strikers. Not only did the major labor groups fail to help, but most state and federal officials were also disinterested.

Not until the 1970s would farm workers succeed in gaining meaningful union representation, and even then they would remain among the most forgotten of the U.S. economy's forgotten men and women.

Strikes and Fights

Even with the federal government lining up solidly behind labor's right to organize and workers' rights to decent wages and working conditions, some big business leaders weren't ready to surrender their old ways of doing things.

Some companies used spies to pose as workers and promptly report on any talk of forming a union. The Pinkerton Detective Agency earned $1.75 million between 1933 and 1936 spying for automakers. "We must do it to obtain the information we need in dealing with our employees," Chrysler Corporation Vice President Herman Weckler told a Senate committee.

When labor trouble appeared imminent, industry could send for the likes of Pearl Bergoff, a burly New York "consultant" who would send a small army of heavily armed thugs with names like "Two Guns" and "Chowderhead" (really!) to act as strikebreakers. Machine guns, billy clubs, and tear gas were standard equipment for Bergoff's men. The Ford Motor Company had its own in-house paramilitary force of 3,000 toughs.

There were other forms of intimidation. Georgia Governor Eugene Talmadge built concentration camps and had them ready, he said, for labor pickets. Pennsylvania mine owners had homes of striking miners bombed. And a textile industry journal editorialized that "a few hundred funerals will have a quieting effect" on labor unrest.

Shutting down cities

All of this anti-union activity was in response to the fact that in 1934, organized labor shook off the torpor with which it had begun the decade. There were 1,800 strikes during the year, involving 1.5 million people. The smallest strikes involved a handful of workers and were over in a day or two. The biggest strikes shut down cities, and often involved violence, as depicted in Figure 11-1.

In Minneapolis, strikes by teamsters in May and July 1934 erupted into battles that pitted the city's employers and police against much of its working class. Two strikers were shot and killed, as were two members of a "citizens' army" organized by employers.

A funeral for one of the striking members drew a crowd of 100,000, and the strikes shut down most of the city's trucking industry. After Minnesota Governor Floyd B. Olson declared martial law in late July and sent in National Guard troops, a settlement was reached, and the anti-union forces' dominance of the state was broken.

Figure 11-1: Unionized strikers fight with a group of nonunion replacement employees as they try to cross the picket line at a factory.

On the West Coast, longshoremen and sailors began an 84-day strike at every major port on the coast in May 1934. Battles between strikers and police or private security broke out in the Los Angeles region's port of San Pedro, where two strikers were killed, and also in Oakland, Seattle, and Portland.

In San Francisco, two more strikers were killed in early July. After the deaths, virtually every union member in the city joined a general strike on July 16. For four days, the city came to a halt.

"No street cars were operating," a journalist reported, "no buses, taxis, no delivery wagons except milk and bread trucks, which were operated with the permission of the general strike committee. No filling stations were open, no theaters, no shops."

Of course, not every newspaper saw it the same way. "The situation in San Francisco is not correctly described as a 'general strike,'" sniffed the *Los Angeles Times*. "What is actually in progress there is an insurrection, a communist-inspired and -led revolt against organized government. There is but one thing to be done — put down the revolt with any force necessary."

Whatever it was called, the strike ended after employers agreed to arbitration, which resulted in the longshoremen being given most of the pay increase they had sought and the right for their union to choose its members.

Sitting down on the job

On December 30, 1936, workers at a General Motors auto plant in Flint, Michigan, shut down the assembly line and sat down. Over the next few days, workers at 16 other GM plants who were members of the two-year-old United Auto Workers (UAW) union followed their lead, and the largest manufacturing company in the world was brought to its knees. Before the strike began, GM was making 2,000 cars a day. During the 44-day strike, it averaged 20.

Unlike most strikes, the GM shutdown was as much about the breakneck pace of the assembly line as it was about wages and hours. "We don't even have time to go to the toilet," complained one GM worker. "You have to run to the toilet and run back."

Also unlike most strikes, the GM workers traded the outside picket lines for the relative comfort of the indoor assembly lines. The sit-down tactic prevented the company from bringing in replacement workers, and it made it harder for police and hired strikebreakers to break heads without risking breaking company equipment.

That doesn't mean there wasn't violence. When police tried to prevent food from being delivered to the strikers, a fight broke out. Using plant fire hoses, the strikers forced the police to retreat. Michigan Governor Frank Murphy, who had just been elected with labor's help, decided not to send in the National Guard. And General Motors, which was losing $1 million a day, gave in.

The UAW, which was affiliated with John L. Lewis's Congress of Industrial Organizations (CIO), won higher pay, shorter hours, and a slowed-down production line. Other auto companies eventually followed, with Ford holding out against unionization longest, until 1941. The UAW's victory helped its membership grow from 88,000 to 400,000 in the first nine months of 1937.

Sit-down strikes became the rage. Unhappy workers adopted the tactic in department stores, barbershops, hotel kitchens, and ocean liners. In March 1937, there were 170 sit-down strikes involving 167,000 workers. Having defeated the auto industry, meanwhile, the CIO took aim at another big industry: steel.

Beating "Big Steel"

In 1934, the Congress of Industrial Organizations (CIO) had won signed contracts from the coal industry, which supplied the fuel to run steel mills. In early 1937, it won the right to organize from the auto industry, which consumed much of the steel mills' product. So CIO leader John L. Lewis decided it was time to go after the steel industry itself, starting with its biggest company, United States Steel. The company had gross earnings of $35.2 million in 1934 ($5.7 billion in 2008 dollars), and yet not a single employee there was considered a full-time worker. The average steelworker was making less than $400 per year in 1937.

"If we can organize here," Lewis said of U.S. Steel, "the rest (of the industry) will follow. If the crouching lion can be routed, it is a safe bet that the hyenas in the adjacent bush may be scattered along the plains."

But Lewis overestimated the "lion" and underestimated the "hyenas." In March 1937, Lewis and U.S. Steel board chairman Myron Taylor stunned the country by announcing agreement on a union contract that had been negotiated quietly by the two men. Taylor, mindful of labor's victory over General Motors, agreed to a contract calling for an eight-hour day and 40-hour week, $5 a day wages, and paid vacations. No strike had been required, not even the explicit threat of one.

Losing to "Little Steel"

The other steel companies, however, proved to be far less agreeable. Called "Little Steel" because of their size relative to U.S. Steel, the firms made it clear they were not in a union mood, particularly if it meant dealing with Lewis and his CIO.

"I won't have a contract, verbal or written, with an irresponsible, racketeering, violent communistic body like the CIO," said Thomas M. Girdler, president of Republic Steel. "And until they pass a law making me, I am not going to do it."

On May 25, 1937, about 76,000 workers walked out of 27 steel plants in seven states. The companies retaliated by bringing in scabs and heavily fortifying the plants with armed guards and "strikebreakers" who alternately urged the strikers to return to work and threatened them.

Before the strike was over, 16 striking workers were killed and hundreds injured. Ten of the deaths occurred on Memorial Day, when police fired on demonstrators in Chicago, shooting many of the demonstrators in the back as they fled.

A Senate investigation into the "Memorial Day Massacre" concluded that "from the evidence we think it plain that the force employed by the police was far in excess of that which the occasion required. Its use must be ascribed to either gross inefficiency in the performance of police duty, or a deliberate attempt to intimidate the strikers."

Intimidated or not, the steel workers lost the battle with Little Steel. They returned to work in July without contracts. (They did eventually win the war in 1942 when they signed contracts with all the Little Steel companies.)

Growing tired of labor strife

One of the reasons the Little Steel strike failed was that President Roosevelt chose not to get involved, despite personal pleas from John L. Lewis.

"A plague on both your houses," Roosevelt said, echoing a line from Shakespeare's *Romeo and Juliet* and signaling that there were limits on the federal government's role in settling labor disputes.

Roosevelt's stance echoed the feelings of many Americans about the almost constant unrest stirred up by labor fights in the decade. There were an estimated 22,000 strikes in the 1930s, involving millions of workers, thousands of injuries, and scores of deaths.

A 1937 Gallup Poll found that 76 percent of Americans favored the existence of unions, but almost as many opposed sit-down strikes as violations of private property rights. (The Supreme Court outlawed them in 1939.) Most people thought unions should have the right to organize, but most people also thought industrialists like Henry Ford should have the right not to let them organize at their companies.

But while the public's ambivalent feelings about labor unions would continue into the 21st century, labor had not only survived the nation's hardest economic decade but also made itself a force in the U.S. economy.

Lessons Learned

Two of the Great Depression's biggest contributions to the U.S. economic culture were the advent of a federal minimum wage and the development of organized labor as a significant force in the financial and political course of the country. Here, I discuss how a missing element in the 1938 minimum wage law has affected its course ever since, and how unions' roles have changed significantly as the economy itself has changed.

Trying to keep pace with the minimum wage

Although the Fair Labor Standards Act was amended 11 times from its adoption in 1938 through 2008, it never included language that would automatically adjust the federal minimum wage to reflect increases in the cost of living.

As a result, increases have always been subject to the whims of Congress and the president, and the wage has been raised only sporadically. From May 1974 to January 1976, for example, it increased three times. But from February 1981 to March 1990, and again from October 1997 to June 2007, it did not increase at all.

Some other facts and figures regarding the federal minimum wage:

- ✔ Since its inception through 2008, the minimum wage has never been enough to lift a family of four above the poverty line if only one member of the family works full-time.

- ✔ The $7.25 minimum wage scheduled to go into effect in July 2009 was less than half the January 2009 average hourly wage of $18.49.

- ✔ States can choose to set a minimum wage higher than the federal level. As of 2009, 27 states had higher rates than the federal government. In addition, more than 100 U.S. cities had adopted "living wage" laws that required companies doing business with the municipal government to pay "living wages" based on the cost of living in the area.

- ✔ As of January 2009, 13 countries had higher minimum wages, in U.S. dollars, than the United States.

Arguments for and against a minimum wage have changed little since the Great Depression. Proponents contend that minimum wage standards reduce poverty and dependence on government aid, stimulate the economy, and help close the gaps between the poor and rich. Increases in the minimum wage, they argue, are also stimulative because they tend to increase other wages.

Opponents insist that raising the minimum wage causes businesses to hire fewer workers, reduce their current payrolls, and raise prices. They also argue that most minimum wage earners are youths and part-time workers whose family incomes are well above the poverty line, and therefore increases in the wage don't help the poor.

Some studies have concluded that there is no clear correlation between raising the minimum wage and job loss, or between raising the minimum wage and reducing overall poverty levels.

Striving to stay relevant in unions

If the 1930s marked the awkward adolescence of the U.S. labor movement, the 21st century could be said to be its faltering old age.

A tectonic shift from an industrial production–based economy to one based on services, retail, and information technology combined with other factors to steadily reduce the size and influence of organized labor in the last half of the 20th century.

At its peak in 1945, union membership encompassed 35 percent of working Americans. In 2008, that number was 12.4 percent. The public sector far outpaces the private sector in union membership: While only 7.6 percent of private-sector workers were union members in 2008, 37 percent of government employees were.

Not all of the decline in union membership can be attributed to a shifting economy or even "globalization." A study of six other industrial countries — France, Japan, Italy, the United Kingdom, Canada, and Germany — found that between 1970 and 1990, union membership in those countries declined from 37.1 percent to 35.3 percent, while in the United States the decline was from 30 percent to 17.6 percent.

In 2005, several major unions split from the AFL-CIO (a federation of unions) to form their own coalition, Change to Win. The unions took nearly 25 percent of the AFL-CIO's membership with them. Optimists pointed out that the last time there was a major split among labor groups was during the Great Depression, when the Congress of Industrial Organizations (CIO) split from the American Federation of Labor (AFL). Overall union membership climbed significantly after the split.

And in 2008, the percentage of U.S. workers in unions made its first statistically significant increase in 25 years, from 12.1 percent to 12.4 percent.

Part IV
Fixing Things

In this part . . .

Americans have rarely elected back-to-back presidents that were as different in as many ways as Herbert C. Hoover and Franklin D. Roosevelt. This part looks at the factors in each man's background that influenced his leadership style; the decisions each made as president during this period; and the unsettled transition from one presidency to the other.

I also cover Roosevelt's New Deal (probably the most ambitious package of domestic measures in U.S. history) and discuss whether the measures worked in whittling down the Great Depression. The part concludes with a summary of what's been learned — and what is yet to be learned — from the era.

Chapter 12

A Tale of Two Presidents

*O*ne was an orphan who made himself a millionaire and became a world-revered humanitarian. The other was born rich but had to rebuild his life after being stricken with a crippling disease. One was a U.S. president who somewhat unfairly has been demonized as a flop in guiding the country during the Great Depression. The other was a U.S. president who somewhat exaggeratedly has been lionized as a savior during the Great Depression.

This chapter looks at Herbert C. Hoover and Franklin D. Roosevelt, the two men who served as president during the period from 1929 to 1941, and how they handled the challenges of the darkest economic time in the country's history. It also covers their campaign against each other in 1932, and how they handled the transition from one administration to the other.

"The Great Humanitarian"

A reporter was said to have asked baseball hero Babe Ruth in 1930 if he thought it was right that at $80,000, Ruth's annual salary was $5,000 more than President Herbert Hoover's. "Why not?" Ruth replied, "I had a better year than he did."

This possibly apocryphal story reflects the reputation of Herbert Clark Hoover, 31st president of the United States, scholar, engineer, life-saving humanitarian — and scapegoat of the Great Depression. No U.S. president ever accomplished as much before he was in the White House — and was so maligned for what he did while in office.

"Once upon a time," Hoover was said to have wryly remarked late in life, "my political opponents honored me as possessing the fabulous intellectual and economic power by which I created a worldwide depression all by myself."

Growing up

Herbert Hoover — his friends called him "Bert" — was born August 10, 1874, in West Branch, Iowa, making him the first president whose birthplace was west of the Mississippi River.

He was part of that generation of Americans who bridged the transition from the country's first century to its second: At the time of Hoover's birth, the Bronx had just become part of New York City; a man named Levi Strauss had just received a patent for "riveted blue jeans"; and Billy the Kid, at 15, was still just a kid.

By the time Hoover was 8 years old, both of his parents had died, and he grew up under the care of an aunt and uncle in Newburg, Oregon. He attended a Quaker secondary school his uncle had helped found, and then he went to a night school where he studied algebra and geometry and developed a love for engineering.

In 1891, despite not having graduated from high school, Hoover was accepted as an engineering student in the first class of a new university in northern California called Stanford. He managed the baseball and football teams, and he met and eventually married another student named Lou Henry, who was the daughter of an Iowa banker. When he graduated in 1895, the 21-year-old Hoover had a degree in geology, $40 in his pocket, and no firm prospects.

Striking gold

Hoover landed a job as a clerk with a San Francisco mining firm, working his way up to become an engineering assistant. In 1897, at the age of 23, Hoover was hired by a British company and sent to Australia to supervise the firm's gold mining operations. By the time he left in 1899 for a new assignment as the chief mining engineer of the Chinese government, Hoover was making $10,000 a year from the mines and was on his way to amassing a fortune of more than $4 million ($85 million in 2008 dollars).

While in China, Hoover helped organize the successful defense of the offices and homes of Western diplomats when a group of anti-Western Chinese attacked them in what was known as the "Boxer Rebellion." In November 1901, Hoover moved to London to become a partner in the mining firm that had hired him four years before.

With London as a base, Hoover traveled to every continent except Antarctica over the next 12 years to oversee various mining projects. But in 1914, the outbreak of World War I effectively ended his life in mining. Hoover volunteered to help more than 100,000 Americans, caught in Europe when the war began, get home.

"I did not know it," he wrote later, "(but) my engineering career was over forever. I was on the slippery road of public life."

Saving lives

When the evacuation of his fellow Americans was finished, Hoover became chairman of the Commission for Relief in Belgium. The group used private donations to funnel food and supplies to German-occupied Belgium. Hoover worked day and night, shuttling across the North Sea between Berlin and London to convince the Germans to allow the supplies into Belgium and overseeing distribution.

When the United States entered the war in April 1917, President Woodrow Wilson appointed Hoover as head of the American Food Administration, responsible for stabilizing domestic food prices, ensuring food got where it was needed, and convincing Americans to cut food consumption (which he did without having to resort to rationing).

After the war, Hoover became chairman of the Allied Food Council and the American Relief Administration. The groups managed food supplies to war-torn countries, including those of defeated enemies. When a British admiral said to Hoover, "young man, I don't see why you American chaps want to feed those bloody Germans," Hoover snapped back, "old man, we can't understand why you British want to starve women and children after they are licked."

Hoover's efforts were warmly applauded at home and in other countries. He became known as "the Great Humanitarian," and *The New York Times* named him one of the "ten most important living Americans."

"He is certainly a wonder," said the Assistant Secretary of the Navy, who was an admirer of Hoover, in 1920, "and I wish we could make him president of the United States. There could not be a better one." The admirer's name was Franklin D. Roosevelt.

Serving presidents

So well-liked was Hoover in 1920 that both major political parties courted him as a possible presidential candidate. He entered the California Republican primary election but finished second and then threw his support behind the eventual GOP nominee, Ohio Senator Warren G. Harding.

After Harding's election, Hoover was appointed Secretary of Commerce. With an engineer's penchant for organization, Hoover used the office to increase efficiency by imposing national size and dimension standards for everything from bed mattresses to bricks to bolts. He pushed for better job safety regulations, promoted international trade, and was a cheerleader for home ownership.

Hoover used his humanitarian skills again by overseeing vitally needed aid to famine-stricken Russia in 1921 and running relief aid to six Southern states in 1927 after huge Mississippi River floods.

In 1923, Harding died and was succeeded as president by Calvin Coolidge. Coolidge did not hide the fact he didn't like Hoover, sarcastically referring to him as "Wonder Boy" and once remarking of Hoover: "that man has offered me unsolicited advice for six years, all of it bad."

Nonetheless, Coolidge retained Hoover as Commerce secretary, in part because of Hoover's widespread popularity. And when Coolidge decided not to run for a second full term as president in 1928, he voiced no public objection to Hoover becoming the Republican candidate.

Serving as president

Hoover easily defeated his Democratic rival, New York Governor Al Smith, in the 1928 presidential race. He assumed the presidency brimming with confidence. "I have no fears for the future of our country," he said at his inauguration. "It is bright with hope."

As president, Hoover had ambitious plans for a progressive, reform-minded program that would make up for the failure of the Harding and Coolidge administrations to do much of anything beyond protect the interests of the business community. He expanded the civil service system, canceled private oil leases on public lands, organized the federal prison system, and planned or launched reforms in social service areas such as slum clearance.

But scarcely eight months into his presidency, the U.S. stock market crashed, presaging the economic disaster that became the Great

Depression. The rest of Hoover's term was completely dominated by trying to fix the financial mess the country found itself in.

It was uncharted territory for a U.S. president. The federal government's role in shepherding the national economy had historically been minimal, so Hoover had no blueprints from which to come up with a plan that might work. He did, however, try.

His attempts included subsidizing agriculture; cutting taxes; increasing taxes; financing public works; making government loans to railroads, banks, and other financial institutions; liberalizing bank credit; and providing federal aid to stave off mortgage foreclosures. He ran up large federal budget deficits in funding some of the efforts to right the economy.

Hoover's efforts won some applause. *BusinessWeek* called his plan to shore up sagging banks "the most powerful offensive force that government imagination has, so far, been able to command." *The New York Times* went further: "The president's course in this troublous time has been all that could be desired. No one in his place could have done more; very few of his predecessors could have done as much."

A good man, a bad politician

But Hoover's efforts were hampered by several factors. One was that it was hard for him to be enthusiastic about governmental actions to which he was philosophically opposed. Hoover believed that government's role in economic matters should be minimal and that direct relief in the form of unemployment aid, old age pensions, or other subsidies to individuals was not the job of the federal government. (See Chapter 5 for more on Hoover's views about direct federal relief to the unemployed and hungry.)

Hoover also suffered from the fact that while he was a very good manager, he was a lousy and inexperienced politician. In fact, the presidency was his first elective office. "Being a politician is a poor profession," he would later write. "Being a public servant is a noble one." That sentiment ignored the fact that the presidency was a political office and sometimes required political skills to build consensus, make compromises, and get things done.

Finally, Hoover lacked the personality to inspire public confidence at a time when the public's confidence was badly shaken. He was somewhat shy and not a good public speaker. When he did talk, he sometimes would say patently absurd things, such as suggesting that "many persons (had) left their jobs for the more profitable one of selling apples" on street corners.

"Hooverisms"

A sure sign that a politician is in trouble is when he becomes the butt of humor, and in the Great Depression, Herbert Hoover's surname was the butt of a lot of bitter sarcasm. The slums of shacks and sheds thrown up by homeless people became known as "Hoovervilles." Broken-down cars pulled by mules were "Hoover Carts." Newspapers used as coverings were "Hoover blankets"; empty pockets turned inside out were "Hoover flags"; and jack rabbits were "Hoover hogs."

The crowning indignity for Hoover came after he left office. A giant dam on the lower Colorado River that had been named for him was ordered renamed Boulder Dam by the Roosevelt administration in 1933. But Hoover got the last laugh on this one: In 1947, after Roosevelt's death, Congress renamed the structure Hoover Dam.

Because Hoover wasn't widely trusted, for example, people continued to withdraw their money from banks and stuff it under their mattresses even after Hoover took steps to prop up the financial industry.

Hoover was also seen as elitist and aloof. He dressed formally for dinner every evening; smoked 20 expensive Havana cigars a day; and declined to visit soup kitchens, bread lines, or any other place the poor and needy gathered.

His national image as a Scrooge in the White House was cemented by the Bonus Army disaster in the summer of 1932 (see Chapter 4 for details). Many Americans were horrified and angered by press accounts and newsreel film of U.S. troops using tanks and bayonets against military veterans who had been seeking early payments of promised service bonuses. The troops' commander, General Douglas MacArthur, had disobeyed Hoover's specific directions and ordered the attack. Nonetheless, Hoover, who had refused to meet with the veterans, was blamed.

Hoover had become so unpopular that an oft-repeated joke at the time had the president asking an aide if he could borrow a nickel so he could call a friend. "Here's a dime," the aide replied, "call both of them." By the time the 1932 presidential election campaign began to pick up speed, Hoover was, politically speaking, a dead duck.

The New Dealer

He could not stand unaided, but Americans accorded him the longest tenure in office of any U.S. president. He was born to wealth and privilege yet was regarded by the down-and-out as a friend to the "forgotten man" and by the rich as "a traitor to his class."

He was so self-confident that an observer joked "he must have been psychoanalyzed by God." He was so optimistic that an aide suggested "he was all light and no darkness." He was Franklin Delano Roosevelt, the 32nd president of the United States and the man often credited with leading the country out of the grip of the Great Depression.

Growing up

Franklin Roosevelt was born January 30, 1882, in Hyde Park, New York. His parents were both from wealthy and established families. Roosevelt's ancestors and relatives included passengers on the *Mayflower* and an opium dealer. He was also related by blood or marriage to 11 U.S. presidents. One of them, his fifth cousin Theodore, became Franklin's political idol.

Roosevelt was educated at a prestigious private boarding school and then graduated from Harvard in only three years. After only a year of classes at Columbia University's law school, Roosevelt passed the New York State Bar exam and took a job with a prestigious Wall Street law firm.

He also married a distant cousin, Eleanor, and had six children. (The marriage was a painful one for Eleanor. Franklin had an affair with her social secretary, broke it off, and then resumed the affair after being elected president. But Eleanor would throw herself into the role of First Lady with zeal and serve as a valuable asset to her husband and the country.)

Starting his political career

After a few years practicing law, Roosevelt grew restless. In 1910, he began his political career by running as a Democrat for a state Senate seat that had been held by Republicans for 26 years. His family name and a generally good year for Democrats carried him to victory, and he won reelection in 1912.

As a reward for working for the election of Woodrow Wilson to the presidency in 1912, Roosevelt was named Assistant Secretary of the Navy. He held the post until 1920, all the while building his standing within the Democratic Party and his popularity nationally.

In 1920, Roosevelt was picked as the vice presidential running mate for Democratic presidential nominee James Cox, the governor of Ohio. But the ticket was thrashed by the Republican pair of Warren Harding and Calvin Coolidge, and Roosevelt returned to practicing law and readying himself for another political campaign.

Losing the use of his legs

In August 1921, Roosevelt was vacationing at the family's 34-room "summer cottage" on Campobello Island in the Canadian province of New Brunswick. After a swim, he began running a high fever and developed a weakness in his legs that eventually turned to paralysis.

His illness was publicly downplayed by the family and reported in the newspapers as everything from a heavy cold to an attack of rheumatism. However it was diagnosed in the press, Roosevelt was consistently reported to be recovering.

But he wasn't. At the age of 39, Roosevelt had been stricken with what was diagnosed at the time as polio, often referred to as "infantile paralysis" because it tended to afflict children more than adults. (In 2003, researchers reported that FDR's disease may have been Guillain-Barre Syndrome.)

Despite grueling and painful efforts, Roosevelt would never again take more than a few halting steps, and then only with the use of heavy leg braces. But in the years leading up to his presidency, FDR would publicly insist that his condition was improving. He never allowed himself to be photographed in his wheelchair or being carried, and he usually gave speeches or made other public appearances standing upright, supported on one side by someone.

Becoming governor

Throughout the rest of the 1920s, Roosevelt kept up his political contacts within the Democratic Party. In 1922, he helped former New York Governor Al Smith win the governorship back. In 1924, Roosevelt made a mesmerizing appearance at the party's presidential nominating convention, giving the nomination speech for Smith, who did not win the nomination.

In 1928, Roosevelt again gave the nomination speech for Smith at the Democratic National Convention. This time, Smith got the party's nod. Roosevelt, who feared 1928 would be a Republican year, did not want to run for anything. But Smith, who wanted FDR's presence on the ticket to help him carry New York, convinced Roosevelt to run for governor. Herbert Hoover slaughtered Smith in the presidential contest, even carrying New York, but Roosevelt won a close race for governor.

As governor, Roosevelt aggressively pushed a program of social services. He won legislative approval of a tax break for agricultural communities in tough economic straits. He also lobbied for old-age pensions funded by workers, employers, and government. "The first duty of a State, and by that I mean government, is to promote the welfare of the citizens of that state," Roosevelt declared.

In 1930, after easily winning reelection, Roosevelt called the Legislature into special session and pushed through a $20 million unemployment relief plan, the first such program by any state.

With the nation's economy going into a tailspin and Democrats growing hopeful of winning the White House for the first time since 1916, Roosevelt's name was increasingly mentioned as a candidate. The mentions, however, were not always flattering. The influential newspaper columnist Walter Lippmann wrote that Roosevelt was "a pleasant man who, without any important qualifications for the office, would very much like to be president."

Running for president

Although Roosevelt had been considered the favorite in many quarters to win the Democratic nomination in 1932, he was not universally acclaimed, in part because people were uncertain whether he was politically conservative or liberal.

"In Franklin Roosevelt we have another Hoover," said the Scripps-Howard newspaper chain. *The New Republic* magazine called him "not a man of great intellectual force or supreme moral stamina." *The Nation* magazine suggested there was "no evidence whatever that people are turning to him as a leader."

Roosevelt's leading opponent was Al Smith, his former political mentor-turned-bitter rival. Smith won the Massachusetts primary, while Representative John Nance Garner of Texas, who was Speaker of the House of Representatives, won the California primary.

When the Democrats met in their national convention in Chicago, Roosevelt found that he could win the nomination only through some wheeling and dealing. After three ballots and no nominee, FDR offered the vice presidency to Garner. Garner, known as "Cactus Jack," accepted the offer. California switched its support to Roosevelt, and he clinched the nomination.

Roosevelt then did something unprecedented in U.S. political history. Flying for nine hours through dangerous headwinds from New York to Chicago, Roosevelt showed up at the convention to accept the nomination in person, starting a practice that was followed in future years by other nominees. After his campaign theme song, "Happy Days Are Here Again," was done blaring, Roosevelt delivered a crowd-pleasing 4,373-word speech. But it was 14 words in the 63rd paragraph that would resonate through the rest of the 20th century:

"I pledge you, I pledge myself, to a new deal for the American people."

Easy Campaign, Hard Transition

The morning after Roosevelt's speech accepting the Democratic presidential nomination, the phrase "New Deal" dominated newspaper headlines across the country.

Neither FDR nor his speechwriter, Sam Rosenman, had any idea that the phrase would catch on as much as it did. It may have been borrowed from a new book called *The New Deal* by economics writer Stuart Chase or from a *New Republic* magazine story by Chase entitled "A New Deal for America."

Wherever it came from, the phrase stuck. An editorial cartoon in the *New York World-Telegram* the day after Roosevelt's speech captured the phrase's appeal. It depicted a farmer looking up at a passing airplane, which on its wings bore the words *NEW DEAL*.

Running to the right

The conservative elements of the Democratic Party weren't quite sure what they had as a candidate. In a speech at Georgia's Oglethorpe University in May 1932, for example, Roosevelt had implied no proposal was too far out to try if it had promise.

"The country needs and, unless I mistake its temper, the country demands bold persistent experimentation," Roosevelt said. "It is common sense to take a method and try it; if it fails, admit it frankly and try another. But above all, try something."

That kind of talk struck some party leaders as being too liberal and capable of scaring off voters who were fearful of "radical" ideas.

"Tell the governor that he is the boss and we will follow him to hell if we have to," Roosevelt's running mate, John Nance Garner, told a messenger. "But if he goes too far with some of these wild-eyed ideas, we are going to get the shit kicked out of us."

Garner and other doubters, however, underestimated Roosevelt's political skills and his pragmatism. "To accomplish anything worthwhile," he said, "there must be a compromise between the ideal and the practical."

In fact, Roosevelt publicly embraced what was a fairly conservative Democratic Party platform. It called for things like a 25 percent cut in federal spending and keeping the country on the gold standard, which would tend to dry up the money supply and make things harder on the poor while protecting the interests of the wealthy.

On the campaign trail, Roosevelt attacked Hoover for "reckless and extravagant spending" and running up federal budget deficits. He also criticized the incumbent for being "committed to the idea that we ought to center control of everything in Washington as rapidly as possible." (Within a year, that statement would ooze irony, as Roosevelt would expand the federal government's role into nearly every aspect of American life.)

Campaigning for a lost cause

In the end, it probably wouldn't have mattered if Roosevelt had worn his underwear on his head and delivered speeches in Urdu. There was virtually no chance voters were going to reelect Hoover, and Hoover knew it. In contrast to the ever-smiling Roosevelt, Hoover's public persona during the campaign ranged from somber to dour. His message seemed to give voters a choice between FDR's "new deal" and his own "same old stuff."

"My countrymen," he said in one speech, "The fundamental issue that will fix the national direction for one hundred years to come is whether we shall be in fidelity to American tradition, or whether we shall turn to innovations."

Hoover didn't begin active campaigning until the month before the election, and it went badly. People threw eggs and tomatoes at his campaign train. He was booed during speeches and greeted with signs that read "Down with Hoover" and shouts of "Hang Hoover." Some Republican candidates for other offices stayed as far away from the Hoover campaign as they could. The crowning indignity may have come in the form of an anonymous telegram to Hoover that said: "Vote for Roosevelt. Make it unanimous."

Winning the White House

As expected, Roosevelt won by a crushing margin. The popular vote was 57.2 percent for FDR and 40 percent for Hoover. Roosevelt received 472 electoral votes, Hoover just 59. In terms of the popular vote, it was the worst defeat ever handed an incumbent president.

That the country had been ready for a change in the White House was obvious. Just what it had changed to, however, was a different story. Newspaper editor William Allen White wrote to a relative of Roosevelt that he hoped FDR "may develop his stubbornness into courage, his amiability into wisdom, his sense of superiority into statesmanship. Responsibility is a winepress that drags forth strange juices out of men."

Roosevelt himself had some doubts. On the night of the election, he told his son James, "you know Jimmy, all my life I've been afraid of only one thing — fire. Tonight I think I'm afraid of something else . . . I'm just afraid I may not have the strength to do the job . . . pray for me, Jimmy."

Handing off the Great Depression

There was a 116-day gap between the November 8, 1932, election and the March 4, 1933, inauguration ceremony, which left Hoover in charge as a lame-duck president. Scarcely a week after the election, he sent a telegram to Roosevelt, asking to meet. Hoover wanted to talk about canceling or modifying European countries' World War I debts to the United States, which was a highly unpopular idea with the American public.

Hoover's motive may have been statesmanlike, but it also may have been politically nefarious: The more the two men were seen to be working together, the less Hoover might be blamed for what was happening. Roosevelt did meet with Hoover at the White House on November 22, 1932, and again in January 1933. But FDR was wary and refused to commit to anything until he was fully in charge.

A frustrated Hoover later said he found Roosevelt "amiable, pleasant, anxious to be of service, very badly informed and of comparatively little vision." He also referred to him as "a very ignorant . . . well-meaning young man," although Roosevelt was only seven years younger than Hoover.

Hoover tried once more to reach some agreement with Roosevelt. In mid-February, he sent FDR a ten-page letter (in which he misspelled Roosevelt's last name) warning him that the country's banking system was on the verge of collapse and asking Roosevelt to make a public statement on what he intended to do. This time, Roosevelt, who was well aware of the banking crisis and had his advisors working on a response to it *after* he was sworn in, ignored Hoover's letter. He later said a secretary had lost it.

The two men met once more on the night before the inauguration, and they rode to the ceremony together (see Figure 12-1), but they would part enemies. Hoover lived for 32 years after leaving office, dying in 1964 at the age of 90. Asked during his retirement how he had handled critics of his role in the Great Depression, he joked, "I outlived the bastards."

Photo by American Stock/Getty Images

Figure 12-1: President Herbert Hoover and President-elect Franklin Roosevelt ride to Roosevelt's inauguration, March 4, 1933.

Avoiding an assassin's bullet

In part to relax and in part to dodge Hoover, Roosevelt took a 12-day cruise in early February 1933 on a yacht belonging to businessman Vincent Astor. On February 15, Roosevelt gave an impromptu speech at a bayside park in Miami from the back seat of an open car. Just after he finished, a crazed 32-year-old unemployed Italian immigrant named Giuseppe Zangara began firing at FDR.

Roosevelt was unscathed, but five other people were hit, including Chicago Mayor Anton Cermak, who had been standing on the car's running board while talking to Roosevelt. The president-elect ordered Secret Service agents to put Cermak in the car and rush to the hospital. Roosevelt cradled the mayor, according to an aide, and told him, "Tony, keep quiet — don't move. It won't hurt if you keep quiet." Roosevelt was apparently unshaken during and after the event. "He had no nerves at all," marveled one of his advisors.

Cermak died on March 6, two days after Roosevelt's inauguration. Zangara, who pleaded guilty to the shootings, was executed on March 20 in Florida's electric chair.

Taking over

While presidents traditionally drew much of their counsel from other politicians or captains of industry, Roosevelt turned to academia. His circle of advisors, tagged with the nickname "Brain Trust," included Raymond Moley, a professor of government at Columbia University in New York; Rexford Guy Tugwell, a Columbia University economist; and Adolf Berle, Jr., a Columbia Law School professor.

Behind the scenes, Roosevelt's advisors and other aides were working on plans to save the country's crumbling banking system. (For more details on FDR's efforts to save the banks, see Chapter 4.) Moley and William Woodin, who would become Roosevelt's first Treasury secretary, met with members of Hoover's Treasury staff to work out details.

Roosevelt, meanwhile, was being told by some people that, if necessary, he should seize more power than the presidency had — just as the German chancellor, Adolf Hitler, was doing at the time. "Even the hand of a national dictator is preferable to a paralyzed state," said Kansas Governor Alf Landon.

In his inaugural speech, Roosevelt did say that to get things moving, he would seek from Congress "broad executive power to wage war against the emergency as great as the power that would be given to me if we were in fact invaded by a foreign foe." Borrowing a line from the 19th-century American writer Henry David Thoreau ("nothing is so much to be feared as fear"), Roosevelt also assured the crowd and the millions listening on radio that it was his "firm belief that the only thing we have to fear is fear itself."

Like the "new deal" phrase in his nomination acceptance speech, the "fear itself" line struck a chord with Americans. But as humorist Will Rogers pointed out, Americans were ready to embrace just about anything the new president did or said.

"If he (Roosevelt) burned down the Capitol," Rogers observed, "we would cheer and say 'well, at least he got a fire started somehow.'"

Lessons Learned

When Americans change presidents, the change is often accompanied by a sense of impatience: Why does it take so long for the old administration to get out of the way of the new one?

Here's a look at how the transition, which used to take even longer, was changed during the Great Depression, followed by a look at how Presidents George W. Bush and Barack Obama handled the hand-off of power during the country's deepest recession since the 1930s.

Changing the wait with the Twentieth Amendment

Under the original provisions of the U.S. Constitution, a newly elected president took office on the March 4 following the November general election. The Congress that was elected in November waited even longer — 13 months — before taking office.

That meant a new congressman elected in, say, November 1884 would not take office until December 1885. It also created the situation where defeated congressmen would remain in office for months, exposing them to the temptation of doing anything they wanted without having to fear voter retribution.

The long wait was considered necessary because counting votes in the late 18th century could take a long time, and a newly elected president would also need time to get his affairs in order and travel all the way to the capital. He could then call the Senate into a brief special session to confirm his cabinet appointees and spend the rest of the year pulling together his administration before the Congress convened in December.

But the advent of trains and telegraphs, and later airplanes and telephones, made the original system hopelessly obsolete. So in 1932, Congress approved the Twentieth Amendment to the U.S. Constitution. The amendment moved the presidential inauguration from March 4 to January 20 and the start of the new Congress to the January 3 after the November election.

But it took until January 23, 1933, for three-fourths of the country's 48 states to ratify the amendment — three days too late to affect the 1932 election. That meant Franklin Roosevelt did not take over from Herbert Hoover until March 4.

Handing off the office from Bush to Obama

There were many similarities between the transition from President George W. Bush to President Barack Obama following the 2008 presidential election and the handoff from Herbert Hoover to Franklin Roosevelt following the 1932 election.

Both occurred in the midst of severe economic crises. In both cases, the banking industry was in shambles, unemployment was climbing, people were losing their homes to mortgage foreclosures, and a popular Democrat was taking over for an unpopular Republican.

But there was also a key difference. In 1932, Roosevelt had badly beaten Hoover after a campaign in which Hoover referred to Roosevelt as a "chameleon on plaid" and Roosevelt had called Hoover "a fat, timid capon." These guys really didn't like each other.

In contrast, Obama, whose opponent was Senator John McCain of Arizona, criticized the termed-out Bush's policies during the campaign but not Bush personally. Bush likewise refrained from personal attacks on Obama.

The result was one of the smoother presidential transitions in modern U.S. history. Obama made it plain that Bush was president until January 20, 2009, and he would not presume to tell him what he should do. In return, Bush graciously conferred with Obama on key issues during the transition.

It was certainly better than when Bush took over from President Bill Clinton in 2001: Incoming Bush aides found that the "W" keys had been removed from many of the keyboards in the Executive Office Building.

Chapter 13

Roosevelt's New Deal

*I*t started at the governmental equivalent of light-speed and ended with a world war. In between was the creation of an abundance of government programs, a fierce fight with the Supreme Court, and new and promising efforts to combat the Great Depression rising from old and failed ones.

Put it all together, as this chapter does, and you had the New Deal: President Franklin D. Roosevelt's attempt to solve an economic dilemma bigger than any the United States had ever seen.

In addition to looking at both phases of the New Deal, this chapter examines FDR's quarrel with an uncooperative Supreme Court and assesses the immediate effects the administration's programs had on the Great Depression, as well as their lasting impact on the country.

Starting Fast: The First 100 Days

On the morning after he was sworn in as president, Roosevelt had himself wheeled into the Oval Office, only to find that there were no pencils or paper in the desk and no buzzer to summon aides. Roosevelt took a deep breath and began bellowing for a secretary. Then he got to work on what would be forever known as the *New Deal.*

The first order of business was assessing just how big a mess the nation's banking system was in. Roosevelt ordered all banks closed so federal regulators could see which ones were sound enough to be allowed to reopen. Within a week, FDR had pushed an emergency banking bill through Congress. (For details on the banking crisis and Roosevelt's response to it, see Chapter 4.)

The swiftness of Roosevelt's action on the banking crisis impressed even those who had been less than impressed by him as a candidate. The influential columnist Walter Lippman, who had criticized FDR in 1932 for lacking leadership qualities, wrote in March 1933 that "in one week, the nation, which had lost confidence in everything and everybody, regained confidence in the government and in itself."

The new president was just getting warmed up. In the first 100 days after taking office, the Roosevelt administration and Congress crafted more than a dozen major pieces of legislation, all of them designed to shore up, patch, revive, or jumpstart some aspect of the national economy. Some historians have labeled the period the busiest three months in congressional history.

"The special session of the 73rd Congress has hung up an amazing record of achievement in its 14-week setting," said *Time* magazine in June 1933. "It was President Roosevelt's do-or-die attack against the Depression."

It often was not the most organized of attacks. One of FDR's top aides, Raymond Moley, once joked that saying Roosevelt's New Deal was planned was like saying a boy's room strewn with chemistry sets and dirty clothes was the work of an interior decorator.

In one instance, Harry Hopkins, FDR's top aide, and Frances Perkins, Roosevelt's Secretary of Labor, huddled under the stairs of a women's club in New York City to draft plans for an emergency relief program. In another case, Hopkins suggested during lunch with Roosevelt that the country needed a public works program to provide temporary employment. Within a week, the plan was up and running under Hopkins's charge, and within a month it had created jobs for 2.6 million people.

When a program didn't work — and plenty of them didn't — the president and his people plucked out its best elements, melded them into a new program, and forged ahead.

In addition, Roosevelt sometimes shot from the hip when it came to picking advisors. For example, his Secretary of the Interior, Harold Ickes, was FDR's third choice for the job, behind two U.S. senators who turned him down. Ickes was a Republican, as were several of Roosevelt's advisors, and had never met the president when he was appointed Interior secretary. Ickes would become one of FDR's most important aides and serve him in various capacities for 13 years.

"Roosevelt is an explorer who has embarked on a voyage as uncertain as that of Columbus," said the British statesman Winston Churchill, "and upon a quest which might conceivably be as important as the discovery of the New World."

An alphabet soup of achievements

Many men in Congress shared Roosevelt's thirst for swift action. More than half of the two houses' 531 members had first been elected in 1930 or 1932; they were sent to Washington with voter expectations that they would do something to knock down the Great Depression. Other congressional members were dazzled by FDR's jaunty confidence or impressed by his enormous popularity. Whatever the reason, most of them voted the way the president wanted, most of the time.

Here's a look at some of the programs that emerged from what became known as *The Hundred Days*.

The Emergency Banking Act

After 35 minutes of debate, Congress passed a measure that gave Roosevelt broad authority over U.S. currency and credit and approved the printing of $2 billion to pump up banks' assets. See Chapter 4 for more on the measure.

The Economy Act

A master politician, Roosevelt loved to "zig" just when his opponents expected to him to "zag." So while many conservatives expected him to run up the federal government's debts for a sheaf of social programs, Roosevelt instead pushed for saving $500 million by cutting pensions to military veterans and reducing salaries for federal workers — including members of Congress. "For three long years," FDR scolded, "the federal government has been on the road to bankruptcy."

The bill passed over the protests of many Democrats in Congress but with support from many Republicans.

The Civilian Conservation Corps (CCC)

Of all the New Deal's projects and programs, this was the one closest to Roosevelt's heart. It established a system of camps for young men who worked in conservation programs throughout the country's national parks and wild lands. For more details on the CCC, see Chapter 8.

The Federal Emergency Relief Act (FERA)

One of the most pressing problems faced by the Roosevelt administration was helping Americans who literally were on the edge of starvation. In May 1933, Congress passed a bill creating the Federal Emergency Relief Administration, and Roosevelt put his top aide, Harry Hopkins, in charge. The program started with $500 million, half of which was passed out to states on a matching basis: one federal dollar for every three state dollars. The other half was designated to go where it was most immediately needed or where the matching fund requirement could not be met.

Even before he had a desk in his office, Hopkins had approved $5 million in grants to six states. He and his small staff alternately coaxed, cajoled, coerced, and threatened local agencies to funnel the funds to the needy as fast as possible. Before the program was absorbed into another New Deal program in 1935, FERA handed out $3 billion (about $48.2 billion in 2008 dollars) to needy Americans.

The Agricultural Adjustment Act (AAA)

At the same time that FERA was being launched, Congress approved a bold program designed to prop up the prices that farmers could get for their crops and livestock by paying them not to plant or raise so much. Take a look at Chapter 6 for more details on the AAA.

The Emergency Farm Mortgage Act and Home Owners' Loan Act

Both measures were designed to provide funds and lending mechanisms that could help people stave off mortgage foreclosures and, in some cases, reverse foreclosures that had already occurred. By 1935, one-fifth of all farm mortgages had been refinanced. The homeowners' program provided loans of up to $14,000 at 5 percent interest. By 1936, the program had made 1 million loans totaling $3 billion.

In 1934, well after the end of The Hundred Days, Congress approved the National Housing Act. The act created the Federal Housing Administration, which insured home mortgages and set up national standards for construction quality and home loans, such as 20 percent down payments for a 20-year mortgage.

The Tennessee Valley Authority (TVA)

The TVA was notable among New Deal programs in that it was designed to make people's lives better in the future — not just to meet an immediate need.

After the United States entered World War I in 1917, the federal government built a dam on the Tennessee River at Muscle Shoals, Alabama. The dam's purpose was to provide cheap hydroelectric power for a plant to manufacture munitions.

But the war ended before the plant was built, and for the next 16 years Congress debated what to do with the dam. Some wanted to sell the project to private interests. Others — most particularly Senator George Norris of Nebraska — crusaded for federal development of the area. With the election of Roosevelt, Norris at last had the powerful ally he needed to realize his quest.

As approved by Congress, the TVA was a seven-state (Tennessee, Kentucky, Virginia, North Carolina, Georgia, Alabama, and Mississippi) organization charged with producing low-cost electricity, developing local manufacturing, enhancing the navigability of the river, providing flood protection, and "improving the economic and social well-being of the people living in said river basin."

By 1940, 21 TVA hydroelectric plants had been completed, providing electric power to tens of thousands of poor rural families who had never had electricity. Many of the project's other goals, such as flood protection, were also reached.

"Ten thousand men are at work, building with timber and steel and concrete the New Deal's most magnificent project, creating an empire with potentialities so tremendous and so dazzling that they make one gasp," federal investigator Lorena Hickok wrote in June 1934. "There's a chance to create a new kind of industrial life, with decent wages, decent housing. Gosh, what possibilities! You can't feel very sorry for Tennessee when you see that in the offing."

Truth in Securities Act and Securities Exchange Act

Not long after the stock market crashed in late 1929, the Senate Banking Committee began looking into just what had happened. Senators listened to tale after tale of legally dubious and morally reprehensible practices by more than a few bankers and brokers.

In May 1933, Congress approved the Truth in Securities Act: a measure that required every new stock issuance to be registered with the Federal Trade Commission and fully disclosed in detail. A year later, the Securities Exchange Act extended the rules to all stocks, required the disclosure of insider trading, authorized the Federal Reserve to set margin rates (see Chapter 2), and created the Securities and Exchange Commission (SEC) to regulate the market.

The Glass-Steagall Act

This measure basically prohibited commercial banks from risking their solvency by dabbling in the securities markets. It also created the Federal Deposit Insurance Corporation (FDIC), which guaranteed personal bank deposits up to $2,500 and was funded by premiums paid by member banks. (See Chapter 4 for more details on the FDIC.)

Roosevelt wasn't crazy about the act because he thought it would prove to be too large an undertaking for the federal government. But he signed it anyway.

"The most far-reaching legislation ever enacted"

After taking over in March 1933, the Roosevelt administration moved swiftly to shore up two of the economy's main pillars: banking and agriculture. On June 16, the last of The Hundred Days, Roosevelt signed a bill addressing a third pillar: industry.

The bill was entitled the National Industrial Recovery Act (NIRA), and Roosevelt somewhat grandiosely called it "the most important and far-reaching legislation ever enacted by the American Congress."

There were two main parts to the act:

✔ One part relaxed antitrust laws, in return for which industries were supposed to huddle up their members and draft workplace standards that would ensure workers a fair wage and decent hours, consumers a fair price, and companies a fair profit. This provision was to be governed by the National Recovery Administration, headed by a hard-drinking ex-cavalry man named General Hugh "Iron Pants" Johnson. There was also a section that guaranteed employees a right to organize and bound industries to minimum wages, maximum workweeks, and the abolition of child labor (see Chapter 11 for details on this part of the NIRA).

✔ The second part of the act created the Public Works Administration (PWA). The PWA was given $3.3 billion and charged, under the direction of Interior Secretary Harold Ickes, to spend it on public works projects that would create jobs and fill needs around the country.

To pay for the measure, Roosevelt adroitly set up a fiscal plan outside the normal federal budget. The plan essentially borrowed money from the public and repaid it with higher taxes on corporations and dividends and a tax hike on gasoline.

While signing the NIRA, Roosevelt declared that "it represents a supreme effort to stabilize for all time the many factors which make for the prosperity of the nation."

He was right about the effort part. General Johnson, lacking the authority to force industry compliance, settled on a dual strategy of convincing industry leaders it was a privilege to be a part of the team and threatening them with consumer boycotts if they didn't join.

Johnson staged mammoth parades and demonstrations in support of the program. He sketched a blue eagle clutching a cogwheel and a sheaf of lightning bolts. The symbol was to be displayed by all companies that were part of the NIRA.

"While every American housewife understands that the blue eagle on everything that she permits to come into her home is a symbol of (her home's) restoration to security," Johnson said, "may God have mercy on the man or group of men who attempt to trifle with this bird."

Initial cooperation was encouraging. More than 2 million employers signed up, including most of the heavy hitters in major industries. (Henry Ford was a notable exception.) But eventually Johnson's cheerleading efforts wore thin. Many industries seized the opportunity to fix prices — at increased levels — but weren't as enthusiastic about abiding by fair labor standards.

Big companies in each industry dominated the drafting of industry codes, so the needs of smaller firms were generally ignored. Price-fixing kept prices high while discouraging incentive for expansion, which in turn meant little or no increase in new jobs.

In addition, some key industries, such as agriculture, were not included. And paperwork for the program was crushing: More than 10,000 pages of rules and regulations governed the NIRA.

The Public Works Administration fared somewhat better. Administrator Harold Ickes was notoriously tight-fisted and released money for projects slowly. He also hated make-work projects, and he refused to "hire men to chase tumbleweeds on windy days."

Home-building efforts by the PWA were fiercely opposed by real estate and construction lobbies and were generally unsuccessful. But in its six years in existence, the PWA did spend $6 billion on more than 34,000 projects that covered parts of virtually every county in the United States. The projects included building aircraft carriers for the Navy, post offices, courthouses, and more than 70 percent of the public schools built between 1933 and 1939. The PWA built the Triborough Bridge in New York City, the Grand Coulee Dam in Washington, and the Port of Brownsville in Texas. Just as importantly, it employed more than 500,000 people per year.

No one likes relief: The Civil Works Administration

With generations-old traditions of self-reliance and individualism imbued in them, most Americans hated the idea of making or accepting handouts, even from the federal government.

That included Roosevelt. When he signed the Federal Emergency Relief Act in May 1933, FDR made it clear that he viewed it as a dire necessity and not a permanent solution. "President Roosevelt is not 'relief minded,'" wrote journalist Gertrude Springer. "He sees relief as a necessary evil to be got rid of at the earliest possible date."

His "deputy president," Harry Hopkins, shared the president's views. "I don't think anybody can go year after year, month after month, accepting relief without affecting his character in some way unfavorably," Hopkins wrote in June 1933. "It is probably going to undermine the independence of hundreds of thousands of families."

So in October 1933, Hopkins suggested to FDR that the government put the unemployed to work over the winter on temporary public-works jobs. Roosevelt agreed, redirected money from the Public Works Administration, and put the peripatetic Hopkins in charge.

The program was called the Civil Works Administration (CWA), and it was hugely popular. In one town, 2,000 people showed up for 155 jobs. In North Carolina, the number of applicants reached 150,000 in one week. The CWA was also popular with state governments, which could hand off projects to it. "This civil works program is one of the soundest, most constructive policies of your administration," Kansas Governor Alf Landon wrote to Roosevelt, "and I cannot urge too strongly its continuance."

Within a month, the CWA had hired 2.6 million people at wages from 40 cents to $1 an hour. Within two months, there were 4 million people working. Much of the work was meaningful. The CWA renovated 300,000 miles of roads and 40,000 schools, and it built 150,000 "privies" in the South.

But some of the jobs were pure make-work. People were hired to hold balloons outside public buildings to frighten starlings. Others were hired to count dogs. A word that had heretofore been used to describe idle cowboys braiding scraps of leather to kill time came to describe some of the CWA jobs: *boondoggle.*

By the spring of 1934, criticism of the program for not creating enough jobs, pressure from businesses that didn't like the competition, and fears that it would become hard to wean people off federal jobs spurred the administration to abandon the CWA.

Starting the Second New Deal

By the end of 1934, the Roosevelt administration's efforts had won widespread public approval. Roosevelt himself — and by extension the Democratic Party — was immensely popular. Democrats picked up 22 more House and Senate seats in the 1934 election, and Roosevelt was lionized in some of the press. "No president in so short a time has inspired so much hope," wrote *The New York Times.*

Forty-one popular songs were written about FDR. Under Herbert Hoover, the White House had received on average about 80 letters a day. Under Roosevelt, the number reached 50,000 on some days. Many people wrote to thank Roosevelt.

"Dear Mr. President," read one letter, "this is just to tell you that everything is all right now. The man you sent found our house all right, and we went down to the bank with him and the mortgage can go on for awhile longer . . . you remember I wrote you about losing the furniture too. Well, your man got it back for us. I never heard of a president like you."

There were more quantifiable measurements of the New Deal's success too. Unemployment had dropped by 2 million, and the gross domestic product was up.

But there was also no shortage of statistics that suggested the programs had not done enough. For example, 10 million people were still out of work in 1935. And there was no shortage of critics. Individuals such as Father Charles Coughlin and Senator Huey Long of Louisiana hammered Roosevelt, as did groups on the left and right of the political spectrum. (See Chapter 9 for more on FDR's critics.)

So Roosevelt recalibrated his efforts. Never a fan of federal spending, FDR nonetheless decided to run up bigger budget deficits to expand federal aid programs. He became more confrontational with big business and pushed for tax increases on the wealthy (known as "soak the rich" taxes) and the closing of tax loopholes. But at the same time he embraced positions favored by those on the political left, he also decided to steer federal aid away from direct relief programs.

"The federal government must and shall quit this business of relief," he told Congress in January 1935. "We must preserve not only the bodies of the unemployed from destruction, but also their self-respect, their self-reliance and courage and determination."

Generating jobs through the Works Progress Administration

In January 1935, Roosevelt's right-hand man, Harry Hopkins, told Congress that if it would allocate the money, the federal government would put millions of Americans to work on public works projects all over the country. (A senator once asked Hopkins if such programs were wise "in the long run," to which Hopkins retorted: "People don't eat in the long run, senator, they eat every day.")

In April, Congress complied, and the Works Progress Administration (WPA) was begun, under the auspices of Hopkins. The WPA was a far more ambitious program than previous federal jobs efforts. Over its eight-year run, the program spent $11 billion (about $170 billion in 2008 dollars) and created 8 million jobs.

The variety of jobs was impressive. The administration oversaw projects from excavating and preserving Native American burial grounds to putting on Shakespeare's *Macbeth* with an all–African American cast. Like other programs, the WPA did a lot of public works construction. Its workers built 110,000 public schools, libraries, post offices, courthouses, and government office buildings. They constructed 100,000 bridges and 600 airports, and they paved 500,000 miles of roads and highways.

The WPA also provided jobs in areas where other public works projects had never ventured. Writers, singers, artists, and actors were employed to write, sing, paint, sculpt, and act. Photojournalists were hired to document the era. When asked if those kinds of jobs were the wisest investment for taxpayer dollars, Hopkins shrugged and said "hell, they've got to eat, just like other people."

Like almost all of the New Deal's programs, the WPA was widely criticized from the right and left. Liberals decried its policy of allowing women and minorities to be paid less than white men. Conservatives scoffed that WPA stood for "We Poke Along" and charged that by guaranteeing the wages of workers, the program eliminated any incentive for them to excel. The WPA was also criticized for being too expensive because its construction costs were often higher than private construction.

In 1939, a nationwide poll asked Americans what they liked best and what they liked least about the New Deal. The answer in both cases was the WPA.

Establishing Social Security

While governor of New York, Roosevelt had explored the idea of a government-run insurance system that would provide some security for senior citizens after they left the labor force. It would also provide a backstop for unemployed people and the dependents of workers who died suddenly. As president, Roosevelt approached the subject cautiously, waiting until the time seemed right to push the idea.

That time seemed to come in 1934. Americans were becoming increasingly enamored with the idea of a government-run old age pension plan. Much of the interest was stirred by an eccentric California doctor named Francis Townsend, who had proposed a simple-sounding but economically nutty pension system. (See Chapter 9 for more on Townsend and his plan.)

"The Congress can't stand the pressure of the Townsend Plan unless we have a real old-age insurance system," Roosevelt told his labor secretary, Frances Perkins, "nor can I face the country" without an alternative plan.

Roosevelt named an "Economic Security" committee to come up with a plan, and in January 1935 he asked Congress to approve the creation of a pension system. It would be paid for in part by employers and in part by a payroll tax deducted from wages, starting in 1937. To build up a reserve, the first payments would not be made until 1942. Provisions were also made for lump-sum payments to survivors of workers who died and for aid to children whose parents died or were unable to work.

Despite furious protests from conservative newspapers and others that the plan smelled of socialism, Congress rather easily approved it, and Roosevelt signed it in August 1935.

The plan had several serious flaws. For one thing, it excluded large groups of workers, particularly those dominated by women and minorities, such as domestic help and farm labor. For another, it was a *regressive* tax, meaning that low-wage earners paid the same rates as high-wage earners, and the tax applied only to the first $3,000 of income.

But even with its flaws, the Social Security Act would prove to be one of the most important legacies of the New Deal. Even detractors were impressed by how quickly and efficiently the act's programs were put into place amid a blizzard of paperwork. Figure 13-1 shows a government ad promoting the program.

Figure 13-1: This 1937 government poster advertised the benefits of the Social Security system.

Feuding with the Supreme Court

While Roosevelt generally had his way with Congress during his first term, he was not so fortunate with the U.S. Supreme Court. Dominated by elderly conservative justices (one was 80 years old, five were in their 70s, and none were under 60), the court overturned several key components of the New Deal.

In a 1935 case that pitted the federal government against a kosher poultry business from Brooklyn, the court ruled that in approving the National Industrial Recovery Act (NIRA), Congress had delegated power to the executive branch in ways "utterly inconsistent with the constitutional prerogatives and duties of Congress."

The Court also overturned the Roosevelt administration's key piece of farming legislation, the Agricultural Adjustment Act. And it threw out a minimum wage law enacted by the state of New York, threatening the administration's plans for a federal minimum wage law.

The court's rulings infuriated Roosevelt, who referred to the justices as relics of "the horse and buggy age." In February 1937, FDR proposed to Congress that he be allowed to appoint a federal judge for every judge that refused to retire after he reached 70. The "court packing" ploy would have raised the number of justices on the Supreme Court from 9 to 15.

"We have . . . reached a point as a nation where we must take action to save the Constitution from the court and the court from itself," Roosevelt explained in a radio fireside chat. "We must find a way to take an appeal from the Supreme Court to the Constitution itself."

Most Americans didn't buy into the idea. "As an American who is a lover of liberty, I cry out against your wicked proposal," wrote the owner of a Cleveland fruit packing company, "to undermine the American institution by packing the Supreme Court, thus making it a puppet under yourself."

Congress eventually rejected the idea. The proposal, however, apparently got the attention of the court. Even before Congress voted the plan down, justices began handing down decisions that upheld New Deal programs that included the Social Security Act, minimum wage laws, labor union organizing rights, and farm legislation. Moreover, most of the court's justices retired, allowing Roosevelt to name their successors.

But the fight left Roosevelt with a political black eye from which he did not fully recover. Republicans made substantial gains in the 1938 elections, which, combined with the country's entry into World War II, generally marked the end of the New Deal.

Assessing the New Deal

Did the New Deal end the Great Depression? No. Did it help end it? Probably not. Did it make things more palatable for Americans living through the period? Probably. Did it have a deep and lasting impact on the United States? Absolutely.

That the New Deal hadn't cured the country's economic blues was obvious as early as 1937. True, the national annual income had climbed from $40 billion in 1932 to $72 billion. But after being re-elected in 1936, Roosevelt had decided that inflation was enough of a threat that it was time to rebalance the federal budget. That meant cutting back on New Deal programs such as the Works Progress Administration.

When federal spending dipped, so did the economy. Unemployment went back up, from 14 percent to almost 19 percent between 1937 and 1938. Steel, automobile, and other industries' production fell, and Roosevelt and Congress responded with a $5 billion spending program that helped start the economy upward again by 1939. But combined with earlier spending efforts, the boost meant that by 1940, the national debt had nearly doubled from the $22.5 billion it had been when Roosevelt took office. Unemployment remained at an unhealthily high 17 percent.

Many, if not most, historians believe that it wasn't until the country began cranking up its production of war materials that the United States finally shook off the icy grip of the Great Depression. (This belief has led to the wry observation that maybe German dictator Adolf Hitler did more to end the Great Depression than did Roosevelt.)

The New Deal did succeed in giving Americans hope during the depression's darkest days. That fact was reflected during the 1940 presidential election, in which Americans gave Roosevelt something no president before him had been given: a third term.

But the real impact of the New Deal went far beyond programs designed to counter a temporary, if lengthy, economic recession. It created the template for much of the modern U.S. political and governmental system.

In the late 1920s, President Calvin Coolidge had noted with no small degree of accuracy that "if the federal government should go out of existence, the common run of people would not detect the difference in the affairs of their daily lives for a considerable length of time."

By the late 1930s, that statement was no longer true. For good or ill, the New Deal firmly established the federal government as the preeminent player in public life:

- ✔ It laid the foundation for the modern safety net of social services.

- ✔ It cemented the federal government's role in regulating the economy.

- ✔ It popularized the idea that the federal government had a duty to provide security for those on the margins of society.

- ✔ It fostered the development of the modern labor movement.

- ✔ It made the government a leading player in U.S. agriculture.

And the New Deal also forged the coalition of interests that formed the core of the Democratic Party for the rest of the 20th century and into the 21st.

Lessons Learned

The New Deal instituted a host of federal government safeguards that ranged from the minimum wage to stock market regulations, and from insured bank deposits to agricultural product price supports. Here's a look at one of the New Deal's biggest legacies — Social Security — and an area it left largely untouched — health care.

Paying for Social Security

In January 2008, a 62-year-old Maryland woman named Kathleen Casey-Kirschling received a check from the Social Security Administration. What made her check unique was that it was thought to be the first paid to one of the *baby boomers:* the estimated 80 million Americans born between 1946 and 1964.

The cost of covering Social Security benefits for all the baby boomers to follow Casey-Kirschling is the biggest worry faced by the system in the 21st century.

Since its inception, the Social Security system was on a pay-as-you-go basis: Current workers paid for the benefits being collected by someone else. Surplus funds were put into a trust account to cover any shortfalls.

The system worked well enough until the mid-1970s, when Congress decided to tie Social Security benefits to increases in the cost of living, with the expectation that payroll taxes to fund the system would keep pace as wages increased. But between 1978 and 1982, inflation soared by 60 percent while wages didn't grow at all. The result was that Social Security experts predicted the fund would be running in the red and forced to dip into reserves within a year or two.

In 1982, President Ronald Reagan and Congress agreed to close the gap by increasing payroll taxes and gradually raising the minimum age for full Social Security benefits from 65 to 67.

In the fiscal year that ended in September 2008, the government collected $785 billion in payroll taxes from approximately 163 million workers to finance $585 billion in benefits for 50 million pensioners. And the trust fund had assets of approximately $2.2 trillion.

But critics of the system point out that while there were 42 workers making payments into the system for every pensioner at the end of World War II, there were only about three workers per pensioner in 2008. And as the baby boomers age, the gap is expected to close to two-to-one. The system is projected to begin running a deficit in 2016.

In addition, critics say, the trust fund consists of assets that amount to little more than IOUs from the federal government, which routinely uses surplus payroll tax revenues for other government operations. Defenders of the system say such criticism is nonsense because all government bonds are essentially IOUs, and the U.S. government backs the special bonds held by the trust fund as it does all government bonds.

But both sides of the debate agree that by the middle of the 21st century, adjustments will be needed to allow the system to cover its obligations. Those adjustments could be further changes in the minimum retirement age, increased payroll tax rates, or lowered benefits.

Closing the New Deal's health gap

Several of President Roosevelt's top aides wanted to include health insurance in the Social Security Act. But "here," according to a September 1935 story in *The Nation* magazine, "the reactionary American Medical Association got busy at once and succeeded in suppressing any suggestion for health insurance."

Roosevelt decided the idea was too controversial and would put the whole bill at risk, so he delegated it to the political limbo of "further study." There it languished for 30 years. Roosevelt's successor, Harry Truman, asked Congress for the establishment of a national health insurance plan. Truman's request went nowhere, and the focus of reformers shifted from covering everyone to covering only those eligible for Social Security coverage.

 In 1965, President Lyndon B. Johnson signed into law the establishment of the Medicare and Medicaid programs. Medicare extended government-sponsored health coverage to Americans aged 65 and older. Medicaid provided coverage for those receiving other safety-net services, such as welfare and aid to children, the blind, and the disabled. Medicaid went into effect on January 1, 1966, and Medicare six months later.

In 1993, President Bill Clinton pushed a massive overhaul of the nation's healthcare system, which had become plagued by soaring costs, confusing programs, and decreasing accessibility to the unemployed and uninsured. But the medical and insurance industries squashed the effort. In 2003, President George W. Bush signed into law a major change in Medicare that created new prescription benefits and other changes.

In 2009, President Barack Obama pledged to seek a universal health insurance system that included elements such as the choice of doctors, protection against financial catastrophe, lower cost growth, and improved patient safety.

Chapter 14

Lessons Learned from the Great Depression

*T*he Great Depression ended roughly with the beginning of World War II. Ever since, it has been the comparative for every burp or bump to come along in the U.S. economy. Nothing like it has occurred in the seven subsequent decades. But could an economic disruption as cataclysmic as the Great Depression happen again?

This chapter addresses that question by first summarizing what happened to the U.S. economy between late 1929 and 1941, and then looking at how the economy has fared since the end of World War II. I consider the similarities and differences between the Great Depression and the recession that began in late 2007. And the chapter concludes with how the lessons from the Great Depression apply to the modern world.

An Overview of the Great Depression

As I point out in Chapter 4, economists and historians have argued for decades about what the precise cause (or causes) of the Great Depression was (or were). It's not just an academic argument.

Knowing what caused the Great Depression to happen could be vitally important in knowing how best to prevent it from happening again. With that in mind, following are summaries of some of the causes and some of the consequences of the Great Depression.

Creating an economic disaster

What do most historians and economists blame for the economic meltdown that was the Great Depression? Here are the most commonly mentioned culprits.

An overabundance of available credit

The development and widespread use of credit to purchase big-ticket consumer items such as cars and refrigerators greatly increased consumer debt in the decade prior to the start of the Great Depression. Consumer debt rose from $2.6 billion in 1920 to $7.1 billion in 1929, a 173 percent increase. When hard times hit, many people found themselves not only short of cash but saddled with debts they couldn't pay. That situation caused trouble not only for them but also for the people to whom they owed money.

A big disparity in the distribution of wealth

Although the 1920s were, overall, a decade of prosperity, the wealth was by no means evenly shared. While the average worker's wages went up only 9 percent, the incomes of the wealthiest 1 percent of Americans soared 75 percent. Much of that wealth was put into luxury items that created few jobs, or into speculative investments that added very little to the economy.

Speculation in the stock market

Although relatively few Americans were directly invested in the market, it nonetheless sucked up a good deal of capital, which drove stock prices far beyond any grounding in real value. The price bubble was inflated on investors' expectations that someone would pay more for the securities than they did. Then the bubble burst in late October 1929, and hardly any buyers could be found.

A shaky financial industry

Many of the country's banks were underfunded, overextended, too deep in speculative investments, and not very well regulated (if they were regulated at all).

Too much stuff

By the end of the 1920s, the country was producing an estimated 17 percent more than it could buy. When the economy slowed down in the wake of the stock market crash, manufacturers with big inventories on their hands shut down production and laid off workers, which stifled consumption even more.

Prescribing the wrong economic medicine

Faced with a massive — and growing — crisis, the federal government took steps that were either wrong or too feeble. These steps included the Federal Reserve Board raising interest rates to stifle speculation, only to have the action restrict the supply of money at the wrong time. President Herbert Hoover and Congress also approved a sizeable tax increase to pay down the federal budget deficit, which also shrank the money supply. And they approved a trade tariff that led to an international trade war.

Dealing with the consequences

Whatever the leading causes of the Great Depression, the consequences were pretty evident — and devastating:

- ✔ Private capital investment fell from $35 billion in 1929 to $3.9 billion in 1933. Adjusted for inflation, the gross domestic product dropped 25 percent between 1929 and 1933, and the national income dropped 50 percent.

- ✔ More than 6,000 banks failed, taking $2 billion in depositors' money with them. Lending came virtually to a halt.

- ✔ Unemployment reached a peak of 24.9 percent in 1933. Many families had only one wage earner, which meant that 30 percent to 40 percent of Americans had no regular income at all.

- ✔ About 300,000 businesses failed between 1929 and 1933 — approximately 14 percent of all the businesses in the country.

- ✔ In 1933, home foreclosures were running at 1,000 per day. By the beginning of 1934, half of the residential mortgages in the country were in arrears.

- ✔ The economic miseries in the United States both complemented and exacerbated the problems in other countries, ensuring that the Great Depression would be global in its reach.

- ✔ Between September 1929 and July 1932, the Dow Jones stock index, a weighted average of 30 major companies' stock prices, fell 89 percent.

- ✔ Prices in general fell 25 percent between 1929 and 1933, making many assets, such as houses, worth less than the money owed on them.

Recessions after the Great Depression

The Great Depression was the King Kong of the U.S. economy's downturns. It easily dwarfed all the recessions before it (although the recessions in the 1870s and 1890s — see Chapter 3 — were pretty grim too), and we haven't seen anything like it since. But that doesn't mean the economy has been all milk and honey since the Great Depression ended.

In fact, according to the official arbiter of recessions — the business cycle dating committee of the National Bureau of Economic Research (see Chapter 2) — 11 recessions have occurred since World War II ended.

On average, the first ten recessions lasted 10½ months. (I can't report the duration of the 11th recession because it wasn't over as of this writing.) On average, unemployment rates increased a maximum of 2.5 percent. And the gross domestic product, adjusted for inflation, dropped an average maximum of 1.9 percent.

Those are relatively mild averages. For example, the average length of 10¹/₂ months is just half of the average 21 months that recessions lasted prior to the Great Depression.

Debating "the Great Moderation"

Some economists have called the post-war pattern of milder recessions "the Great Moderation." But because economists like to argue about nearly everything, there is disagreement about what caused the more moderate recessionary periods.

One theory is that better information-gathering techniques allowed the Federal Reserve Board (see Chapter 2) to stay on top of the economic situation and ease up or tighten interest rates. Doing so has allowed the money supply to increase when recessions hit and decrease when inflation is a threat.

Another theory is that the expansion of service industries' role in the U.S. economy made it less prone to the ups and downs of an economy based heavily on manufacturing. At the same time, the theory goes, manufacturers and retailers did a better job of maintaining inventories at levels that neither flooded the market nor starved it.

And some people believe that an expansion of credit following World War II enabled people to adopt buy-now, pay-later spending patterns instead of everyone stopping spending when times get rough. The monthly credit card payments helped keep things rolling.

Looking at post-war recessions

Whatever the reasons, the result is that nothing like the Great Depression has come along in the post-war United States — so far. Here's a look at the 11 recessions that have occurred since 1945.

1948

Economists say this 11-month downturn, which began in November 1948, was a "natural down cycle" caused by the economy adjusting to post-war production. The unemployment rate reached 7.9 percent; the gross domestic product (GDP) dropped by 1.8 percent.

1953

Beginning in July 1953, this ten-month recession has been attributed to the Federal Reserve Board (the Fed) tightening money supplies in an effort to head off inflation following the end of the Korean War. The federal government diverting more money into national security intensified the problem. Unemployment climbed to 6.1 percent, and the GDP dropped by 2.7 percent.

1957

This recession lasted only eight months, starting in August 1957, and was attributed to the Fed tightening money supplies. Unemployment climbed to 7.1 percent, and the GDP dropped by 3.7 percent. Interestingly, the Dow Jones Industrial Average dropped 19 percent during this recession after holding steady in the more severe 1953 recession.

1960

A ten-month recession that began in April 1960 was triggered by a combination of high inflation and growing unemployment (which reached 7.1 percent). Increased government spending ended it. The GDP dropped 1.1 percent.

1969

This relatively mild 11-month recession that began in December 1969 was again caused by increasing inflation and declining employment. Unemployment peaked at 6.1 percent; the GDP dropped by 0.2 percent.

1973

This one was a nasty bugger, beginning in November 1973 and lasting 16 months. It was caused by a combination of factors. The Organization of Petroleum Exporting Countries (OPEC) quadrupled oil prices as a consequence of war in the Middle East. Inflation soared, partly as a result of federal spending (on the Vietnam War and social service programs) and partly because the United States went off the gold standard (see Chapter 7).

President Richard Nixon imposed wage-and-price controls, which kept prices so high that demand fell. The result was *stagflation,* a relatively rare economic condition that combines recession with inflation. Unemployment reached 9 percent; the GDP dropped 3.1 percent.

1980

This recession was actually just a preview of a much nastier one that began in 1981. The 1980 version started in January 1980 and ended in June.

1981

This 16-month-long recession began in July 1981 and was widely considered to be the worst since the Great Depression. It's usually attributed to two causes:

- ✔ A revolution in Iran that resulted in sharply higher oil prices.

- ✔ Interest rates that were raised to the highest level since the Civil War in an effort to fight inflation.

Unemployment soared to a post-Depression record high of 10.8 percent, and it stayed above 10 percent for ten months. The GDP dropped 2.9 percent.

1990

This relatively mild eight-month recession that began in July 1990 was most probably a result of a crisis in the savings and loan industry the year before.

2001

An eight-month recession that began in March 2001 was sparked by a severe downturn in Internet businesses (the "dot-com industry") and aggravated by the terrorist attacks of September 11. Unemployment hit 6 percent, but the GDP dropped hardly at all.

2007

This recession began in December 2007 and, as of March 2009, was entering its 16th month. That duration made it at least as long as any recession since the Great Depression.

The causes of what was sometimes wryly referred to as "the Great Recession" were rooted in the bursting of a real estate bubble in the United States.

Simply (and simplistically) put, lenders made home loans to a large number of people who couldn't afford them. The loans were "bundled" together and resold as securities. When the borrowers began defaulting on the loans, the securities lost value. Major lenders and other firms that dealt in the mortgage-based securities, from banks to the world's largest insurance company, went belly up or were financially crippled.

The collapses and crippling, in turn, shocked the stock market. The market lost almost 50 percent of its value between December 2007 and March 2009. Unemployment reached 8.1 percent, and the gross domestic product dropped 2.2 percent.

How Things Have Changed since 1929

Once upon a time, the U.S. stock market fell sharply. Financial institutions that had made unwise and highly speculative investments began to teeter; some collapsed. Home mortgages were foreclosed at an accelerating rate. Some people had dangerously overextended their credit and were facing debts they couldn't pay.

Other people feared times would get worse, so they quit spending. That action caused manufacturers to produce less and lay off workers, which raised unemployment levels, which increased fears of an economic collapse, which led to even less spending.

The economic mess was precipitated by, in the words of a prominent economist at the time, "an abundance of greed and an absence of fear (that) led some to make investments not based on the real value of assets, but on the faith that there would be another who would pay more for those assets."

"At the same time," the economist continued, "the government turned a blind eye to these practices and the potential consequences for the economy as a whole."

"[E]ventually however," he said, "greed gave way to fear . . . it is the transition from an excess of greed to an excess of fear that President (Franklin) Roosevelt had in mind when he famously observed that the only thing we have to fear was fear itself."

The economist was Lawrence Summers, who was Secretary of the Treasury not under Roosevelt but under President Bill Clinton, and who was named director of the National Economic Council by President Barack Obama.

Summers wasn't speaking in 1933 about the Great Depression. He was speaking in mid-March 2009 about a worldwide recession that began in late 2007 and was on to the verge of becoming the longest economic downturn in the United States since the Great Depression.

The numbers from the 2007 recession were indeed sobering:

- ✔ $50 trillion in wealth was erased worldwide between late 2007 and spring 2009, $7 trillion of it from the U.S. stock market and $6 trillion from U.S. real estate.

- ✔ The gross domestic product decreased and the unemployment rate increased at the fastest rates in more than half a century; at least 4.4 million jobs were lost in the United States alone.

In addition, the net worth of many Americans suffered a double whammy, as securities in the form of stocks, mutual funds, and retirement programs such as 401(k) plans took a big hit at the same time that real estate valuations headed south in a hurry.

In a speech in early March 2009, Christina Romer, the White House chief economist, acknowledged she had found herself "uttering the words 'worst since the Great Depression' far too often: the worst twelve month job loss since the Great Depression; the worst financial crisis since the Great Depression; the worst rise in home foreclosures since the Great Depression."

But, Romer noted, for as many similarities as there were between the Great Depression and the recession that began in late 2007, there were probably more key differences.

That's "trillion," with a "T"

According to the online news archive Nexis, the term "trillion dollars," or close variations of it, appeared in U.S. newspaper stories 410 times in all of 1989. It appeared 1,918 times in the month of February 2009.

That analysis is borne out by comparing some of the numbers from the two periods:

- ✔ The Dow Jones Industrial Average fell 89 percent between September 1929 and July 1932. The drop between December 2007 and March 2009 was 49 percent.

- ✔ The economy contracted 25 percent between 1929 and 1932. Between 2007 and 2009, it contracted about 6 percent.

- ✔ The unemployment rate during the Great Depression peaked at 24.9 percent in 1933. In March 2009, it was at 8.1 percent. Moreover, there were far more two-income families in 2009 than in 1933, which helped ease the sting if one of the wage earners lost his or her job.

- ✔ While an estimated 50 percent of all home mortgages were in arrears in 1933, the figure was 12 percent in early 2009.

"If what we have now is a rainstorm," economist and writer Amity Shlaes said in a January 2009 appearance on National Public Radio, the Great Depression "was a (Hurricane) Katrina."

The Legacy of the Great Depression

The impacts of the Great Depression on 21st-century America are measurable in several ways. One way is that, for good or ill, the Great Depression significantly enhanced the role the federal government plays in the U.S. economy. When economic trouble hits, most Americans look quickly to Washington to see what the government is going to do about it.

Much of that expectation is based on the legacy of federal government programs that were first created in response to the Great Depression itself and exist today as safeguards against some of the worst blows of a recession.

Those programs include federal insurance against the loss of bank deposits; insurance against unemployment; a federal pension system for the elderly and disabled; and programs that provide food, shelter, and financial aid to the needy.

Those Great Depression legacy programs have been joined in the decades since by other "safety net" components such as federal health insurance for senior citizens and the poor, and safeguards such as checks on abuses of the stock market and increased vigilance over the money supply.

The public's expectation of government intervention has also engendered a feeling of obligation in most post-Depression governments to act quickly — if not always wisely — in the face of economic problems. For example, after taking office in January 2009, President Barack Obama quickly launched a three-pronged attack on the deepening recession that had begun in 2007:

- ✔ Less than a month after taking office, Obama signed the American Recovery and Reinvestment Act (ARRA), the largest economic stimulus effort in U.S. history. The $800 billion act included funds for everything from income tax breaks to extended unemployment benefits to money for state programs to financial incentives for buying new cars and first homes.

- ✔ The second prong was called the Financial Stability Plan, which included elements that ranged from the government buying up or refinancing mortgage, student, and small business loans as a way of getting non-bank lenders back on their feet, to injecting federal funds into stressed banks.

- ✔ The third prong was the Helping Families Save Their Homes Act, which was designed to make it easier to modify home mortgages and reduce the rising numbers of foreclosures that were mainly a result of the real estate bubble bursting in 2007.

"The president is committed to an approach that moves aggressively on jobs, on credit, on housing," said Summers, Obama's chief economic advisor, in a March speech to the Brookings Institute. "In this effort, he has insisted that we be guided by the recognition that the risks of overreaction are dwarfed by the risks of inaction."

The final lesson to be learned from the Great Depression is that all bad things, like all good things, come to an end. While historians and economists argue as to what, if anything, worked to help end the Great Depression, the inescapable fact is that it did end.

"If we continue to heed the lessons of the Great Depression," noted economics historian and presidential adviser Christina Romer in March 2009, "there is every reason to believe that we will weather this trial and come through to the other side even stronger than before."

Part V

The Part of Tens

The 5th Wave   By Rich Tennant

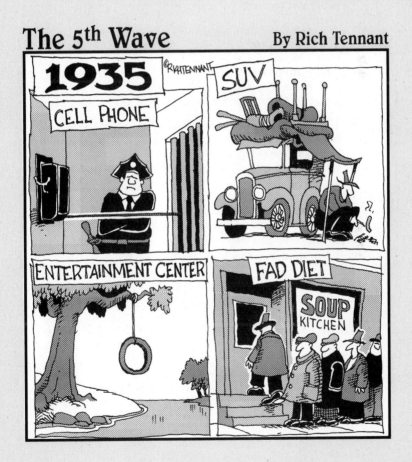

In this part . . .

No book *For Dummies* is complete without The Part of Tens. This part features lists of ten good movies either made or set in the Great Depression, ten things that were invented or popularized in the period, and ten things that weren't all that depressing about the Great Depression.

(Someday there oughta be a book *For Dummies* with nothing but Parts of Tens. . . .)

Chapter 15

Ten Good Movies Made in or about the Great Depression

· ·

*T*housands of movies were made during and about the Great Depression, so it's tough to pare the list down to just ten good ones. My chief criterion was that they tell viewers something about what the period was like.

The Public Enemy (1931)

Stars: James Cagney, Jean Harlow. **Director:** William Wellman. Cagney plays Tom Powers, a working-class kid who "wises up" and becomes a bootlegger and hoodlum, only to get gunned down at the end of the film.

Although Cagney's character is supposed to be a bad guy — in one famous scene he mashes half a grapefruit in the face of his girlfriend — Cagney was so charismatic that many people in the audience felt bad when Tom Powers was killed. The film, a hit at the box office, was made before Hollywood established its self-censorship board in late 1934. It was one of the reasons the censorship code, which effectively banned gangster movies, was adopted. (See Chapter 9 for more on gangster films during the 1930s.)

I Am a Fugitive from a Chain Gang (1932)

Stars: Paul Muni, Glenda Farrell. **Director:** Mervyn LeRoy. Based on a real-life story, the film follows a guy (Muni) who is wrongfully charged with a crime and sentenced to hard labor on a Georgia chain gang. He makes a daring escape and lives a successful life under an assumed name for seven years. He is eventually tricked into surrendering with the promise of lenient treatment, only to find himself back on the chain gang. He escapes again, and as the movie ends, he is still on the lam.

This film was controversial when it was released because of its depiction of the way prison inmates were treated. It also disturbed audiences because its ending was neither happy nor conclusive. In the final scene, when his lover asks how he lives as a fugitive, Muni's character says, "I steal," as he slips into the darkness. Great Depression audiences undoubtedly felt great empathy with the injustice of Muni's character's situation.

Gabriel Over the White House (1933)

Stars: Walter Huston, Karen Morely. **Director:** Gregory La Cava. This is one weird movie. Huston plays Judson Hammond, a new U.S. president who is a good-time guy and stooge for political party bosses. Then he has a car accident, gets a visit from the archangel Gabriel, comes out of a coma, and assumes power as dictator. He takes over Congress, finds public works jobs for the unemployed, rounds up gangsters and has them shot, and bullies other countries into paying their debts to the United States and signing an international peace treaty. He dies a hero to the world.

The film was based on a novel by an ex-British general and brought to the screen by newspaper baron William Randolph Hearst. It was produced with the approval of Roosevelt, whom Hearst backed in the 1932 election. Hearst apparently meant it as something of a guide for FDR to follow. Roosevelt called it "an intensely interesting picture." It was a big box office hit in 1933 but faded into obscurity, as did Hearst's support for FDR by the end of 1933.

Gold Diggers of 1933 (1933)

Stars: Dick Powell, Ruby Keeler. **Director:** Mervyn LeRoy. A 1933 critic called it "an imaginatively staged, breezy show, with a story of no (great) consequence." That was fine with Depression-era audiences. Musicals offered an escape for people who came to see the lavish song-and-dance numbers — not to gain insight into the human condition.

Based on a hit Broadway play, *Gold Diggers* actually had two directors: LeRoy for what little plot there was (struggling actresses and songwriter get big breaks on Broadway), and showman Busby Berkeley for the musical numbers. There is one politically charged song, "Remember My Forgotten Man," that's about the World War I vets who had hit hard times. (Read more about them in Chapter 4.)

Dead End (1937)

Stars: Joel McCrea, Humphrey Bogart, Sylvia Sidney. **Director:** William Wyler. This film is set at New York City's East River, where residents of luxury apartments view the river while trying to ignore the slums along its banks. A gang of poor kids bully and then accept a rich kid; gangster Bogart tries to kidnap the kid; out-of-work architect McCrea kills Bogart; and one of the poor kids does the right thing and turns himself in for stabbing the rich kid's dad.

The film was spawned from a hit Broadway play. It's notable both for its depiction of inner-city life during the Great Depression (*The New York Times'* review called it "disturbingly accurate") and the debut of the Dead End Kids, a group of young male actors who would go on to star in nearly 90 low-budget films through 1958.

The Grapes of Wrath (1940)

Stars: Henry Fonda, Jane Darwell. **Director:** John Ford. Based on John Steinbeck's novel (see Chapter 8 for more on the book), the film is the story of the Joads, an Oklahoma family that has been forced off its farm and migrates to California. At the end of the film, the eldest son (Henry Fonda) kills a man and leaves the family, presumably to fight social injustice.

The film tones down the novel, as well as injecting extra optimism. "They can't wipe us out and they can't lick us," says Darwell as the matriarch of the family. "We'll go on forever Pa, 'cause we're the people." Despite its somewhat exaggerated portrayal of the "Okie" migration, the movie is often listed as among the best of all time.

They Shoot Horses, Don't They? (1969)

Stars: Jane Fonda, Michael Sarrazin, Gig Young. **Director:** Sydney Pollack. Based on a 1935 novel, this film tells the story of people in a dance marathon, which people participated in (along with other types of endurance contests) because they were desperate for money in the 1930s. (See Chapter 4 for more on endurance contests.) As the marathon drags on, an unscrupulous emcee comes up with gimmicks that entertain the audience while adding to the dancers' misery.

Although the film takes place almost entirely within a ballroom, it does give audiences a glimpse into how the desperate circumstances of the Great Depression led to desperate efforts by some people.

Sounder (1972)

Stars: Cicely Tyson, Paul Winfield, Kevin Hooks. **Director:** Martin Ritt. Based on a young adults' book, the film concerns an African American family of sharecroppers in Louisiana during the Great Depression. The father (Winfield) is arrested after stealing food for his hungry family and is taken off to a labor camp. The son (Hooks) goes off in search of his dad and winds up at the home of a schoolteacher (Tyson), who encourages the boy's desire for an education. Sounder? He's the family dog.

While a bit schmaltzy, the movie affords a view of how tough things were for rural African Americans in the 1930s. For more on that topic, see Chapter 5.

Bound for Glory (1976)

Stars: David Carradine, Ronny Cox. **Director:** Hal Ashby. This film is based on the life of folk singer/political activist Woody Guthrie. Guthrie lived the life of the people he sang about: the hardest-hit victims of the Dust Bowl and the hard times. (See Chapter 6 for more on the Dust Bowl.)

The film is based on a 1943 autobiography and follows Guthrie (Carradine) on his trek to and around California in the late 1930s. Unlike *The Grapes of Wrath,* the film shows what life was like for "Okies" in both rural and urban settings.

Cinderella Man (2005)

Stars: Russell Crowe, Renée Zellweger, Paul Giamati. **Director:** Ron Howard. This biographical film traces the life of James J. Braddock, a promising boxer in the late 1920s who gets hurt and is forced to take menial jobs just as the Great Depression is beginning. Desperate to feed his family of five and forced to go on relief, Braddock (Crowe) goes back to boxing and beats long odds to become the heavyweight champion.

The movie accurately depicts Braddock as the hero of millions of other Americans down on their luck in the 1930s, and it shows how close to disaster so many people's lives were in the Great Depression.

Chapter 16

Ten Things Invented or Popularized in the Great Depression

• •

*N*ecessity is the mother of invention (and laziness the father), and there was certainly a lot of necessity during the Great Depression. So maybe it's not surprising that a lot of stuff was invented, improved, or popularized during the period. Here's a look at just ten such things.

Sliced Bread (1930)

Ever hear the saying "It's the greatest thing since sliced bread" and wonder how long that actually means? In 1930, the Continental Baking Co. began marketing pre-sliced Wonder Bread around the country. A reliable slicing machine had been perfected in 1928, making the mass production of pre-sliced bread possible.

Sales lagged at first because consumers were suspicious of anything so convenient. But by 1933, 80 percent of bread sold in the United States was pre-sliced and wrapped. For a brief time during World War II, the federal government banned the sale of pre-sliced bread because the Feds thought it would save on waxed paper used to wrap the sliced loaves. But the ban was rescinded when the government realized it really wasn't saving money and was just irritating the bejabbers out of a lot of sandwich makers.

Twinkies (1930)

As long as we're in the bakery aisle: One day in the spring of 1930, James A. Dewar, an official for the relatively new Continental Baking Co., realized that equipment the firm owned for making strawberry-filled "Little Short Cake Fingers" was being used only when strawberries were in season. So Dewar tried filling the cakes with a banana-flavored crème, and it worked.

Inspired by a billboard advertising Twinkle Toe Shoes, Dewar named his confectionary creation "Twinkies." They sold in a package of two for 5 cents (64 cents in 2008 money). Because of a banana shortage during World War II, the company switched to a vanilla-based filling. In 2007, the corporation that now owns the brand was cranking out 500 million Twinkies a year.

Scotch Tape (1930)

One of the handiest household items was invented by a banjo player who had a job with a sandpaper company. The musician/inventor was named Richard Drew. He worked for the Minnesota Mining and Manufacturing Co., which had started out as a mining business but switched to making sandpaper products.

In 1925, Drew invented masking tape so auto painters could more easily use two colors without the border between them getting messy. In 1930, he came up with a variation on the tape, using transparent cellulose. The new tape became a big hit in the Great Depression because it allowed people to mend things rather than replace them.

The name? The first version of the masking tape was light on adhesive and fell off. A frustrated auto painter told Drew to tell his "Scotch" (a pejorative for *cheap* or *stingy*) bosses to put more stick'em on their product. Drew's employer, better known as the 3M Co., not only did so, but it also trademarked the name.

Alka-Seltzer (1931)

So, in 1928 this guy walks into *The Elkhart Truth,* an Indiana newspaper, and notices no one is sick from the flu that's going around. The editor tells the guy it's because of a mixture of aspirin, bicarbonate of soda, and lemon juice that he whips together for the staff.

Fast forward to 1931. The guy, whose name is Andrew H. Beardsley, is chairman of the Dr. Miles Medical Company. He has his chief chemist come up with an effervescent tablet with ingredients similar to the newspaper elixir. They call it Alka-Seltzer, and by 2005 they were selling 300 million tablets a year. Which is a lot of burping.

Fritos (1932)

Nineteen thirty-two didn't seem like a really good year to start a business, especially in the snack food field. Undaunted, a Texan named Elmer Doolin borrowed $100 from his mom and bought a recipe, 19 retail accounts, and an old handheld device called a "potato ricer." With it he churned out ten pounds a day of salted corn chips that he sold for a nickel a bag.

Eventually, Doolin expanded his production facility from the kitchen to the garage and got some better machinery. By the 21st century, the company he started was the largest salty snack company in the world. The Frito Pie? Some say Doolin's mom invented the combination of chili, cheese, and Fritos. Others say a Woolworth's in Santa Fe, New Mexico, invented it. Fortunately, Alka-Seltzer had been invented by then.

Toll House Cookies (1933)

Ever started baking something and found out you lacked a key ingredient? Thankfully for cookie lovers everywhere, that's what happened to Ruth Graves Wakefield. The owner of a lodge in Massachusetts called the Toll House Inn, Wakefield was making cookies one day when she found she had run out of baker's chocolate. So she took a semisweet chocolate bar a fellow named Andrew Nestle had given her and cut it into tiny chips.

When the cookies were done, she found the chips hadn't melted. Everyone loved the cookies anyway. In 1939, Nestle began making semisweet chocolate morsels. Milk has never been the same.

The Laundromat (1934)

Fritos weren't the only thing to come out of Texas in the Great Depression. In 1934, a fellow named J.F. Cantrell looked around his Forth Worth neighborhood and noticed that many of his neighbors lacked a washing machine. So he went out and bought four electric washing machines, installed them in a building, and charged people by the hour to use them.

Thus was born the "washateria," later to be known as the laundromat. Cantrell's customers were provided with hot water, but they had to bring their own soap. Variations on laundromats over the years have included restaurants, bowling alleys, and even a topless nightclub. I don't know whether you had to bring your own soap to that one.

Tampax (1936)

In 1931, a Colorado doctor named Earle Haas invented a new kind of tampon that used a telescoping cardboard tube applicator. He called it "Tampax," which he said was a combination of "tampon" and "vaginal pack." Unable to sell his invention, he sold the patent and trademark to a business group that began marketing it in 1936.

Naturally, one of the big hurdles was to promote a product no one wanted to talk about. So the company tried to closely tie its product to the medical community. Its first ad proclaimed it was "accepted for advertising by the American Medical Association." That last part didn't mean it was endorsed by the AMA, just that it was accepted as an ad in the AMA journal. Never mind, it worked. Tampax eventually cornered 55 percent of the worldwide tampon market.

Nylon Bristle Toothbrush (1938)

In 1930, DuPont Chemical Company scientists came up with a substance that stretched and had a silky texture. And that's why you probably don't brush your teeth with hair from a Siberian boar.

Toothbrush bristles were usually made from boar's hair up until 1938. But in that year, Dr. West's Miracle Tuft Toothbrushes came along, with bristles made of something called nylon. They were hard on gums at first, but scientists eventually found a way to soften the bristles. And the folks at DuPont were so excited with their new substance that they came out with another nylon product the very next year: women's stockings. It caught on.

Rudolph the Red-Nosed Reindeer (1939)

In 1939, executives at the Montgomery Ward department stores asked Robert L. May, a company advertising copywriter, to come up with an original story they could give away at Christmas. May came up with a story about a red-nosed reindeer. The reindeer's original name was Rollo, then Reginald. Finally, with the help of his 4-year-old daughter, May settled on Rudolph.

The story was an immediate hit, and the company distributed 2.4 million copies in the first year. The story and character were turned into lots of products. And in 1949, a cowboy star named Gene Autry recorded a song written by May's brother-in-law, Johnny Marks, about Rudolph. You may have heard it.

Chapter 17

Ten Not-So-Depressing Things about the Great Depression

- -

The overall impression many people have about the Great Depression is that everyone was pretty depressed all the time. But as I explain in Chapter 10, Americans didn't walk around with their chins dragging for an entire decade. Here's a list of ten things about the Great Depression that were pretty cool, then and now.

Marx Brothers Movies

The Marx Brothers may have been the perfect comedic tonic for the Great Depression. On-screen (and sometimes off it), the Marxes (Marxists?) did what they wanted, went where they wanted, and said what they wanted (except for Harpo, who never spoke on-screen).

For people who had been beaten down by forces they didn't understand and couldn't control, the brothers' (yes, they were really brothers) fresh and funny anarchy was a great way to strike back at "the system," even if only vicariously. "Practically everyone wants a good laugh right now," observed *Variety* of the brothers' 1933 anti-war, anti-government film *Duck Soup,* "and this should make practically everybody laugh."

The Marx Brothers starred in 11 films during the Great Depression, including two that were versions of their Broadway plays *The Cocoanuts* and *Animal Crackers.* Among the others were such gems as *Horse Feathers, A Night at the Opera,* and *A Day at the Races.*

Shirley Temple

At less than four feet tall, Shirley Temple was the biggest thing in Hollywood for much of the Great Depression. Little Shirley wasn't vertically challenged. She was just a child, born the year before the 1929 stock market crash.

But what a child. For four straight years, from 1935 to 1938, the curly-haired moppet was the biggest box office draw in the country. Her relentlessly cheery disposition and big smile were the perfect antidotes for the Great Depression blues, and she was a walking, talking, dancing, singing goldmine too. Besides making $5 million a year for her studio (Twentieth Century Fox) and $300,000 a year for herself, Temple spawned merchandise that included dolls, soap, baby carriages, and ribbons — and a hair style that was mimicked by hundreds of thousands of little girls.

When she grew up and eventually left show business, she didn't do badly either. Temple became a U.S representative to the United Nations and the U.S. ambassador to Ghana.

The Golden Gate Bridge

On May 28, 1938, President Franklin D. Roosevelt pressed a telegraph key at the White House announcing to the world that something of a miracle had occurred in San Francisco: A public works project had been completed under budget and ahead of schedule.

Okay, so the real news was that the Golden Gate Bridge had opened, connecting San Francisco and the eastern side of San Francisco Bay by stretching across 4,200 feet of open water. That made the structure the longest suspension bridge in the world at the time. Construction took a bit more than four years and cost $35 million (about $5.4 billion in 2008 dollars), paid for through a bond issuance by six northern California counties. It also cost the lives of 11 workers.

The bridge actually opened to foot traffic the day before FDR hit the telegraph key, and 178,000 people poured across the Art Deco structure in both directions. *Time* magazine called the bridge "the world's greatest by practically every measurement — length of span, height, difficulty of achievement." Not a bad Great Depression legacy.

The Wizard of Oz Movie

This film is one of the Great Depression's legacies that was more appreciated in later years than it was at the time. Released in 1939, the film got good, but not great, reviews. *The New York Times* suggested that it was "all so well-intentioned, so genial and so gay that any reviewer who would look down his nose at the fun-making should be spanked and sent off, supperless, to bed." *Time* magazine noted that the pure fantasy parts were great, but "when it descends to earth, it collapses like a scarecrow in a cloudburst."

The film, which was based on a beloved 1900 children's novel by L. Frank Baum, cost Metro-Goldwyn-Mayer (MGM) a bit less than $2.8 million to make ($42.7 million in 2008 dollars) and took in a bit more than $3 million when it was originally released. But it did quite well when it was re-released in 1949, taking in another $1.5 million.

And after it began running on television in 1956, the film's popularity soared, as did its standing in film history. In 2008, the American Film Institute named *The Wizard of Oz* the best fantasy film of all time and the film's song "Over the Rainbow" as the best movie song of all time. I guess they just didn't appreciate winged monkeys during the Great Depression.

"Wrong Way" Corrigan

Douglas G. Corrigan had some solid aviation credentials when he climbed into the cockpit of his airplane on the morning of July 17, 1938. He had been flying for 13 years, had helped build the plane in which Charles Lindbergh became the first man to fly solo across the Atlantic Ocean, and had himself flown across the United States solo.

On this particular morning, Corrigan had filed a plan to fly from New York to California. Less than 30 hours later, he landed in Ireland. Corrigan explained to bemused customs officials that it had been foggy when he left New York and he had misread his compass and had flown east instead of west. Everyone had a good laugh over the mistake. Corrigan and his plane were put on an ocean liner and sailed back to New York, where he received a good-humored ticker-tape parade attended by an estimated 1 million people.

"Wrong Way Corrigan" became a nationwide phrase synonymous with going in the wrong direction. But there's a big question whether the pilot really did go in a direction he didn't intend. Turns out Corrigan had been denied permission to make the dangerous trans-Atlantic flight for three years before he made his trip. Many people suspect that he was dodging aviation bureaucrats with his "wrong way" story. If so, Corrigan, who died in 1995, never confessed.

The Debut of Bugs Bunny

The first screen appearance of the cartoon character the Encyclopedia Britannica called "the most celebrated and enduring lagomorph in worldwide popular culture" came in 1938. Lagomorph? It's the mammalian order to which rabbits and hares belong. Anyway, the wisecracking, carrot-chomping rabbit showed up in a cartoon starring Porky Pig called "Porky's Hare Hunt." He was, however, a mere shadow of the rabbit that movie audiences would come to know and love.

In 1940, the bunny first uttered "Eh, what's up doc?" and in 1941 was formally christened with the name "Bugs." The appellation came from the nickname of animator Ben "Bugs" Hardaway, who had drawn a casual sketch of the character that was labeled "Bugs' Bunny" by a colleague.

The rabbit quickly became a favorite of late Great Depression and World War II audiences. Bugs sometimes emulated the on-screen persona of another period favorite, Groucho Marx, using a carrot the way Groucho used a cigar, making jokes directly to the audience, and even using a Groucho line: "Of course you know, this means war!" It must've worked: In 2002, TV Guide named Bugs the number-one cartoon character of all time.

Baseball's All-Star Game

Baseball fans around the country picked up newspapers on July 7, 1933, and read about a new version of the national pastime, played the day before in Chicago: "Out of the shooting stars of baseball's dream game blazed the mighty war club of the one and only Babe Ruth," the Associated Press reported, "to hoist the American League to a spectacular 4–2 triumph over the National League in the first all-star game in the majors' history."

The game, which had been played at Comiskey Park before a crowd of 49,000, was the brainchild of *Chicago Tribune* sports editor Arch Ward. Ward had a two-fold purpose: to have a big sporting event to go along with the city's "Century of Progress" World Exposition, and to raise money for a pension program for veteran ballplayers.

The game couldn't have gone better if Ward had scripted it. The teams were selected by fans, who voted on ballots provided at the nation's ballparks and in newspapers. Ruth, the greatest player the game ever produced, and who was near the end of his career, hit a two-run homer and made a game-saving catch against the right-field wall in the eighth inning. Initially planned as a one-time event, the All-Star Game has been played every year since and has become a midsummer staple.

The Introduction of Muzak

If you've ever been on a long elevator ride and wondered whom to blame for the music being played, it was George Owen Squier. Who? Squier. He was a World War I two-star general who had the distinction of being the world's first airplane passenger when he flew for nine minutes on a Wright Brothers plane in 1908. He also invented a device that could be used to measure the speed of a projectile.

But Squier's lasting claim to immortality — or ignominy — was something he came up with in 1922. It was a way to transmit phonograph music over electric power lines. That same year, he sold his invention to a firm called North American Company. Twelve years passed before the firm began to market the invention, which Squier had dubbed "Muzak," a cross between "Kodak" (cameras were all the rage then) and "music."

Unfortunately for the company, in the dozen years it had taken to get Muzak to the market, commercial radio had caught on, and there wasn't much call for Muzak in private homes. Plus, it was the middle of the Great Depression. Undeterred, the firm turned its attention to public places, such as restaurants, office buildings, and yes, elevators.

The product was helped along by several more-or-less scientific studies in the 1930s that concluded low-volume, unobtrusive music increased worker productivity, decreased absenteeism, and even made cows give more milk and chickens more eggs. As of 2009, Muzak was piping 2.6 million different songs into tens of thousands of stores, offices, and elevators around the world, with a daily listening audience estimated at 100 million. So feel free to sing the praises of the Great Depression's George Owen Squier. Or curse his name.

The World's — and Other — Fairs

As I note in Chapter 10, Depression-era Americans were crazy about motor trips, and among the period's chief destinations were various fairs and expositions around the country. And not just any old fairs and expositions.

In 1933, Chicago celebrated its 100th birthday by putting on a "Century of Progress" World Exposition. The fair, on the banks of Lake Michigan, showed off ultra-modern architectural styles, as well as old-fashioned fair attractions such as hoochie-coochie dancers like Sally Rand and "Little Egypt." It also featured the wonders of electricity with what was billed as "the world's largest display of electric lighting." The expo drew 10 million people.

In 1935, San Diego hosted the California Pacific Exposition, exposing tens of thousands to the wonders of Southern California. The following year, both Texas and Michigan staged lavish fairs, followed by the Golden Gate Exposition in San Francisco. But the coup-de-decade was the 1939–40 New York World's Fair.

Developed on 1,216 acres that had previously hosted an ash dump, the fair featured everything from a 250-foot parachute jump to the broadcast of a speech by President Roosevelt over a medium called television. (About 1,000 New Yorkers saw it.) There were pavilions hosted by various nations, including one that promoted the establishment — some day — of a Jewish state in the Middle East. There was a gigantic diorama of future life in the United States, complete with 500,000 individually designed homes, a million miniature trees, and 50,000 miniature vehicles. (They somehow forgot to include any churches and, after a lot of complaints, were forced to add a few hundred.)

While the fair drew more than 45 million visitors during its two-year run, it actually lost quite a bit of money. That's what happens when you sandwich a world's fair between a Great Depression and a world war.

Superman

Yes, Superman! Strange visitor from another planet, with commercial, promotional, and mass-merchandising powers far beyond those of mortal comic book heroes!

Or something like that. In truth, Superman was from Cleveland, or at least his creators were. It was 1933, and two 19-year-old guys named Jerry Siegel and Joe Shuster were looking for a career path. They came up with a cape-wearing superhero and for the next five years shopped their idea around. Finally, in June 1938, the Man of Steel made his debut in Action Comics No. 1 (a mint copy of which was appraised at $340,000 in 2006).

The following year, Superman got his own comic book, and the year after that, his own radio show. The radio show, in fact, was where his fans first met Daily Planet editor Perry White, cub reporter Jimmy Olsen, and Police Inspector Bill Henderson, all of whom became regular members of the Superman family. It was also on radio that Superman first encountered Kryptonite, the debris of his home planet that is deadly to him.

Lois Lane? He met her in Action Comics No. 1. Even asked her on a date. Well, he *was* faster than a speeding bullet.

Appendix

For Further Reading

*I*f you've been with me since the opening pages of this book, you may recall I point out in the Introduction that more books have been written about the Great Depression than any other period in U.S. history, except for maybe the Civil War.

Well, here's a list of some of them. They range from new to older, and from general histories to tomes that laser in on a particular facet of the time.

✔ **Best, Gary Dean.** *The Nickel and Dime Decade: American Popular Culture during the 1930s.* **Praeger Publishers, 1993:** From fads and crazes to shirt styles, a somewhat scholarly look at some breezy, yet interesting, aspects of the Great Depression.

✔ **Congdon, Don (editor).** *The Thirties: A Time To Remember.* **Simon and Schuster, 1962:** An engaging and entertaining collection of essays and articles about the Great Depression, both contemporary and historical.

✔ **Egan, Timothy.** *The Worst Hard Time.* **Houghton Mifflin Harcourt, 2006:** A tale from Pulitzer Prize–winning journalist Egan of those who were caught up in the Dust Bowl — and persevered. Reads like a novel.

✔ **Gerdes, Louise I. (editor).** *The 1930s.* **Greenhaven Press, 2000:** A nifty collection of contemporary and modern essays and excerpts about issues and cultural events during the era.

✔ **Green, Harvey.** *The Uncertainty of Everyday Life, 1915–1945.* **University of Arkansas Press, 2000:** Provides a look at how Americans made their way through life, including what they ate, what they did for fun, and how they got old.

✔ **Kennedy, David M.** *Freedom from Fear: The American People in Depression and War, 1929–1945.* **Oxford University Press, 2001:** The gold standard for history books on this period. Eminently readable, sweeping in scope, and highly detailed.

- ✔ Kyvig, David E. *Daily Life in the United States, 1920–1940.* Ivan R. Dee, 2004: A nifty balance of the vital and the trivial. Examines life in the 1920s and 1930s and includes a more detailed look at daily life in six U.S. cities, large and small.

- ✔ Lash, Joseph. *Dealers and Dreamers: A New Look at the New Deal.* Doubleday, 1988: Not so much a recitation of the New Deal's programs as a story of the men and women who helped President Franklin D. Roosevelt put his visions to work.

- ✔ McElvaine, Robert S. *Down and Out in the Great Depression: Letters from the "Forgotten Man."* University of North Carolina Press, 2007: Just what the title says — a collection of letters written to the White House during the 1930s.

- ✔ McElvaine, Robert S. *The Great Depression: America, 1929–1941.* Three Rivers Press, 1993: McElvaine takes an unflinching look at the period and critiques some other historical interpretations of it. Authoritative, if a bit cranky.

- ✔ Rothermund, Dietmar. *The Global Impact of the Great Depression, 1929–1939.* Taylor & Francis, 2007: A thorough, if a trifle tedious, look at how the rest of the world fared during the period.

- ✔ Shlaes, Amity. *The Forgotten Man: A New History of the Great Depression.* Harper Perennial, 2008: Shlaes, a conservative economist and columnist, explores the era by recounting the roles played by a diverse cast of characters that range from Herbert Hoover's treasury secretary to the kosher butchers from Brooklyn whose court case ultimately ended one of the biggest New Deal programs.

- ✔ Watkins, T.H. *The Hungry Years: A Narrative History of the Great Depression in America.* Henry Holt and Co., 1999: An excellent and thoroughly readable overview of the period that focuses less on what went on in Congress and more on what went on in the homeless camps.

Index

• *M* •